Love's Leading Ladies

Love's Leading Ladies

Kathryn Falk

PINNACLE BOOKS   NEW YORK

LOVE'S LEADING LADIES

Copyright © 1982 by Kathryn Falk

An original Pinnacle Books edition, published for the first time anywhere.

First printing, February 1982

ISBN: 0-523-41525-7

Cover photos courtesy of:
Mary Cornelison (Shirlee Busbee)
Peter Gruseon (Barbara Cartland)
Nancy Rica Schiff (Janet Dailey)
David Brisco (Patricia Matthews)
Thomas Victor (Janet Louise Roberts)

Text designed by Michael Serrian

Printed in the United States of America

PINNACLE BOOKS, INC.
1430 Broadway
New York, New York 10018

CONTENTS

To my mother, Grace Christman Falk, who loved romantic novels and passed them along to me.

*INTRODUCTION by Tom E. Huff**

Romance is dead, the cynics say, and, indeed, in this age of credit cards and computers it has become quite scarce. Gorgeous damsels in low-cut satin gowns no longer captivate cossacks and cause kings to lose their thrones. Dashing scoundrels in buckskin breeches are extinct, and the last handsome pirate with smoldering eyes and active libido has long since sailed away into the sunset. Heathcliff may still haunt the Yorkshire moors, but he is merely a shade now.

In today's world of tension and taxes, inflation and inequality, life is fraught with pressures, and men and women alike seek escape through vicarious experience. Men have the brilliant and chilling espionage novels of Nicholas Guild, the thundering adventure novels of Robert Ludlum and Wilbur Smith, the Westerns of Louis L'Amour, and women have the novels written by the ladies profiled in this volume. Romantic fiction is the most popular, fastest-selling genre in the book industry today, a veritable bonanza for publishers, but it was not always this way.

A woman browsing in a bookstore or examining paperback titles at the local drugstore in the '50s and early '60s was hard put

---

*Tom E. Huff is author of the critically acclaimed *Marabelle*. For seven years he did weekly reviews, wrote celebrity interviews and conducted a column on paperbacks for a major Texas newspaper. He has published over twenty novels of romantic suspense under various pseudonyms and, as "Jennifer Wilde," has written *Love's Tender Fury, Dare to Love* and *Love Me, Marietta*.

to find suitable reading material. With the exception of paperback reprints of stalwart bestsellers like Edna Ferber and Frances Parkinson Keyes, the racks were packed with three major categories, all male-oriented: Westerns, the hard-boiled detective novels of Mickey Spillane and the like, and novels known in the trade as "Skin Books," books concerned primarily with flesh, the steamier the better. Although statistics showed that 80 percent of books bought were bought by women, publishers were slow to pick up on it.

Victoria Holt, Mary Stewart and Dorothy Eden changed all that, and by the mid-'60s male fiction was being crowded aside by hundreds and hundreds of romantic novels featuring on their covers a frightened damsel in a diaphanous nightgown, her hair streaming behind her as she flees a dark, spooky mansion with one light burning in an attic window. (Always just one light, always in the attic, don't ask me why.) The Gothic boom was on, and there was a dramatic change in the publishing world.

With the exception of the ever-popular Louis L'Amour, Westerns virtually disappeared. Spillane and his dozens of imitators diminished in popularity, and superb, sexy story-tellers like Irving Wallace and Jackie Susann who wrote for women as well as men made Skin Books passé. The racks were now packed with books aimed at the female reader, and when, inevitably, Gothics became a glut on the market and began to lose steam, new genres appeared to satisfy the thirst for vicarious romance.

The Harlequin Romances started small, selling steadily but receiving very little attention from anyone but the thousands of women who bought them regularly. The thousands became millions, and other publishers began to introduce similar lines, books designed for women who, as girls, had sighed to the novels of Emily Loring and Grace Livingston Hill. The heroines were always very pure, usually with names like Fern and Amelia and Janice, while the heroes were young and handsome and noble, usually lifeguards at the summer camp where the heroine worked as youth counselor. (He invariably turned out to be a millionaire's son, working as a lifeguard to prove to Dad that he could Make It On His Own.)

These "light romances" grew a bit racier—the hero was allowed to stroke the heroine's breast after a while—and, with ERA, the heroines became more independent and self-reliant, working as nurses, lawyers, archeologists, photographers for top news magazines. Fern, Amelia and Janice were supplanted by Sue, Jane and Phyllis, the handsome young lifeguards by dynamic business executives, moody brain surgeons and virile oil tycoons. Summer camps were out, exotic locales in.

A shy, extremely demure secretary in Fairfield, California was largely responsible for the next big boom in romantic fiction— the most popular, the most profitable of all. As a girl she had thrilled to the novels of Rafael Sabatini and Rosamund Marshall, had loved *Forever Amber,* and she wondered why books like that were no longer being written. Rosemary Rogers decided to write one herself. Doing research during her lunch hour, reading dozens of weighty tomes for background material, she filled hundreds of spiral notebooks with her tale, going through five complete drafts before she decided *Sweet, Savage Love* was ready for publication.

Accepted immediately, published with considerable fanfare, the book was a phenomenal success, and the "historical romance" was born. (Born anew, we might add. Scarlett, Amber and Kitty had practiced their wiles decades earlier, and Yerby's *A Woman Called Fancy* had enthralled millions in the early '50s.) It quickly became the hottest-selling genre in the country, the best—those written by Miss Rogers, Kathleen Woodiwiss, Shirlee Busbee and one or two others—selling in the millions, their imitators doing remarkably well and causing cash registers to ring steadily, making music that delighted publishers' ears.

Romance may be dead, as the cynics declare—women are too busy fighting for their rights in the business world to don low-cut satin gowns, too busy changing diapers, cooking meals and managing busy households to captivate cossacks and cause kings to abdicate—but the *spirit* of romance lives on, and more and more women are reading romantic fiction.

Why? The answer is simple. The tired businessman trudges home, tosses briefcase aside, loosens his tie and picks up a Louis L'Amour novel to dwell for a while in a simpler age where men could fight for justice and were rarely browbeaten by bureaucratic employers or harassed by tax auditors. After a long day of coping with broken washing machines, kindergarten car pools, temperamental lawn mowers and rising food prices, a day of working twice as hard in an office in order to earn considerably less than the man working at the next desk, women seek release in novels that permit them to vicariously don those gowns and captivate those magnetic heroes they're not likely to meet during their coffee breaks or at the local supermarket.

Mr. L'Amour, Nicholas Guild, Robert Ludlum et al are performing a marvelous service for the men who read their books, and the ladies profiled in this volume are doing the same for women. Often ignored by reviewers, usually denigrated by critics of "serious" fiction (the kind raved about but rarely read, remaindered for 98¢ on sale tables), these women are the ones who have kept the book industry solvent during difficult times. They're to be commended for it, one and all.

**** **** **** ****

Who better than Kathryn Falk to profile *Love's Leading Ladies?* A vivacious auburn-haired beauty with languorous brown eyes and provocative mouth, Miss Falk might best be described as a combination of Auntie Mame and Ann-Margret. She is "The Den Mother of Romance Writers," if one can imagine a den mother in sequinned Galanos gown, a martini glass in one hand, an editor's pen in the other. Miss Falk has led a life that would put most romantic heroines to shame, and she may well be the world's leading authority on romance—or will be when Zsa Zsa retires.

When asked to do a profile of my friend Kathryn, I was tempted to write a racy, vastly informative exposé. Better judgment prevailed. Suffice it to say that Miss Falk has an impressive portfolio in the romance department. She has had a long, tempestuous relationship with a very handsome, very gifted Academy Award-winning actor. A Prince of India, wildly infatuated, longed to whisk her off to India and make her his Maharani—and that's not the half of it. After a number of years of romantic adventures that would make delicious copy for any

Kathryn Falk

tabloid, Miss Falk has found True Love at last with the brilliant and extremely personable Kenneth Rubin, whom she eventually plans to marry.

Miss Falk and Mr. Rubin live in a lovely, cobblestoned neighborhood in Brooklyn Heights, sharing a pale yellow turn-of-the-century carriage house with white shutters and balcony. The home is actually a museum, filled with Mr. Rubin's fascinating collection of antique coin-operated machines of all shapes and sizes. He is the foremost authority on such unusual novelties, and his book, *Drop Coin Here,* is the definitive volume on the subject. It is amidst these nostalgic, somewhat eccentric surroundings that Miss Falk publishes *Romantic Times,* a bimonthly newspaper devoted exclusively to romantic fiction, Mr. Rubin serving as her business manager and calming her down when her enthusiasm threatens to soar into orbit.

Romantic Times had its premier issue in July, 1981, and quickly became "The Bible of Romantic Fiction," providing readers with a lush cornucopia of lively information about the people who write, produce, illustrate and publish romance novels. It contains reviews, exclusive interviews, gossip columns and a wide variety of special features to enchant fans of the genre. Miss Falk does for romantic fiction what Rona Barrett does for Hollywood—and then some.

She devotes "twenty-four hours a day" to talking long distance with dozens of romance writers, maintaining bulky files on hundreds of same, contacting publishers, constantly adding to her vast storehouse of knowledge on romance fiction. Miss Falk knows everything there is to know on the subject—including a lot of wonderfully racy bits she's not allowed to publish. She has a nation-wide network the FBI would envy and, as the Official Spokesperson of the genre, has been the subject of a veritable blitz of public attention, her looks, personality, pizazz and intellect making her the darling of the media.

Reared in the lovely suburb of Grosse Pointe, Michigan, with idyllic summers spent at the family ranch in Canada, Miss Falk was a romantic, precocious child, devouring romantic novels by the hundreds and dreaming of the glamorous, exciting life she was determined to lead. The precocious child bloomed into a lovely young woman with suitors by the score, but Miss Falk was not content to marry the captain of the football team and retire to suburbia with two kids, a station wagon and a membership at the local spa. Brainy and ambitious, she wanted more.

At the University of Detroit, she was involved in "all sorts of outside activities." She was Miss Bond Bread for one semester. Being Miss Bond Bread was, one assumes, quite an honor, and she was dubbed "quite a cupcake." She was, of course, a cheerleader, and she conducted a dancing and cheerleading school on the side. She also had her own radio and TV show on campus. Her mother was determined that she become an English teacher, but the errant Miss Falk had Other Ideas.

Deserting academia for livelier fields, Miss Falk moved to Greenwich Village where she did modeling, dabbled in acting, did public relations work for a major corporation and held "various odd jobs" before going into business for herself. It is rumored that she once appeared in a Wild West show at Madison Square Garden, riding bareback in silver shorts and Stetson, but I have been unable to confirm this. It's the sort of thing she would have done, yes, but I flatly refuse to believe that she once sold chocolate-flavored bagels on Wall Street while attired in red can-can dress and fishnet stockings.

Miss Falk eventually established and ran a chain of stores devoted to doll houses and miniature furniture. The business was extremely successful, and Miss Falk, "America's foremost dollhouse authority," penned the recently published *The Complete Dollhouse Building Book*, which tells readers everything they always wanted to know about same.

Amidst her multitude of professional activities and her extremely crowded social calendar, Miss Falk continued to read romantic novels and was consumed with curiosity about the authors. What was Kathleen Winsor really like? Where did Anya Seton live? Why was Victoria Holt able to produce so many books while Gwen Bristow produced so few? She decided to find out. After meeting Kenneth Rubin—on a riverboat in the middle of the Mississippi River where, contrary to rumor, both were attending a convention and Miss Falk was *not* entertaining as a professional tap dancer—she sold her various businesses, moved to Brooklyn Heights and began the gigantic research project which has resulted in this volume and *Romantic Times*.

So, as we have seen, Kathryn Falk is one of Love's Leading Ladies herself and is more than qualified to write about the others. Several of the ladies profiled herein are close personal friends of mine, and I can truthfully say that they're a fascinating group, entertaining storytellers all. Long may they reign.

Violet Ashton

But now Irina suspected that her husband was rekindling the flames of his early love for Tanya. She could not blame her friend. Tanya was not evil. She just loved life. She was beautiful and she exuded an aura of sensuality which aroused the sleeping tiger in all men.

—*Love by Fire*

The small, fair-haired girl sat quietly, her head bent over the coal-oil lamp, as she read children's classics of the past glories and follies of famous people long dead. On snowbound nights, her family would gather around the dining room table, ignoring the harsh winds howling outside across the arid plains of Saskatchewan, Canada, and tell family stories.

"I grew up on history," says Violet Ashton. "My mother would tell such wonderful stories. At the age of six she stood at the knee of a great aunt who recalled the French Revolution and told how her father stood beside the cart which wheeled Marie Antoinette to the guillotine. I'm sure it was no accident that my first book would be set in the Napoleonic era."

Violet talks with pride of an old photograph on her living room wall. It shows her mother, Harriet Abbot Brown, as she looked at twenty, elegantly dressed for her presentation to Queen Victoria. "My mother's gown was of satin with tulle headdress and egret feathers," Violet explains with painstaking

1

detail. "They were always worn at presentations of that day—1889. Queen Victoria never attended balls or parties of any kind after Albert's death. She merely 'received' the debutantes who bowed the knee and passed onto more exciting things such as dancing and parties."

Violet Ashton believes she writes historical novels because of her mother's glamourous and exciting background—"the kind I never had or knew, but grew up on. Tales of London celebrities and social life were my favorites, but then these were the illustrious family forebears." A great-aunt, Dinah M. Craik, was the author of *The Little Lame Prince* and the lyrics to "God Rest Ye, Merrie Gentlemen;" Jonathan Swift, the greatest genius in the family, was the Irish satirist; a cousin wrote "Great Earl of Kildare" before his death at twenty-eight, and Violet's grandmother penned essays and was presented with a prize by Charles Dickens. Among her family heirlooms is a copy of Milton's *Paradise Lost*, autographed by Dickens.

"I was born in Saskatchewan," recalls Violet, "on February 5, 1908. Mother married an Englishman, a man of good yeoman stock whose father used to judge sheep all over England—he later bought and ran The Three Pigeons, an inn for working men on the outskirts of London. Saskatchewan was a dry, bleak part of the world and sometimes the temperature dropped to 56 degrees below zero and we remained snowbound for weeks. But growing up on an isolated farm provided ample time for reading. At the age of nine, I had mastered all the classic literature for children. My greatest childhood thrill was the arrival of *A Child's Book of Knowledge* at the farm. The purchase must have been at great personal sacrifice to my parents, I realize now. I recall jumping up and down with impatience while my father untied the boxes, and carefully removed all knots from the twine, because nothing was wasted in those days."

In 1924, Violet left the cold part of the north and emigrated to the United States, married a charming "trickshot golfing artist," and raised a family of three children in sunny California. "But even during my most harried years, seldom a day passed that I didn't do some writing," recalls Violet. "I had drawers of writing. I submitted short stories to a San Diego publication, a few of my bylines appeared through the years in California papers." No novel had as yet appeared on the bookshelves, though there was a longish manuscript in the back of the writing drawer. She'd scribbled a title on it, *Delphine*, and the setting was the Napoleonic era.

"I think one reason I was a 'late bloomer' was that the Depression of the thirties kept me desperately attempting to rear three children and it took me years to get over that terrible experience. I think of myself as an ordinary woman who has always been a feminist and ahead of my time regarding women's rights.

"I am an Aquarius—very independent and merrily we go to hell all the way! When most women were blushing and simpering, I was forging ahead determined to live my own life—as all of you do now—and caring not a fig for the 'genteel and overly-refeened' fainting robins of my day! Like my mother, I inherited a strong sense of the unfairness and brute stupidity of men generally towards women. A man I knew once told me, 'You have a good mind—you think like a man!' 'Thank you for nothing!' I told him. 'I have a good mind and I think like a WOMAN!' Exit me. I lived a life of hard work, but always very cognizant of Who I Was." She smiles and adds . . . "My mother was born to money. I have had to dig like HELL for mine!"

Violet's life took a sharp personal turn in 1953 when she was forty-five years old. She and her husband parted as friends. "I didn't want to be a burden on anyone," she admits now, "and found a job at a doughnut shop, in Huntington Park, California.

"Without my writing and books, I would have died of mental starvation." She describes those days with words like "blood, sweat and tears," but makes it clear that life was not all bad. "I met some lovely people," she says. "And although standing behind the doughnut counter was exhausting, I felt it was an excellent vantage point from which to observe the human scene."

Violet Ashton joined a local writers' group—Writer's Workshop West—in 1974. Two years later she was inspired to take out the manuscript, *Delphine*, revise it, and send it off to a New York agent.

A few months later Violet hung up her apron for the last time and said good-bye to her many good friends and coworkers at the doughnut shop. She was retiring after seventeen years, because of the letter she received from the Fawcett's Gold Medal publishers. It was near the date of her sixty-eighth birthday.

"When the mailgram came I was shaking so bad I couldn't open it," recalls Violet, who still wears her hair in soft ringlets. "My daughter was with me at the time and said a publisher wouldn't send bad news in a mailgram."

She was pleased to learn *Delphine* was accepted, but the title would be changed to *Love's Triumphant Heart*. Next, she wrote a sequel—*Love's Rebellious Pleasure*. Violet's third and fourth novels have entirely different settings. "I chose the pre-revolutionary period in Russia for *Swansong*. The sequel to this was titled *Love by Fire*." What would her mother have thought of her novels? "My mother would have referred to them as 'penny dreadfuls,'" chuckles Violet. "That's the English phrase for inexpensive novels."

What is the piece of philosophy she would pass onto others, based on her long and now fruitful literary life? "Enjoy yourselves while you can. The years pass and one regrets passing up so many things regarding romance that we might have indulged in!"

In her own San Jose, California, garden, Violet grows spectacular-looking tomatoes, corn, and potatoes, which she presents as gifts to her friends and family, who live near her "ordinary house with two bedrooms and small study," where, contrary to some opinions, she does not live out her own romantic fantasies. "If I did I'd have been raped in every country of the world!" she declares with a lovely smile.

Her favorite childhood foods were a delicious Irish sodabread and an Indian curry which her mother learned to make when she lived in India for three years. She doesn't have the recipe for either, although "I remember the sodabread had plenty of raisins in it." She does have a favorite and dearly loved recipe for her readers:

4

ENGLISH BUTTER TARTS

Enough pastry for two-crust pie

2 eggs
1 cup brown sugar
½ cup light corn syrup
1 tb. vinegar
1 tsp. vanilla
½ cup *butter*—not oleo!
½ cup currants (You can use raisins, but they're not as good)
½ cup chopped nuts (Any kind)

Set oven at 425 degrees. Use ordinary muffin pans or tart shells.

Beat eggs slightly, add sugar, syrup, vinegar, vanilla, and butter. Stir in currants and nuts. Fill tart shells 2/3rds full. Bake 15 to 20 minutes until well browned and set.

Rita Balkey

*Like the wind we rode all night,
Lothar in front, I behind him, my
arms wrapped around his waist,
hands clenched together in front.
The large black stallion snorted long
puffs of white breath into the clear
mountain air. A freezing rain fell as
we entered the rocky gorges and steep
mist-shrouded peaks of the Black
Forest. My cheek pressed against the
coarse wool of Lothar's cloak, receiving the strong thrust of his powerful
muscles as he guided the stallion up
the mountain path.*

—*The Prince of Passion*

The modern romantic author usually includes an orphan girl
in one of her stories. In fact, it's an old favorite Gothic
technique. (Remember *Jane Eyre!*)

Rita Balkey, the author of *Prince of Passion* and *Tears of
Glory,* is probably the only romantic author who actually was
an orphan! Her birth was humble and her upbringing hard.
She was born in the 1920s. "I was six when the market crashed
on Black Monday. I knew nothing but poverty and bad luck for
many years—my mother dying, my father disappearing, and my
childhood spent for the most part at St. Joseph's Home for
Orphans in Pittsburgh."

The author's birthdate is October 26, the sign of Scorpio.
Determination, intensity, and courage suggest the basic characteristics of the passionate Scorpio people. They surmount all

7

obstacles when they gear for action. Their intuition gives them a chance to seek high goals as time goes on.

Rita took full advantage of the favorable aspects of her birth sign. "While in the orphanage," she recalls, "I received an excellent grounding in reading, writing, and arithmetic. Most important, I was encouraged to read and write there. I had a twin sister with whom I was very close and she loved romantic novels and stories, as did I. One of the few things I remember about my mother is her love of love story-type magazines and romantic novels. They helped her survive. I resolved that one day I would write the kind of fiction my mother and sister and I loved."

Now she writes romantic novels full-time. "I am a romantic by nature," says Rita. "A novel which does not have a love interest of some kind doesn't interest me."

Rita's first writing was in college in the 1940s when she was editor of the Seton Hill (PA) newspaper and literary magazine. She wrote short "mood pieces, nothing strongly slanted toward love, because mine was a small liberal arts 'arty' place." After graduation she wrote some confession stories. "I thought the field could be easier to break in," she says. "I received encouraging letters and made one sale. But, like many others, I decided I wanted real-life love and marriage and children more than a tough uphill battle to become a writer. I got married, worked in an office to help out, got pregnant, and my writing career died a slow but sure death."

This happened because Rita is a homemaker at heart. After living in an orphanage, she longed for a home of her own. "I do not regret putting off my writing career for so long," she says sincerely. "I enjoyed raising my four lovely daughters and pouring my creativity into motherhood and my marriage. I became adept at cooking, especially at making soups and homemade bread. To me, good cooking is simply common sense and experience."

When Rita's children were in school, she decided that in order to have some financial independence, she must go back to college and get a Master's degree, which would in time lead to a teaching job. "I guess, because I was considered such a good student, I was asked to teach a composition class. This experience reawakened my own writing interest, and I had numerous feature articles published in the *Los Angeles Times* about my orphanage days, and mythical and biblical topics."

Between the years of 1964 and 1979, she continued teaching, earned her Ph.D., and became a professor of English at California State University in Fullerton. She was divorced in 1969. "In 1979, I took a disability retirement (due to my failing health) with emeritus status in order to write full-time. I finally realized that I could not teach and write and do justice to both. I now knew that writing would occupy the rest of my life.

"I had already published three text books on the Bible as literature, but I had never tried my hand at the romantic writing I had always dreamed of doing. I knew my first effort would have to have a historical background. I infinitely prefer a story of other times."

Rita chose the mid-nineteenth century in America and Bavaria for her first historical romance, *The Prince of Passion*. She used her considerable research in the period when St. Joseph's orphanage was founded because she wanted to include the fascinating background of the founding nun, five sisters of Notre Dame from Bavaria. "During my research I read the chronicles of the orphanage from the 1850s. In the first chapter of my novel, the soon-to-be deposed King Ludwig bestows a bag of money on five nuns for their journey to America. Not only did the king actually give them this money, but continued to support them in part after their arrival in America. Many orphanages and schools were founded with the generosity of this doomed monarch.

"The eroticism and passion in my novel revolves around the illegitimate daughter of King Ludwig. Sieglinde is a Valkyrie no virile man could resist," says Rita with a smile.

"My gratification comes from the triumph of creation," the five-foot, blonde, blue-eyed author says. She adds that she always wanted to be "tall and beautiful and well endowed, with many lovers and an adoring public. Doesn't any author? I live with a heroine for months before I begin to describe her," explains Rita. "I know her better than I know myself."

Rita's first novel, *The Prince of Passion*, included a genuine historical character, Rudi Stammler, who ran a popular cafe in Greenwich Village. "This soup recipe (which follows) made his customers roll their eyes in ecstasy. It's a Bavarian favorite, ridiculously simple to prepare. Once the trick of rolling out noodles is learned, you will never buy another pack of the store-bought variety. Homemade noodles have real character and nourishment," says Rita knowingly.

GOLDEN CHICKEN SOUP

Simmer a fat stewing chicken to tenderness, along with whole carrot, whole stalk of celery, and onion (halved). Keep white meat out of water if possible. One quart of water is usually enough for a two or three pound fryer. Add salt and pepper, bay leaf, and rosemary to taste.

Drain chicken, place in bowl or platter for picking meat off the bones. While chicken is cooling, cut up vegetables into bite-size chunks, and add liquid, which you have saved in the soup pot. Fresh chopped parsley and chopped green pepper may be added now. Do not overdo—you don't want vegetable soup. (And don't use the chicken giblets in this recipe!) If you're afraid of fat, you may cool soup liquid and drain off excess fat.

HOMEMADE EGG NOODLES

These are made previously to the soup, of course. If you can roll out a piecrust, you can roll out noodles.

Mix 2 eggs and flour (about 2 cups), ½ tsp. salt in a deep bowl, until mixture is of a consistency to roll out. For yellower noodles, use just the yolks and a little water.

Let the ball of dough rest about ten minutes before rolling. Flour your board or cloth, and keep a little flour handy for insuring that the dough will not stick. Roll from the center out, patching up any holes with dough from the edges. Allow the rolled dough to dry before attempting to cut any, and a good spatula will lift them up. Make the noodles as thin as you like, but thick noodles are the best, in my opinion. About ⅛ inch is my favorite thickness.

Let rolled-out dough dry on board for about half an hour.

With a sharp knife, cut into strips. Allow to dry overnight. You may place them in a low oven for about ten minutes or so, if you're in a hurry, but don't brown them. That ruins the flavor.

Add noodles to soup and cook about 15 to 20 minutes.

Iris Bancroft

The tenderness grew slowly into a surge of passion. Her body was hot, burning, on fire with a desire she had not known she could feel. She tried once to collect her thoughts, to remember that this man was her enemy, to remember that he threatened her peace. But the thoughts would not come. All she knew was the closeness of his embrace, the pounding of her heart, the pulsating of her longing.

—*Rapture's Rebel*

Nothing about Iris Bancroft is typical, especially her birth. It was exotic—and tragic. She was born of missionaries in King Chow, Hupeh Provence, China, on May 26, 1922, a time of great unrest. Her parents were sent there by the Swedish Covenant Church to work with the Chinese converts. Her life comes full circle in one of her historical romances, *Love's Burning Flame,* when the heroine spends some time in Imperial China, where savagery, especially to women, was very common.

Iris was one and a half when she left that turbulent continent, and her father died shortly thereafter. Her mother brought her to Chicago, where Iris spun youthful dreams of becoming a choir director. "I know now," confesses the romantic Iris, "that at the time I had a crush on the director of the choir at Fourth Presbyterian Church, where I sang."

In the early 1940s, she fell in love with a sailor whose religious background differed from hers. By mutual agreement, they stopped seeing each other before they got too serious. Then came World War II. "I married in 1945, and my husband went into the navy. At the war's end he returned, and we had two sons, William and Walter. I must admit now to not being completely honest in that marriage and in 1961 I asked for a divorce. I left my sons with their father because I felt it would be best for them if I did."

After her second marriage in 1961, Iris taught school and also sold insurance with her new husband, Keith Bancroft. Then a big change came over her life: in 1963, the West Coast beckoned.

"We moved to California to work for nudist publications as photographers and writers, and later, as editors," recalls Iris. They continued to work for publishers of such magazines until, in 1977, they both quit their steady jobs to work as writers. Since then, she's made their living from her books. Iris now boasts of seven published novels, using the pen-names of Iris Brent and Andrea Layton, along with her own.

But was the switch from writing nudist articles to historical romances a smooth one? "I transferred to books rather natural-ly," recalls Iris. "There are things I want to say in books, and I knew I'd need to learn a great deal about writing before I could sell anything. However, I was fortunate. My first two books, *Swinger's Diary* and *My Love Is Free*, based on the lives of two women I met in Los Angeles, gave me the chance to discover that I could carry a story to completion. Still, I had a good job as an editor of a magazine, and so I spent most of my time writing articles for magazines. Then I became impatient with such work. I suppose it was just time for me to change—to do what I had in one way or another been preparing myself to do for so many years: I started writing historical romances. I felt I could do them well, and I loved history. I try, in all my romances, to include a good deal of real history—to make my characters take an important part in the affairs of their days."

Iris believes that the way romances will move a reader—if they are to become anything but a momentary entertainment—is for them to become as realistic as possible. "I think most readers enjoy learning something about history while they enjoy a good

14

story, and books that give them both entertainment and realism will last longer and give greater satisfaction to the readers—as well as to those who write them."

Her novel, *Rapture's Rebel*, takes place during the 1710 war between Sweden and Russia—a war that was fought for the most part in Finland. The Finns suffered greatly, losing one-quarter of their population to war, plague, famine, and to conscription of entire villages to work as slaves in Russia. Her latest book, *Rebel's Passion*, is set near Philadelphia between 1792–95. The plot revolves around the first tax revolt in America. She's currently working on the life story of a woman who lived for seventeen years in China as the wife of a missionary.

Like many a Gemini writer, the 5'5" brunette, with luminous blue eyes, is a marvelous hostess and usually the life of the party. She also dabbles in painting and clay statues—she made erotic statues in the sixties. Then, there's the viola; she plays in the Burbank Symphony Orchestra and in the La Mirada Symphony Orchestra, two community orchestras that accept nonprofessional players. Her husband, she says, plays in them both, too, but he is a pro, and is the leader of the trombone section in both groups.

Neither Iris nor her husband are part of the Hollywood scene, though they are presently members of MENSA, and the Mystery Writers of America. She also sings regularly at St. Stephen's Lutheran Church in Mission Hills, but is not a member of any church.

Their California ranch-style home is in Granada Hills, twenty-five miles south of Los Angeles. "The neighborhood children consider us the 'gurus' of pets, and when they get a new pet, or have a problem with any they own, they call on us. We have raised birds they brought us, and helped search for lost dogs. However, our latest adventure tops all of that. We recently had one of our cats—the playful one—bring home a goldfish, which I found on our doorstep where he customarily leaves dead mice, and other unmentionables. The goldfish turned out to be very much alive, though he wasn't moving when I found him, and he now is settled in a new home—a tank we had put away

15

when we gave up the tropical fish! We consider ourselves unique in that we have the only stray goldfish in (possibly) the world!"

Iris considers her literary success only moderate, at least so far. "We live on the money I make, but only because we are frugal people. Keith is still just starting out as an author (of nonfiction books on photography), and so his contribution is not large yet. However, we recognize that we want very little that we don't already have. We still travel around the U.S., we visit with our friends, and we enjoy our beautiful home and our pets. We also enjoy each other. Ever since my marriage to Keith, we've worked together a great deal, and I am still delighted in his company."

Since Iris loves the natural things best in life, her favorite recipe is one for natural whole bread. She got it from a booklet that accompanied her Vita Mix, and altered it to satisfy her taste.

IRIS'S NATURAL WHOLE BREAD
2 cups hard Western Wheat (kernels)
¾ cup soy beans (dry)
½ cup nuts

Beat in Vita Mix until it all turns into flour. Add 2 packages dry yeast and mix lightly (a few turns of the mixer). Add 1¾ cups cold water, mix by forward and reverse strokes of Vita Mix until dough is well mixed. Add water, if needed, or some whole wheat flour, if dough is too wet.

(Iris generally adds the following ingredients with the water—3 tablespoons molasses and 1½ tablespoons vegetable oil.)

When bread begins to come together and rises in mixer, she removes it from the mixer and puts it into a bread pan. She permits it to rise to the top of the pan, and then she bakes it 30 minutes at 375 degrees and 30 minutes at 300 degrees.

Bread cooked in this manner is a high-protein bread, made with the freshest possible ingredients. AND NO SALT.

Jennifer Blake

His mouth held the heady taste of whiskey and the firm sweetness of desire. Serena stood disarmed in his close embrace, enthralled by the cool touch of his flesh on hers, enraptured by the sure strength of his arms that held her and the devastating tenderness of his touch. Her heightened senses crowded out thought and reason in the recognition of pleasure long denied, long despaired of.

—*Golden Fancy*

Readers may know her best as Jennifer Blake, the author of tender, passionate historical romances. But she's also established herself with the pen-names of Elizabeth Trehearne, Maxine Patrick, and her own name Patricia Maxwell. With more than twenty romantic novels to her credit, she just started work on a three-book contract with Fawcett Publications, and her schedule is filled with plans for another "royal" series.

Patricia Anne Ponder was born March 9, 1942, in a 120-year-old raised cottage built of hand-pegged cypress with a "mud-daub chimney and a roof of hewn shingles," she recalls. "The home of my maternal grandparents in Goldonna, Louisiana. My grandmother, a locally famous midwife, delivered me by the light of a coal oil lantern, following a pattern that had begun when my ancestors settled in that remote back country swampland of Louisiana in the early 1830s, and did not change until well into the decade after World War II."

When Patricia was two, her father bought an eighty-acre farm in the rolling hills of North Louisiana twenty miles away, and so she was raised as a country girl with a creek to paddle in and woods to roam in. "I was an outdoor type," she claims, "but as I grew older, I often worked in the library during study hall hours, and as far back as I can remember, I was constantly reading; indoors and outdoors, it made no difference."

She believes she had an ideal childhood. "I was healthy, happy, confident, part of an extended family of grandparents, aunts, uncles, and cousins. My parents made me feel special; attractive, intelligent, loved. My mother was energetic, as apt to paint a room or repair a broken rake as bake a cake, though her favorite relaxation was reading. My father was easy-going, well read; the kind of person who takes pleasure in collecting odd and unusual bits of knowledge. Only the Great Depression prevented him from going on to major in journalism in college," she says with regret in her voice. "But, so great was their support and interest that I always felt there was nothing I could not do or be if I set my mind to it."

In most southern climates, the women develop and mature early; Patricia was no exception. During the fifties, when she was growing up, there was a definite movement of women back into the home, a retreat from the major role women had played during World War II. "Careers for girls were not actively discouraged," Patricia admits, "but the atmosphere for them was not favorable. Most girls were quietly groomed to become wives and mothers, and there seemed no reason to delay. The fall I was fourteen, I began receiving anonymous poems. How could I, given my temperament, resist such an approach? I met my poet, Jerry Maxwell, a few weeks later, and the summer I was fifteen, we were married.

"By the time I was twenty, I had three pre-school age children, and had spent five years doing nothing except caring for them, cooking, cleaning, and—reading. (Patricia quit high school when she married but did complete the requirements for a GED diploma.) At that time, I devoured seven or eight books every week; Gothics, Westerns, historicals, classics, romances of every category. They were like a narcotic, something I craved,

18

something so necessary to me I literally could not do without them," she remembers.

Then the day came when she began to be vaguely dissatisfied. As she read she could see ways that, to her, the stories could have been made better, more interesting, more satisfying. One day she threw a book down with those famous last words: "I could do better than that!"

Over the next five years she tried her hand at short stories, newspaper articles, poetry, and one abortive novel. She joined the North Louisiana branch of the professional organization for women writers, and The National League of American Penwomen. "At that time the Penwomen were compiling a book of Louisiana landmarks," she explains, "and each member was asked to submit two suggestions for places of interest for inclusion. I chose two old plantation homes in my area, visited them, talked to the owners, researched the backgrounds, and wrote the pieces which were subsequently published in *Vignettes of Louisiana History*."

Patricia had always enjoyed reading Gothics and had a good idea of the requirements. Visiting the old houses, and learning their stories stirred her interest, and the result was *Secret of Mirror House*. "It took a year to write," she recalls, "a year during which I had another child. When it was finished, I took a long, hard look at it, and at my level of ability, and decided to submit to the paperback original market. With high hopes, I mailed it off. It came right back unopened because I had sent it to a publisher who did not take unsolicited manuscripts, one of the many lessons I had to learn."

Instead of writing the required query letter, Patricia selected another publisher who did look at unsolicited material, Fawcett Gold Medal Books. "They took it," she says blissfully, "bless them, spelling errors, atrocious typing and all, with the provision that I add thirty pages to the manuscript. Since the editor had made definite suggestions as to where the additions could be made, this was no problem. By the time the book appeared in 1970, I had completed a second novel that was also bought by Fawcett."

After such an auspicious beginning, Patricia hit a snag. She agreed to collaborate with a friend, Carol Albritton, on a book idea she had worked up using Hurricane Camille, the killer hurricane that struck the Gulf Coast in 1969. The book, using a modern background, was rejected by Fawcett as not suited to their list, then she sent the manuscript to Ace Books and it was published under the pen-name for the combined authorship, Elizabeth Trehearne.

"Before I realized the prejudice against modern Gothics," says Patricia, ever the psychic Pisces woman, "I had written another. But it was at this time that I saw the need for someone to help me avoid such pitfalls, in a word—an agent. I wrote to the well-known Donald MacCampbell and was accepted as a client on the basis of my previous sales and, so he says, the beguiling enthusiasm of my letter!"

Patricia published four more Gothics, gradually establishing herself a style deliberately rich in color and historical detail. Then, during the recession of 1974–75, the Gothic as a book category went into a decline. "Nobody," she sighs, "would buy one at any price. I tried a murder mystery, an ante-bellum romance, and a modern romance, none of them very successful. At about the same time, the first of the so-called Sweet/Savage historical romances was published. Suddenly the appetite of the public for this type of book was overwhelming. The originators of the genre could not begin to fill it. Every publisher wanted to try at least one for his list. My agent contacted me on behalf of a well-known publisher, and I agreed to work up an outline for approximately double the advance I had been getting for Gothics, and also to submit a pen-name that would be exclusive to this publisher. The name selected is a combination of a first name I had always liked and my grandmother's maiden name, to form Jennifer Blake."

Patricia did the outline, and the publisher accepted it, giving her the go ahead to write the book. Six months later, the manuscript, all 520-odd pages and 150,000 words was delivered. But the road to romance isn't always smooth. "Back came a four-page letter of disparagement from the editor," says Patricia. "Fault-finding and including suggestions, that if followed, would mean a complete rewrite of the book. So destructive was the criticism that, though I had grown fairly tough-skinned over the years, I didn't write a word for three weeks. The condemnation was so wholesale, in fact, that it was apparent the letter was designed with the specific purpose of persuading me to withdraw my manuscript. For whatever reason," she adds, "the publisher had decided against coming out with this type of fiction.

"My agent assured me that there would be no difficulty in placing the book elsewhere, and so, though I was under no obligation to do so, I refunded the money already paid me, and asked to have my manuscript withdrawn. The book, *Love's Wild Desire,* was bought by Popular Library and became a national bestseller for them," she recalls gleefully. "Within a week after it hit the bestseller list, the editor from the first publisher called, offering five times the amount of the advance I had received previously if I would do my next book for them. Informed of the offer, Popular Library matched it, and so, replete with satisfaction, I continued with them. I will admit however that I found some of the suggestions in that debilitating letter useful, and have not hesitated to put them into practice. I am also aware that I owe the sudden, dramatic increase in my advances to that editor and her letter!"

As a change of pace from the long, enormously complicated plots of the historical romances, and because she was wary of being caught again in a category that might not endure, Patricia began writing in the sweet romance genre between her bigger books. To save reader disappointment, a further pseudonym was suggested, and she became Maxine Patrick also. To date there are more than four million books in print under Patricia's various names, and they have been translated into more than six foreign languages.

Through all of her ups and downs in becoming a best-selling author, Patricia has managed to raise a wonderful family. "My eldest son is a graduate of LA Tech University in Computer Science, and our second son works with his father in real estate and the automobile businesses we own. One daughter is married and the youngest is a pretty high school student," she says proudly.

The Maxwells are using some of her royalty monies to finish up the building of their new home in Jonesboro, Louisiana, the Old Southern planter's cottages with one and a half stories, a wide central hall, ten-foot ceilings, long front gallery with columns and railing, fan-lighted doorway, etc. "Considering the type of books I write, it could be right out of one of my plots," she smiles. "In addition to the money I receive, though nice in itself, my books have given me something intangible—a marvelous feeling and a great boost to my ego."

A favorite recipe is one handed down through several generations of Patricia's family. Her version is slightly modernized.

SWEET POTATO BISCUITS
Bake two or three sweet potatoes or yams. Cool and peel. (Leftover potatoes are usually used.) Mash.

Sift together in a large bowl:
2 cups self-rising flour
1 tsp. baking soda

Add:
1 cup sweet potatoes, well-packed
1 cup buttermilk

Mix well. Form into biscuits, using your favorite method. Place in well-greased pan. Bake at 475 degrees until they begin to brown on top. Serve with plenty of butter. The more potato you add, the stickier the biscuits get, and the better!

Parris Afton Bonds

"Lario was a simple man. A man capable of great tenderness and gentleness despite his savage Navajo blood." Rosemary stared down into her glass, not seeing the ruby wine but images of a time never to be repeated. "I used to think of him like the fierce dust devils—you remember the way the sand would get in your eyes so you couldn't be seeing anything else? Lario was like that, except he got in my heart and mind so there was nothing else."

—Dust Devil

Everyone asks Parris Afton Bonds the same question: "How do you manage to write with five boys in the house?"

Contrary to ordinary thinking, the boys (who range in age from two to fourteen) enable her to produce both better quality and a greater quantity of manuscripts. How? "They vacuum, wash, and fold clothes," she explains, "dust and clean bathrooms *and* fix dinner in the evenings. I admit that the youngest is not fully trained yet; and does take up a lot of time, and that my seven-year-old's antics, such as drying the cat in the microwave, can be distracting!"

But these very same antics, she believes, help her to keep writing in perspective. "The boys pull me away from the typewriter and force me to take a new look at an old theme when I return. There have been times when I was certain that a room needed to be reserved for me at our local sanitarium . . . and yet I would not change one minute of my day. I'm doing something I absolutely love—and I'm getting paid for it. And, best of all, I am able to be at home with the people I love!"

Home for Parris is a Spanish hacienda on a remote Texas farm. For the first three years that Parris wrote novels, her bedroom served as her office. Then the Bondses built their own home on what she calls their "twelve-acre mini-farm, raising chickens, cows, pigs, horses, ducks, cats, dogs, and, of course, sons." Parris made certain that she had her own office for escape purposes. From her windows she can visualize Indians and buffalo pounding over the rolling hills by her property. "When my boys ask what they can do for entertainment, I tell them to go outside and battle the raiding Comanches," says a smiling Parris, who is a 5'4", sexy green-eyed brunette.

Parris, the type of pretty Texas female usually seen in the Westerns, loves the Southwest region of the United States because she believes it alone had true romance since women were so rare and valued. Another reason for Parris's love of the Southwest is that she lived in Mexico (two sons were born there) and came to appreciate the culture and the people who were largely responsible for settling this part of the world. "The women pioneers were such strong women with strong characters, which is good material for any kind of novel. The weaklings rarely survived the journey west. I love the fact that these women weren't put on pedestals."

"My novel, *Dust Devil*, is about just such a pioneer woman—Rosemary Rhodes, a young Irish girl, who comes West to create a kingdom, to fall in love with a man of the forbidden race—an Indian—and to live a hundred years to see her grandson, who is three-quarters Indian, become the first Indian governor of the state of New Mexico."

Parris was born on July 21, 1944, in Tampa, Florida, the eldest of four. She's on the zodiac cusp between Cancer and Leo, which accounts for her natural parental instinct and enjoyment of home life, and her extreme emotional swings.

"I am a very emotional person, with mountain highs and *low* lows," admits Parris. "My husband, Ted, is extremely easy-going. He makes my life with him so content that I am able to

24

channel all the energy that would be spent on wasted anger and depression toward writing. Whatever success I have had at writing is due in half to Ted. He relieves me of as much responsibility as possible so I can meet my deadlines."

In 1980, some writers in Texas banded together to form the charter chapter of Romance Writers of America, of which Parris is a member of the Board of Directors. "Most of my close friends are writers. By telephone, all over Texas and even New Mexico, we share our ups and down in writing, we scream and curse and cry and console. And rejoice. Two or three times a year we all get together at someone's house for one of those old-fashioned slumber parties where we can talk until dawn about the horrors and rewards of writing."

Which brings up the personal discussion of Parris Afton Bonds's own writing. "In a way," she says cautiously, "I find my approach amusing, because as a tyro at writing romance I found it very difficult to justify sexual intercourse between two unmarried characters and still remain true to my Christian tenets. (Parris is a born-again Christian.) As a result I often had to resort to 'rape' between my hero and the heroine in order to juggle the sex and romance! I feel I've matured some now, both in my walk with my Christian faith and my writing.

"I believe that God gave us sexual organs and the intelligence to recognize that sex should not be promiscuous, that sex is best when it is celebrated within the boundaries of marriage. But any historical buff knows there were times, especially on the American Western frontier, when the circuit preacher was not available, and a man and woman had to make their own declaration of marriage."

Heroines who hop from bed to bed, she believes, have no respect for themselves. "As a reader, I have no respect for them and soon lose interest in the story. But a strong romance between one man and one woman—with or without that fabulous sex—can't be beat!"

Sometimes Parris is asked for advice about writing, and her answer is, "Our Heavenly Father, who lovingly made each of us, gave us a talent. He wouldn't cheat any one person or give one person more—He gave each of us an equal talent measure. If you feel you *have* to write, then writing is probably *your* talent. How you develop the talent is up to you—get busy writing!"

Parris began writing at six, and her mother still has her first typewritten three-page story—with a "horrendous" title of "The Blackhawk Raiders." "Since then I wrote compulsively, but not consistently, until we moved to Mexico nine years ago. Then I began writing professionally for magazines and newspapers—not much money, but, oh, the experience! Worth four years of college. In 1976 I wrote my first novel, *Sweet Golden Sun*, and sold it the first time out. I've now finished my eighth, with one more to go on a contract with Popular Library," she adds happily. Parris also finds the time to write contemporary romances for Silhouette.

Parris's hobbies are flying (she holds a student pilot's license), tennis and chess.

If and when she's in the mood to cook, she has a favorite instant Jello salad that seems to please all palates around her large dining room table.

INSTANT JELLO SALAD

One 6 oz. package Jello, mixed dry with 1 small carton of cottage cheese, a container of Cool-Whip, and a can of drained fruit. Chill and serve.

Barbara Bonham

*Then he was kissing her, and the
desire that had obsessed her spread
like a flash fire through her body.
Kirk's hands tore at the fastening of
her robe and moved over her naked
body; at his touch, she moaned softly
into his mouth. In turn, her hand
sought and found him and her pelvis
curved instinctively towards his.*

—Passion's Price

The students at Creighton University Law School in Omaha
would never suspect Barbara Bonham of writing historical
romances for Playboy Press. She appears to be a sedate, middle-
aged woman, who is comfortable in her role as wife to her
husband-student.

"My husband, at age fifty-three, after seven years of retirement, has entered law school," she's proud to say.

While Max is in school, Barbara has *plenty* of time to
compose more historical romances and increase her fame in
one of the raciest genres of romantic fiction.

No one would guess that this sensible-looking lady is the
author of *Passion's Price,* and other torrid titles.

"I know they use an amusing nickname, 'bodice rippers,' for
my type of historical romances, but," assures the white-haired
author, "my works are not all *that* erotic. I do treat sex in an
adult manner but use restraint," she adds. "I stay within the
bounds of good taste."

Presently she's working on a straight historical novel, covering one family's experiences through three generations (from about 1870 to 1918). This is her greatest undertaking thus far, and includes the history of the founding of a settlement in Nebraska's Republican River Valley, and leads up to the year 1918, with the town at the highest point of its development.

Barbara Bonham is particularly interested in Nebraska's pioneer period. "Because my two sets of great-grandparents were homesteaders," she explains. "One set of grandparents arrived by covered wagon to settle seven miles from the place where I was born and reared, and only a few miles from the farm near Naponee, where I presently live with my husband—when we're not away at school."

Barbara knows Nebraska well. She was born in Franklin, Nebraska, and attended public school there, and later, for a time, the University of Nebraska. Following college, she worked for four years as a nurse in the community. She gave herself a present on her twenty-first birthday, and enrolled in a correspondence course in writing. Three years later, she sold her first story.

"The correspondence course itself didn't help," recalls Barbara, "but it started me writing." Through an advertisement in a writer's magazine she found an agent who marketed her stories for her. Always interested in history, Mrs. Bonham sketched out a prairie pioneer novel, while writing confession stories. Her agent said it was more appropriate as the basis for a children's book. So she wrote *Challenge of the Prairie*, which is still in print. Then came *To Secure the Blessings of Liberty,* on how the Constitution was written; *Willa Cather,* a biography for ages ten to fourteen; *Heroes of the Wild West,* based on the television show, "Bonanza"; and several other juveniles. She also wrote three nurse novels: *Diagnosis: Love, Army Nurse,* and *Nina Stuart, R.N.* Certainly, Barbara's four years as an office nurse for her stepfather helped authenticate the settings.

During this time, she vacationed in Sausalito, California, in a small hotel that looked like a French country inn and was inspired to write a Gothic novel, *Sweet and Bitter Fancy.* At that point, she also changed literary agents, and her new agent urged her to try writing historical romances, since they were a new and popular market.

"I guess I got in on the ground floor," Mrs. Bonham recalls. "I wrote four novels of this type, the first being *Proud Passion,* which was published by Playboy Press as their first historical romance."

All of her novels are intensely researched. "I don't think there's any better source than an old newspaper file to get the feel of a period and everyday details—to understand what an ordinary day in an ordinary life was like. A reader is interested in people, in what happens to them, their problems and how they solve them. The reader expects to be transported into another world, another reality."

If her new novel, a Nebraska saga, is successful, then the historical West is the area of writing where she wants to stay. Pioneer history, she says, turns her on and she has to be "turned on to her own plot and characters, her own ideas, to write well. "I have to be moved intellectually or emotionally by situations or characters." One of her biggest problems in writing the confessions had been that she didn't "have a lot of sympathy for the heroines. They got into trouble that I thought any sensible person wouldn't!"

It's not unusual for a Virgo such as Barbara (she was born on September 27, 1926) to be unsympathetic to girls who get into careless situations. Virgos prefer a controlled life, and they're concerned with the fine details, such as fashion and style. Costume details are particularly vivid in Barbara's novels.

Inspiration for her characters, plots, and settings comes from real-life people, situations, and places, but they are transformed when they enter her novels. She starts rewriting immediately, finding that roughing out chapters and then polishing them keeps her book moving. She also does a complete plot outline before she starts writing. "I write with a pen because I don't like typewriters, and I aim for 1,000 words a day. I start writing at nine, and on good days, I'm through at three P.M. I'm finally beginning to write the way I'd like to write, after thirty-two years at it. There's a thin line between the amateur and professional writer. It's a thin line, but oh, my, what you have to do to get up to that line."

Proud Passion revolves around beautiful and brave Odette, who was a woman destined for great love and high adventure, both of which she finds when she comes from France to the savage frontier wilderness of the Ohio River country. *Passion's Price* is set in nineteenth-century America, and the heroine is Beata Winfield, lovely young widow, and *Dance of Desire* is the account of a great nineteenth-century flamenco dancer, Nicaela Gallard, who involves herself in treacherous intrigue.

The spinner of these sultry plots says she is accurately characterized "as a loner" who doesn't mind solitude. When not writing she walks, gardens, or swims in her indoor pool.

"I used to think writers were a breed apart," she sighs. "I didn't know they were just ordinary people."

With Max in school, there's *too* much activity around them both to even think of food. They eat out a lot and home-cooked meals are best left unmentioned. Hence, no recipe!

Rebecca Brandewyne

*As long as she lived, she would
remember this wild reunion of their
bodies upon the high seas, separated
from each other for so long, feverish
with hungry passion. The feel of
Rian's weight as he lay atop her,
driving her senses into a heady rapture that swirled up and engulfed her
in the flickering darkness; her sweet
cry of ecstasy proclaiming her surrender as she quivered, trembled,
exploded beneath him like a savage
wind in a raging storm . . .*

—*No Gentle Love*

Rebecca Brandewyne, a blonde, sloe-eyed Kansas author, who
dreamed of becoming another Margaret Mitchell, sold her first
historical romance novel at the ripe young age of twenty-five—
making her one of the youngest published authors in the
romance field today.

Born Rebecca Wadsworth, she selected her own pen-name,
and later made it her legal name, when her first book, *No Gentle
Love*, was sold. "I wrote the book with that name and I love it,"
she explains. "I wanted a name with a historical flair and one
that was unique. I wanted a name that would stick in the minds
of readers," she emphasizes.

No Gentle Love took her two years to complete. At the same
time she was holding down a secretarial job in Wichita to
support herself. The nearly 600-page novel was altered in plot

and characterization through six major rewrites and numerous smaller overhauls.

"A lot of people think historical romance is simply adventure. But it has a story line that revolves around real events. What happens to characters could not happen if that particular phase of history had not occurred," she explains.

The characters in *No Gentle Love* live in the Regency Period, between 1812–1817 in England and Ireland. The plot touches on the Napoleonic Wars, the Irish Revolution and slave trade. It's an era with which she was extremely familiar because of her college minor in history. (Rebecca holds several university degrees and is also a member of MENSA.)

To guarantee authenticity, she absorbs history books, searching for minute details which will enhance her plot and characters, and she studies photographs of a likely setting thoroughly enough to add colorful description to her scenes. Next year she anticipates a trip to Scotland, England, and Ireland to see at last the land about which she has written so well and so successfully.

Originally, Rebecca didn't want to be a writer. She wanted to be a dancer in the Metropolitan Ballet, but her mother wouldn't let her take lessons. "My mother, I think, had ballet confused with weight-lifting; she kept warning me what it would do to my muscles! Now, because I sit at a typewriter all day, my muscles have atrophied, and I'm having to take ballet to build them up again! What a lark! I also belly dance, which is wonderful exercise and lots of fun." (Rebecca wrote for the *Binty Baladi*, the Middle-East magazine for belly dancers around the world.)

Although Rebecca has not yet danced a solo number, she has progressed enough to become a member of a local belly dance troupe. For the first time, at a Wichita dance seminar, she heard her stage name, Ishtar, called out. "Ishtar, in history, was the Babylonian goddess of love and war," explains the author-dancer, "and means morning star. I discovered her in a book— naturally!—and knew that I must take her name for my own at once. She seemed so much like me in the novel I read, and I think every performer should choose a name which represents the spirit of her or his own style of dancing. I hope within the next few years to write a novel in which a belly dancer is the heroine, thereby combining my two loves."

Rebecca's career is running smoothly by comparison to her formative years and adolescence. Her high school years in Wichita were miserable. "My father left Mother and me and my younger sister," she recalls. "There was ten dollars in the house at the time. I didn't have pretty clothes or a car. I wasn't a cheerleader, or anything like that. I was shy. I didn't have many dates. I was in drama classes, but I was never in any of the plays. Once when we were doing *Glass Menagerie* as a class project, I got to play Laura, but I was never in a real production. My grades weren't very good."

Her grades improved sensationally when she entered Wichita State University as a journalism major—"I worked and studied when I was in WSU. I was so busy there wasn't time for anything else. I was secretary to the chairman of the journalism department. At night I worked as a desk clerk at the Ramada Inn East, and on weekends I worked for my mother, who's an insurance broker."

While Rebecca was studying effectively enough to graduate cum laude with departmental honors (she believes she is the first WSU journalism major ever to do so), she worked as a sports writer on the student newspaper; she was secretary-treasurer and later president of Women in Communication; vice-president of Sigma Delta Chi, the professional journalism society; and she was a homecoming queen finalist.

"When I graduated I was offered a job as an intern sports writer with United Press International in New York, but I turned it down because I wanted to stay in the Wichita area, my favorite place in the world. I applied for a job at the *Eagle*, Wichita's newspaper," she says. "But they offered me a job to write obits, and, of course, I turned that down, too."

Instead of starting at the very bottom of the journalistic ladder, she became executive secretary to three IBM marketing executives (they made their own coffee, she says firmly) and began writing a novel in her free time at night.

Rebecca started to write a Western, but after twenty-five pages she abandoned it. "I didn't know anything about Western life," she said. "I set my next attempt in Regency England, in 1812, and I felt comfortable. My second novel, *Forever My Love*, is a historical romance also, but set in Scotland during 1472-1495, a period I could handle. My third novel will again be a historical romance, but this time set primarily in West Texas during 1848-1866. It's not completed yet," she says and sighs. "Once you start writing, it's awful, you have all these novels and all these characters inside your head and they want to get out!"

She's now quit her day-time job. She has an agent, two books are in print, and she's personally publicizing her novels. She also has a boyfriend. "He's quite unique," is all she will say. But it is a fact that he went into the B. Dalton store in Wichita and bought out every copy of her first novel, after which he proceeded to distribute them to *all* his friends. These same friends presented her with a T-shirt that said: #1 WITH US, NO GENTLE LOVE.

However, even with romance alive in her life, Rebecca plans to remain a writer-dancer. "I'm not interested in marriage. I want to develop my career. I'm twenty-six now and there's plenty of time to think about love and that sort of thing later."

Years ago, she had her horoscope charted (Rebecca was born March 4, 1955) and was told that her Piscean sun-sign included a grand trine that indicated success in publishing. "I have since cut my forecasts out of the paper," she says. "You wouldn't believe some of them! On the day of my first autograph party, my horoscope said, 'Today you will produce work you will be proud to sign your name to!' How about that, all you skeptics?"

Rebecca makes absolutely delicious Cornish hens stuffed with wild rice and mushrooms and basted with Amaretto di Saronno, but she's one of those people who cooks to taste—a pinch of this, a dash of that—so her recipe, regretfully, remains secret.

Dixie Browning

*Before she could arrange her de-
fenses in an impregnable barrier, he
had leaned over and gathered her up
in his lap and under the sensuous
impact of his direct gaze, she melted,
throbbing foot, aching head, and all.*

*"How the hell am I supposed to
talk to you when you sit there with
your hair falling around your head,
your lipstick all eaten off, chocolate
on your shirt and a bandaged foot
and all I can think of is how I'm
going to manage to get you in my
bed?"*

—*Renegade Player*

One look at Dixie Browning's marvelous watercolor paintings makes one wonder why the dark-haired author ever
switched to literary endeavors. She has painted all her life, won
dozens of awards, had numerous one-woman shows and exhib-
ited from New York to South Carolina, as well as in traveling
shows across the country. She has taught art, juried shows,
illustrated books, and helped found and served on the board of
directors of one of the oldest co-op galleries on the East Coast.
She also helped organize and served as first president of the
Watercolor Society of North Carolina. Her works hang in
collections throughout the country.

Why did Dixie turn to writing after achieving such notable
success in art? "I was bored," she confesses. "Not being
ambitious, I had no desire to conquer new territory as an artist,
and writing provided the opportunity to start at the bottom and

35

work my way up again . . . plus the satisfaction of creating with a new medium—words." So the spunky lady has pulled in her work from the galleries where she used to exhibit, and her art supplies dry up. She no longer paints; her lovely large studio goes unused. A loss, one would say, but then there's the reading world's gain.

Instead, she sits in front of her typewriter in the living room—pine paneling, fireplace, oriental rug, floor-to-ceiling paintings, sculpture, blown glass—and weaves her glowing romances. She begins soon after seven A.M. and writes for a couple of hours at a stretch, interspersing creativity with household chores, during which she does her thinking. She slows up in the afternoon and seldom writes at night. Dixie reads constantly. "Before, after and almost during my writing," she says with a cheerful grin. She is critical of some authors, envious of others, and stimulated by all in one way or another, she insists.

Between 1980 and 1981 alone, Dixie's name appeared on five Silhouette romances. It's a little known fact that under the name Zoë Dozier she had published two romances for another publisher.

Dixie was born on September 9, 1930, in Elizabeth City, North Carolina, in her grandmother's house. Her father, Maurice (Dick) Burrus, was a professional baseball player at this time. Dixie's mother, Rebecca, flew with her six-week-old daughter to watch him play in Atlanta, and Dixie had the first adventure of her life—the small plane lost a wheel and made a forced landing in a cornfield! But all survived.

Eventually, the family moved to Hatteras, where Dixie's father's ancestors had lived since the year 1700. "My grandfather, Captain Ethelbert Dozier Burrus, who had retired from the sea, shared his home with us. Daddy was a Texaco distributor with irons in a lot of different fires and Mama was, and is, a very lovely, patient woman," Dixie reveals. The family grew. Dixie soon had a brother, Steve, and later on, two sisters, Sara and Mary.

"We grew up on Hatteras Island before the highway was built, before Oregon Inlet was bridged, and before the National Park Service took over much of the land," says Dixie, recalling those halcyon days. "I spent a good part of my early life either in or on the water, and was graduated as valedictorian in a class of three," she sums up.

Dixie's first love, art, was her foremost study for a year at Mary Washington College in Fredericksburg, Virginia, and another year in Richmond. Then, it was a year of nurse's training in Winston-Salem, North Carolina. "It was a random choice," she admits, "which I soon learned was fate! Had I not been there, I would not have met Lee Browning on a blind date. I came home after a day spent in the Blue Ridge mountains and woke up my roommate to tell her I was going to marry him. That was in September, and he didn't ask me until the following March! *Agony!*"

After thirty years of marriage the glow is still there! Dixie says firmly: "I love *Love* more than anything, and my husband more than anyone!" She rapturously recalls their early married years. "We were married in October, 1950, after spending months clearing the land he had bought outside town and building our house. After the honeymoon, we moved into our home—no inner walls, outer walls of insulating board. We sat on stacks of lumber and cooked on a hotplate and *slowly* finished the house," she pauses. "As a matter of fact, it's not finished yet.

"Lee is an electrical engineer, a ramblin' wreck from Georgia Tech, who came from Birmingham originally and has worked for R.J. Reynolds Tobacco Company in Winston-Salem for some thirty-five years. He's a handsome man, a romantic, tender, strong, humorous man and I adore him," she adds lovingly, her brown eyes gleaming.

The couple have two children. Elizabeth, twenty-eight and Leonard, twenty-five. Leonard, dark, bearded, and handsome, lives in Frisco on Hatteras Island, where he built a vacation home from the ground up for his parents. Elizabeth recently met and married Randolph Fox of Durham, North Carolina. It was a storybook romance, Dixie says. In fact, their story gave her another idea for a novel. "After my daughter graduated from the University of North Carolina, she remained in Chapel Hill to work, and at age twenty-seven finally bought her own house in a small town called Bynum, some thirteen miles from Chapel

Hill. I wrote a story about a woman, my Elizabeth's age, who got sick and tired of being match-made by friends and family and bought herself a three-room house in Bynum and subsequently met and married the hero. It's called *Island on the Hill,* and Silhouette bought it.

"I enjoy writing about familiar locations, as well as familiar occupations," she emphasizes. "I can then concentrate on the interaction between hero and heroine and spend less time on research and travel."

Dixie's birth sign, Virgo, signifies the realization of hopes. People dominated by this influx are frequently calm, confident and contented. They are also likely to be reflective, studious, and extremely fond of reading—all of which may be said to apply to this charming author. Also for ten years she explored the occult extensively. "I did astrological charts for years, in order to prove to myself, one way or the other, its validity," she says. "I'm now a believer, but not a fanatic. I believe in the Edgar Cayce phenomenon, in reincarnation, and also that most of what's been written about those subjects in the recent past is bunk, ground out to editorial specifications."

Dixie seldom, if ever, cooks with recipes. She loves to cook seafood and one of her favorite dishes is baked fish. She is happy to share her method.

BAKED FISH

A large flounder or sheepshead or other baking fish, cleaned, scored deeply on either side and placed in a baking pan, is seasoned well with salt and papper and surrounded by whole potatoes and onions. Strips of bacon or thinly sliced salt pork are placed on top and water is added about halfway up sides of vegetables. Lid is placed on for first half of cooking . . . some 30 or so minutes, depending on size of fish . . . then removed so that meat on top browns. Baste occasionally as it bakes at 350 degrees until potatoes are done.

Serve with coleslaw, made with coarsely chopped cabbage, dressed with mayonnaise, vinegar, salt, pepper and dill weed, and with hot buttered cornbread.

Shirlee Busbee

*She was incrediby desirable to him,
her body an alabaster and pink altar
that he paid homage to, his own
body hardening and tightening with
delicious hunger to feel himself lost
again in the hot silken sheaf of her.*

—*Renegade's Lady*

When Shirlee Busbee was a secretary at the County Parks
Office in Fairfield, California, she had a friend in the secretarial
pool, a dark beauty named Rosemary Rogers, a divorcee with
several children. Although Shirlee was married she had no
children, but the two women had another subject aside from
family to discuss on their lunch hours and coffee breaks. For
example, they were both avid readers of romantic novels.
Rosemary, however, was actually trying to write a romantic
book, at her daughter's suggestion, and often Shirlee watched
her typing some of her manuscript on the office typewriter.

"One day," recalls Shirlee, "Rosemary came to the office and
announced the sale of her first novel to Avon Books. I was so
excited for her. That was when I decided that I should get
around to writing a book. I'd dreamed about it for years. My
husband had encouraged me to join the Famous Writer's
Correspondence School, but I took only five lessons in three
years!"

Rosemary couldn't have been more helpful. "When I finally finished my first book, *Gypsy Lady*, I dedicated it to Rosemary because she nagged the devil out of me to finish it."

The Parks Director of Fairfield County now claims he's going to buy the typewriter that both women used in the office and put it in his own private museum. "He's going to buy the desk, too," reports Shirlee merrily. "And he has Rosemary's old white office sweater that she wore. I kept my old white sweater, but he looked so crestfallen when I took it, I may relent and let him have it! I can see it now—The Rogers-Busbee Historical Museum. See the Famous Typewriter! See the Good Luck Sweaters! See all for fifty cents! Groups any size a dollar! Not really," she adds, "but sometimes I wonder. . . ."

Shirlee was born in San Jose, California, on August 9, 1941. She has all the traits of Leo—broadminded, generous, and brave, and not afraid to follow her own intuition. Leos are said to have a special affinity with Sagittarians, and not only is her husband Howard (a strong, blond Clint Eastwood type) a Sagittarian, but so is Rosemary Rogers and several other friends in the romance world, such as Kathryn Falk and Bertrice Small. The group stays in close touch by phone.

Shirlee's home in Fairfield is orderly but creative. She has two loving men in her life who support her career and keep her life running smoothly—her husband and her father, Gat Egan, a perfect Southern gentleman and a fabulous cook—but that isn't the end of the household. "For the rest of the crew, there are three schnauzers; Schatzy, who started it all; Fritz, my father's dog; and Baron, who is the result of Schatzy and Fritz becoming romantically involved. Then there is Gypsy, a shepherd-coyote mix, so named because she appeared like a gypsy in the night, and old Winters, a golden labrador. There is also a calico cat who only appears after dark and whose only entrance into our house is through the bedroom window."

Shirlee leads a quiet life. "I think most writers do—if life is too exciting there is no time to write!" Shirlee declares. "Up until about three years ago, Howard was an upholsterer, but now he is my manager, errand boy, secretary, and Man-Friday. Without him, it would be impossible for me to write one word.

We work very much as a team, Howard proofreading the rough drafts of the manuscript, and lately even typing up the final draft for me. He is a man of many talents. For instance, he just finished adding on what we call simply, 'the room.' It is a room for all reasons—my desk and typewriter are out there, my reference bookcase, his reading chair, my stereo and records and a couch for me to stop and grab a quick nap if I wish. It has skylights, a woodstove, and paneled walls—makes you feel you are in a small cabin in the woods. Schatzy and Baron keep me company, and I guess provide some light relief when I get too deeply involved in a book. It is very hard to concentrate when a little black nose is suddenly shoved under your arm and a rubber bone is dropped in your lap."

While Shirlee is working on a book she usually has classical music playing in the background. "My very favorite selection is a piece entitled *Concierto de Aranjuez*. I have several different recordings of it, and I put them all on at the same time and listen over and over and over again," she says and sighs. Her hazel eyes take on a dreamy quality.

"Writing is not something that I trained for," admits Shirlee. "It is something that just happened. My good friend Tom Huff (readers know him as Jennifer Wilde) says I do it by osmosis—I haven't decided whether he is paying me a compliment or not. At any rate, I have been a voracious reader all of my life. When I was about twelve, my mom used to send me to the store to pick out her reading materials, because as she said, 'You know what I like.' I always picked out historicals—Frank Yerby, Frank Slaughter, Jan Westcott, etc. And I guess because of that it isn't surprising that I wrote historicals."

Shirlee's favorite period of history is hard to pin down. But it would have to be either the Regency era in England or the Norman invasion of England. "I love English history. I think in one of my other lives I must have been an Englishwoman—of the nobility, naturally!"

Writing a book is an agonizing experience for her. She worries continuously. "I am always wondering," she confesses, "if the story is exciting enough, will the readers like it as well as the previous one, etc. And my characters drive me wild—they all

41

have minds of their own and there are times I could cheerfully strangle them for being either too arrogant or for the women being such complete ninnies! I try very hard to be accurate with my history, from the events that take place, to the clothing and furniture, and I spend a fortune on research books—always thinking of the next book ahead. The book I just finished, *Renegade's Lady*, dealt with the Council House Massacre in San Antonio, Texas, in 1840. Well, not really, that's just the background," she continues. "It really deals with Rafael Santana, a part-Comanche, part-Spanish hero, and Beth Ridgeway, an aristocratic Englishwoman. Plus Sebastian Savage, Jason's youngest son (Jason of *Gypsy Lady*). He is also on the scene, certain that he is in love with Beth. Rafael just happens to be his cousin—sort of!" she adds, with her delightful smile. (Shirlee has the famous Lauren Hutton tooth gap.)

As each book progresses and gets nearer and nearer to the rough draft being finished, everyone at the Busbee household gets involved with it. "If it weren't for the two fabulous men in my life I wouldn't get *anything* done! I don't even have to worry about such mundane things as dinner dishes—Howard and Dad argue whose turn it is and I merely waft my way out of the kitchen and let them decide. Obviously, I *never* cook dinner, either," she says and grins. In a writer's world, Shirlee seems to have the best of everything. So far her earnings have enabled her to invest in a beautiful spread of wilderness in northern California, presently their vacation spot. They have plans to develop the property and perhaps go into animal husbandry.

Shirlee is constantly on a diet. "I bet I've lost 500 pounds and gained it back too! I am lazy, incredibly so! My idea of heaven is a stack of Harlequins, a chaise, and a Diet Pepsi." Within the family she is known as "Bunny," but not because she is small and cuddly—"I'm 5'10" and, well, chubby," reports the curvaceous brunette—"but because there happens to be *two* Shirlee Busbees, well not quite . . . there is Shir*lee*, me, and Shirley, Howard's brother's wife. So to save confusion, I was nicknamed Bunny because of the time when I was raising Giant Flemish rabbits."

As for her future, Shirlee "Bunny" Busbee hopes that when she is eighty she will still be writing books.

One of Shirlee's favorite recipes is a particular dish served to Beth, in *Renegade's Lady*, when she is visiting in New Orleans. "My heroines always eat so well," Shirlee comments with a grin.

CHICKEN DUXELLES

8 chicken breasts (wing
  attached)
2 tbs. lemon juice
2 tsp. thyme
Salt to taste

Freshly ground black pepper
½ stick butter
¼ cup Madeira (optional)

DUXELLES:

12 oz. fresh mushrooms, finely
  chopped
2 tbs. butter
3 tbs. finely chopped onions

2 tbs. finely chopped parsley
Salt to taste
Pepper to taste

SAUCE:

Butter that remains in baking
  dish
2 tbs. flour
1 beef bouillon cube

1½ cup whipping cream
1 cup slivered almonds,
  toasted
Garnish: parsley and paprika

Prepare and season chicken at least 1 hour before cooking. Skin and debone breasts, removing 2 pinions but leaving main wing bone. Rub with lemon juice, thyme, salt and pepper. Preheat oven to 400 degrees and melt ½ stick butter in a large, shallow baking dish. Arrange breasts in a single layer; turn each breast once to coat with butter. Add Madeira, cover lightly with wax paper; cook 10–12 minutes. Transfer chicken to warm serving dish, wing bone down. Reserve butter.

In a skillet prepare duxelles by combining mushrooms, butter, onions, parsley, salt, and pepper. Cook until mushroom liquid disappears, approximately 10 minutes. Spoon duxelles onto chicken pieces equally. Keep warm while making sauce.

43

To baking dish add 2 tablespoons flour; stir and cook 3 minutes without browning. Add boullion cube and cream, and boil rapidly to thicken, stirring constantly. Spoon over chicken; top with almonds, parsley, and paprika. Serve.

Barbara Cartland

As the music of the waltz grew more insistent, Gisela put her arms round Miclos's neck and he crushed her against him until it was hard to breathe. Then he lifted her onto the bed and a moment later was lying beside her, his lips on hers; the violins were playing very, very softly: "My heart is dancing, now you are mine!"

—The Waltz of Hearts

Some pass her books by; some can't get enough of them. But it's impossible to be neutral about Barbara Cartland, the standard bearer of true romance and perhaps the most prolific author alive.

There is something undeniably cheerful in an octogenarian who favors Norman Hartnell pink gowns and white Rolls-Royces, and who recently had a pamphlet printed to inform the curious press of her life's achievements, not the least of which is herself. Close up, she looks a little like a sugarplum fairy. Her hair is platinum, her eyeshadow delicious turquoise, and her mouth the proverbial rosy lips most living legends favor. Her visual flamboyance is very appealing as though she has stopped the clock at an hour that suits her person admirably. Her fifty-two-year-old daughter, Raine, still calls her, "Mummy," and it is through Raine—a divorcee, she married Lady Di's divorced daddy and became Countess Spencer—that the doyenne of romantic novelists has become a step-grandmother of the Royal Family.

If Princess Diana of Wales did not exist, Barbara could have easily invented her, a lady of unsullied reputation, an archetype, in fact, of every Cartland heroine in every one of her romances (sales reached 150 million last year). All Cartland heroines are virgins, nineteen, and ready to open up like flowers, but only on the wedding night in the last chapter. And then, of course, a discreet veil is drawn over the actual act, which takes place, doubtless, under piles of snowy sheets, and lacy nightgowns.

As she said recently, "You can't get more naked than naked. These days people are quite worn out with pornography, poor darlings. They're terrified that they're abnormal if they don't have intercourse upside down swinging from a chandelier."

Miss Cartland says, too, she feels very sorry for young girls at the moment because now, "If a man buys a girl a good dinner he expects her to bounce into bed with him. She's supposed to give her all for an evening out—in my day we expected a bit more than that."

She insists vehemently that women's liberation won't admit that men can enjoy sex like a good meal and forget it, whereas women get emotionally involved and miserable.

"That's why I'm selling millions of paperbacks to women who are on Valium because they're having such a rotten time in real life. They don't want to read about the kitchen sink, they can look at that any time they're peeling potatoes. I'm their escape. I give them glamor, beautiful clothes, and the marvelous attentive men they are starving for."

Though Barbara writes primarily for female readers and rarely hesitates to speak for all womankind, she is no friend of feminists. "I don't like most women," she admits without hesitation. "I can't bear ugly women who sit about doing nothing but waiting to play bridge. All my life I have thought men were something very special. It is a treat to be alone with them. I prefer a dumb man to an intelligent woman."

If Barbara Cartland is dated—"some sort of marvelous British heirloom" by her own description—her value in the market-place is still soaring. Her books have been sold to TV and the movies, her name appears on a romantic line of perfume, fabric, and home decorating items, and her home and the Spencer estate are part of a special tour.

What is it like to be Barbara Cartland? To live at Canfield Place, the fourteen-room mansion in Hertfordshire, England, the former playground of Beatrix Potter? Here's a typical day in the life of this successful author of romantic fiction.

"I wake up at 8:00 A.M., when the gardener buzzes me so he can take Duke, the black Labrador, out. He is one of the Queen's Sandringham strain and always stays in my room at night. The Pekinese, Twi-Twi, sleeps at the end of my four-poster.

"My old maid, Purcell, who has been with me for thirty-three years and is now in her eighties, comes in about 8:45 A.M. with breakfast which Reeves, the butler, has carried upstairs for her.

"I get up, do my hair and put on makeup simply because I like looking nice and I believe in self-discipline. I complete my face in a much more complicated way after my bath at 10:45 A.M. I don't mind admitting I wear false eyelashes!

"I eat the same thing for breakfast every day: an egg, my bran—I'm a great believer in bran—a tablespoonful of honey, and ginseng tea. I take all my vitamin pills—usually seventy or eighty. I read six newspapers.

"I answer all my letters when Mrs. Waller, my chief private secretary, arrives at 9:00 A.M.—there's no question of me staying in bed because so much has to be done and everyone depends on me to keep things working. We deal with telephone calls and my urgent things. Today it was doing the week's menus with the chef, Nigel Gordon. Then I see the other secretaries, and Mrs. Elliott takes the 8,000 or so words I dictated to her the previous afternoon to be xeroxed. We have to photostat everything at least seven times.

"Really, the mornings here are like a bad Noel Coward play. Telephones, secretaries, and dogs all demanding attention.

"My maid organizes what I wear and my hairdresser comes in several times a week. I wear a lot of what Sir Norman Hartnell calls 'Cartland Pink.' It is a warm, happy color when you get old. I hate beiges, they make a woman look like a baked potato.

"After my bath I use ice on my face. It is so much better than a

47

facelift. Not on the cheeks (it breaks the veins because it is too strong) but on the eyes and under the chin.

"I use what I call a working girl's makeup, which lasts all day, and I don't necessarily have to touch up in the evenings. I have a sun-proof cream as a foundation from Elizabeth Arden and special powder from Cyclax—who are the Queen's suppliers—because my skin is so pale.

"At night I always use a vitamin FF cream, which is the only thing I know that takes away the crepiness on the eyelids.

"I take the dogs out for a walk before lunch, and do my yoga breathing to freshen my mind. I lunch alone; today it was cold cuts, mixed salad, and Brie washed down with water.

"At 12:45 I shut myself away with Mrs. Elliott to whom I dictate whatever chapter I am doing. I dictate or write between 6,000 and 9,000 words by 3:30 P.M., lying on the sofa, swaddled in a white coverlet. I then think about what I want to write and ask my subconscious for a plot—and one is provided. I always find the first chapter the most difficult to write. Toward the end of a chapter I will ask Mrs. Elliott, 'How many words?' The Labrador (a gift from a longtime friend, the late Lord Mountbatten) and Peke recognize the sentence and almost immediately jump up, and we go for a walk through the kitchen garden where Peter Rabbit lived. The hole in the wall is still there exactly as it was in Beatrix Potter's day when her grandfather owned the house.

"We have tea at 4:00 P.M.—usually a biscuit and some cake. Then I work through until 7:00 P.M. researching. I have a hot bath—two hot water bottles put in my bed—and I retire after putting on my FF cream and putting in my Lady Jane flat curlers. I go to sleep about 10:30.

"I don't go out much in the week except perhaps sometimes for a television interview. The weekends I reserve for my family, (two sons, one daughter, and their offspring. Son Ian acts as her personal business manager). Yes, I work very hard, but what else does someone of my age do? I don't play bridge or golf, and with four permanent and six subsidiary secretaries, several dogs, a house and estate to run, I just keep working."

Like her fictional heroines, Barbara Cartland was a virgin

("Of course!") when she married wealthy Alexander McCorquodale at London's fashionable St. Margaret's, Westminster, in 1927. "In those days we were all terribly innocent and pure," she says. "Remember, there was no such thing as the Pill. The difference between the lady and the prostitute was enormous."

A certain soap opera plotline ran through her own wedding. It was at the ceremony that the bridegroom's cousin, Hugh McCorquodale, first saw Barbara and, as she tells it, fell in love with her on the spot. The marriage of Barbara and Alexander "was disastrous." When she sued for divorce five years later, he cross-petitioned, citing Hugh as corespondent. The allegation was dismissed in court. She calls it a "spiteful, dirty trick." She and her second husband Hugh enjoyed a wonderful romance, and were "blissfully happy" until his untimely death twenty-seven years later.

Barbara Cartland lives up to her title, the Queen of Health, in England. Not only does she write and promote her books on health, nutrition, menopausal replacement therapy, but she practices what she preaches. Every day she swallows more than seventy vitamins, special calcium tablets, and her own formula for "brain pills"—vitamin E, vitamin B6, and ginseng.

The English press and television have always treasured her, but now it seems she's becoming somewhat of a national landmark, too. Recently, she and her blonde curls were encased in a life-size, waxlike substance at Madame Tussaud's museum, although the resemblance could stand improvement. At the unveiling, the museum director explained why they chose Barbara Cartland: "We at Tussaud's today have a difficult time trying to find suitable feminine lady figures even in these days of feminism and women's lib."

When all is said and done, this remarkable woman, a cross, some say, between the Queen Mother of England and Zsa Zsa Gabor, will probably have the last word. She admits that in reality the kind of romance in her books might be a crashing bore in real life since it all turns out the same. "But," she stresses, "romance in life makes an important difference. Never, *never*, run away from it."

Meanwhile, her virgins are still big business, so says Miss

Cartland, who has other reasons for choosing her historical settings. "It's difficult to portray virgins in modern dress," she admits. "Furthermore, I prefer a period when men were not wearing wigs. It's unattractive to have a young man taking off his wig in bed!"

The one question on the lips of every Cartland fan is, "Has she known such men as romantic as her heroes?" The answer is "Never! I always liked the dark, handsome cynical type. But all I ever got were the fair-haired, blue-eyed stupid ones," she says, turning her beautiful jewellike eyes from the chilly prospect and gazing at her reflection in the Victorian mirror, ensconced by the blazing log fire and surrounded by her favorite Pekineses.

Barbara Cartland was born July 9, 1901, under the sign of Cancer, ruled by the moon. It's not surprising that Barbara is content in domestic situations of all kinds, real and fantasy. This sun sign's almost extreme domesticity can place them among the happiest of marriage partners, for they like to have houses as much as human ties. Cooking goes hand in hand with their love of hearth and home. Barbara's chef, Nigel Gordon, prepares a wonderful French Strawberry Shortcake, which Barbara recommends as food for lovers.

SABLEE AUX FRAISES
(French Strawberry Shortcake)

2 cups plain flour
7 ozs. sugar
13 ozs. unsalted butter
1 egg yolk
2 tbsp. of heavy cream
1 qt. strawberries (or raspberries)

Mix first five ingredients together. Working with the palms of the hands, not the fingers. Place the mixture in the refrigerator for at least an hour. Roll it out to a thickness of an eighth of an inch and cut into three round pieces. Place each piece on a baking tin and put into a 400 degree oven. Be careful, as the pastry should bake in 4 to 5 minutes. Allow it to cool. Clean the strawberries or raspberries thoroughly. Mix them into some raspberry sauce consisting of raspberry seedless jam mixed with some syrup. Alternate the three layers of shortcake with two layers of strawberries or raspberries. Spread the rest of the sauce on top and cover with cream.

Jayne Castle

He was provoking her now with little darting forays of his hand and tiny, almost-painful kisses. She was no longer sure which of them was trying to drive the other insane and she wasn't sure she cared...

—A Man's Protection

With her long brown tresses parted in the middle and gently sloping over her shoulders, her wide-eyed look of innocence, and her pretty dimpled face, Jayne Castle looks more like a naive teenager than a successful author. But she is. Very much so. Yet she is young in her outlook and attitude. Ask her what she likes, and she will list her first choices: "Jeans, Country-Western music, pasta, wine, the stockmarket, and the color yellow." Of course, no need to mention that her first love is writing; in particular, romantic novels for the Ecstasy series.

"The Ecstasy series is based on a sensuous, passionate approach to the romance, one that accepts that red-blooded heroes and heroines do make love before the last chapter and sometimes before they're married! It's absorbing and exciting to create one of these stories, and I thoroughly enjoy it," she says. Interestingly, Jayne finds it difficult to describe the overpowering urge she feels to put her romantic fantasies on paper. Nor does she have any desire to write other types of material. In college, Jayne admits, she found it was an effort to put together a twenty-page paper. "But when it comes to romantic fantasy, I can put together a twenty-page chapter in a day.

"I went through the changes produced by the Women's Movement in the late sixties and early seventies and I came out of it with very strong notions of equality and free choice," Jayne reveals. "But it didn't kill the fantasies in my head." Obviously, she is enchanted by the fantasy world, which she enters and leaves at will. When she is working on a novel, she becomes temporarily fascinated with whatever absorbs her heroes and heroines.

Jayne has two younger brothers and finds that their delightful senses of humor occasionally show up in her heroes. In addition—and rather to her surprise—the father of the heroine in her first book for the Ecstasy series, *The Gentle Pirate*, bore more than a passing resemblance to her father, Donald H. Castle, a marine and holder of a Navy Cross from World War II. "Everything I know about marines and put into that book probably came from him by osmosis," she says laughing. Her father noted the resemblance, and commented that he could have taught the hero, Simon, a few things.

The vivacious Jayne lauds her busy mother, Alberta, who has retired to Tucson, Arizona. "I have the greatest admiration for her, having set about creating a whole new life after raising three kids. Her interests are as varied as any of my heroines," she says.

Although Jayne read voraciously as a child, she insists that she wasn't "one of those precocious kids who keep diaries and write poems." She received her Bachelor's degree in history from the University of California and a Master's in librarianship from San Jose State University in 1971. She worked as a librarian before quitting to write full time, and supposes she chose that profession initially because it provided the perfect excuse for delving lightly, or deeply, into all sorts of information, literature and philosophy.

Romantic that she is, Jayne and her husband, Frank A. Krentz, an engineer, eloped to Canada in 1971. Jayne admits that she has drawn upon his expertise on more than one occasion when writing about unfamiliar fields. "He doesn't always agree with the way my heroes behave," she grins bemusedly. "I'll never forget his remarks after reading a bedroom scene in which I had the hero gallantly walk out and leave the heroine alone for the night. He told me that wasn't very realistic, that a man in love with a woman would *never* have walked away from a provocative situation like that. I told him we romance authors don't worry *overmuch* about realism."

If anyone complains about the "sameness" of romantic novels, she has a ready and reasonable response. "A good romance can incorporate a variety of the more interesting and powerful of human emotions, from humor and love to hate and desire. It doesn't really matter if some themes are repeated over and over again because that's *exactly* what our own inner fantasies do—repeat themselves in different guises."

Jayne willingly confesses that she has been a romance addict since 1972 when she discovered that there was a genre much more suited to her particular fantasies than Gothics. Up until then she had stuck with science fiction and adventure novels, which she hasn't completely abandoned, though there is no question that romance novels play a special role in her life. She began writing in 1973—a romance which never sold—and kept her ego intact by selling a few trade articles and some confession stories. The sale of her first romantic novel occurred in 1979, and was followed with four other successful romances in rather quick succession. "From 1973 to 1980, writing was a fairly unsuccessful hobby. Now it's a satisfying career," Jayne says happily.

Seated at her typewriter in her lovely apartment, Jayne can look across Lake Washington at Mercer Island and the city of Seattle. "The Northwest is a young, vigorous place and we're enjoying it very much, volcanoes and all," she says, her bright hazel eyes sparkling. She and her husband have lived in a variety of places, including the Virgin Islands, the Southeast, the Pacific Northwest, and California. But the state of Washington has a very special appeal to both of them.

Cooking also appeals to Jayne, particularly when she prepares the following:

PAELLA

This is a *Spanish* dish, not to be confused with the food of Mexico or the Southwestern United States. Serve it with a good California Chardonnay wine on the table and some sensuous classical guitar on the stereo. A crisp salad and hot sourdough bread go nicely.

1 cup cooked chicken, cut in 2-inch pieces
4 cups hot chicken stock
¼ cup olive oil
1 clove garlic
2 cups uncooked rice
As much saffron as you can afford. The stuff's expensive.
   (1–2 tsp.)
1 cup fresh peas
6–8-½ inch slices of chorizo or other zesty, hard sausage
Approximately 1½ lbs. raw shrimp
18–20 clams in their shells

PROCEDURE

In a large, lidded casserole or *paellero*, heat the garlic in the olive oil. Remove garlic. Over moderate heat add the rice, stirring until lightly browned. Dissolve the saffron in the hot stock and add the stock to the rice. Add the peas, sausage, and chicken. Cover and bake at 350 degrees for 20 minutes or until most of the liquid has been absorbed. Add, arranging attractively, the shrimp and clams. Cover and steam until shrimp is pink and clams have popped open—about 10 minutes.

Serves 4 to 6 people.

Elaine Raco Chase

The friction of hard flesh against silken skin brought tremors of pleasure washing over Casey like a warm slow tide. She felt the hardening intrusion of his male body and eagerly let her pliant form absorb the bold thrust of his virility.

—*Double Occupancy*

Elaine Raco Chase writes romances that feature "spunky, competent, witty" women. The heroines she creates "can take care of themselves in any situation." Where does this author find her inspiration for such dynamic characters? She readily admits to being just as able as any of the women she writes about.

"I've had a lot of interesting things happen in my life," she says, blue eyes flashing. "I've beaten up a mugger; broken two feet at the same time; crashed into my husband's car with my own; blown up stoves, coffee pots, and a television." In addition, she can scuba dive, ice skate, ski, surf, and fish. She has even gone up in a hot air balloon and climbed a mountain, and though she decries violence, she has shot a gun and a bow and arrow.

Elaine doesn't have to travel for excitement. It seems she gets plenty right in her own home town, which presently is Ormond Beach, Florida. You are likely to find her there, dressed in

T-shirt and jeans, if not writing, then possibly doing house-work, painting, or cooking for her family: husband Gary D. Chase, and children Marlayna Ruth, seven, and Gary Marc, ten.

"A lot of people ask how my husband has handled all this," the blonde, 5'7" author smiles. "Well, trying to be a housewife-mother-author and wife is 'Stress City.' When I first started writing romances I got no encouragement at all—not even from my own mother. My husband was always saying it was an unrealistic dream. Even when an agent picked me up, he was skeptical. He didn't even admit he might be wrong after I had signed my first contract and received an advance. But things have changed," she says with a grin. "Now he'd like to chain me to a typewriter."

With her usual humorous outlook, Elaine jokes about her neighbors' reaction to a successful author in their midst. "Most of my friends and neighbors seem disappointed in me," she chuckles, recalling her spicy plots. "They expect a romance writer to wear chiffon and pearls and to eat chocolates." But Elaine prefers to be her own informal self—no airs for her.

Like many girls, Elaine was a late bloomer. "I went through high school without attending any of the proms and having only one date," she reveals. After graduation, however, she found herself catapulted into the working world, and a whole new dimension of life opened up before her. Leaving her home in Rotterdam, New York, she traveled to New York City, where she found life far more exciting and challenging. Working at an advertising agency, her career as a professional writer began— her talents focusing on the task of selling a product in sixty seconds or less.

As a result of taking a journalism course, she started to put together her first contemporary category romance, *Rules of the Game*. Since she had done very little traveling, her first novel was set in upstate New York, where she was raised.

Elaine does a lot of research on her novels, and not just on locales. "I read magazines like *Psychology Today, New Woman, Self,* and *Ms.;* those that can tell me what women want to hear about, what they feel and what their problems are. I also read some men's magazines to get their point of view. It helps to make fictional characters become so alive that people actually feel they know them."

Each new novel becomes a fascinating challenge for this talented writer, though she readily admits to getting the fabled writer's block when confronted with "250 blank pages that must be filled with cleverness and sensuality," as she puts it. When she begins to question whether it's all worth the blood, sweat, and tears that she puts on each page, Elaine is likely to receive an encouraging letter from someone she's never met who has read one of her novels. "And that makes it all worthwhile," she says.

Elaine and her husband and children recently moved from New York to Florida and had a home built with a den just for the writer, filled with bookcases on two walls, a typing desk, a working desk, and a telephone that, she says, "is answered under protest."

It's a neat, efficient kind of arrangement, well suited to Elaine's quiet, methodical and reliable Virgoan personality. Born August 31, 1949, Elaine considers herself "a true Virgo." Characteristic of her sign, Elaine frequently knows what her children are going to do *before* they do it. "They think I have ESP," she says.

Though Elaine hates interruptions when she's writing, she does keep the television set going. "Even as a busy student with homework (she graduated high school with top honors) I always had the television on," she says. "I love to listen to the daytime 'soaps'—their dialogue makes *mine* seem like jewels!"

As the author of contemporary romances, she finds it difficult to read other authors of that genre. "I was weaned on detectives and mysteries and am still an avid fan," she confides. In fact, she has been working on a major suspense novel that takes place in Miami and the Keys.

Elaine tries to type ten pages a day. "They may not all be gold, but it keeps the creative juices flowing and makes writer's block less habit forming," she says. "I try to keep regular hours, but I'm a great procrastinator," she admits. "I once hung twelve rolls of wallpaper just as an excuse not to write that day." Usually the meticulous Virgo author cleans and tidies her

59

house, throws in the laundry, dusts, etc., and finally hits the typewriter about ten each morning. "My son arrives home from school at noon. I break for lunch with him and we chat; then I work until four composing directly on the typewriter." Research notes are done in longhand. "I get very involved with each book," she confesses, "doing hours of research not just on locales but reading articles on character traits that involve my heroines and heroes."

Success hasn't changed her life, she insists. "I still do all my own cooking, cleaning, redecorating, gardening, and shopping," she says without complaint. When it comes to food, Elaine admits a penchant for seafood—clams, oysters, and rock shrimp, although she recently fell in love with Chicken Napoli, which she describes as "pounded baked boneless breast of chicken smothered in mozzarella and strips of bacon." Full recipe upon request!

Marion Chesney

Constance finally freed her mouth and whispered, "Here? I—I m-mean . . . you can't want to . . ."

"Oh, yes I can," said Philip, lowering her onto the floor. His hand ran down the length of her body, making her shiver, and stopped at the lace of the pantalets. "Do these peculiar things go very far up?" he whispered with his mouth against her breast.

"Only as far as the knee."

"Good," said Lord Philip Cautry, "because I mean to go so much further than that. How easily they come undone! Perhaps a sensible fashion after all."

—*The Constant Companion*

Marion Chesney—who is "domiciled" now in Brooklyn, but still retains the delightful traces of a Scottish brogue—is better known by some of her other Regency pen-names. When closing a letter to an admiring reader, she inscribes at the bottom of the parchment, "From all of us! Jennie Tremaine, Ann Fairfax, Helen Crampton, Marion Chesney, and Marion Gibbons."

Like her heroine Jean in *Regency Gold*, who always dreamed of taking part in a romantic situation, Marion, too, was always a bit of a Walter Mitty. As a child growing up in Glasgow, Scotland, she lived a good part of her life between the pages of books, the heros and heroines seeming more real to her than anybody in the outside world.

61

Marion was born under the zodiac's communication symbol —Gemini (June 10, 1936)—and destiny always led her toward a writing career. But the thrill of being a novelist was not hers until an accident of fate—the cost of her young son's tuition— changed her life as she neared her fortieth birthday.

"When I was nineteen," explains Marion, "I had my start in writing by being thrown in at the deep end. I was working as a bookseller in a book shop in Glasgow, and during my coffee break at a local restaurant, I was joined by one of my customers. She said she was features editor for the *Scottish Daily* and needed a reporter to cover an amateur show out in the sticks because the editor's nephew was in it. Trembling, I said, 'I'll do it for you.' She said, 'Have you done any writing?' 'Oh, lots,' I said, lying in my teeth. She looked doubtful, but it was beginning to snow and all the reporters were in the nearest pub, so I got the assignment. That was the beginning. I worked my way up to leading theater critic of the paper.

"I left my job to get married," continues Marion, and she proceeds to weave a tale as exciting and perilous as a plot of her novels! "My husband is a man named Harry Scott Gibbons, who was a spy for British Intelligence in the Middle East, back in '57, but that, as Rudyard Kipling would say, is another story. He was offered the editorship of the *Oyster Bay Guardian*, of all things, and we moved to America and ended up in Brooklyn— broke. My husband was working on the tabloid, but what with inflation and so on, we could not raise the money to pay St. Ann's (a private school in Brooklyn Heights) for my child's education."

The headmaster had given Marion a year to pay, but she couldn't find a job in 1977, no matter how hard she tried. "I was even turned down by the local supermarket!" she recalls. To escape from all this harsh reality, she began reading Regency novels by the ton.

"I had always been a fan of Georgette Heyer," explains the fair-haired, gray-eyed author in a sincere breathless, low voice. "And I found some of the language in the American ones very strange and unconvincing. For instance—'Let us walk, the house is but a few blocks hence,' says the Duke to the Duchess.

So I said—very arrogantly, I admit, and you'll have to forgive me but it was the arrogance born of sheer desperation and a wilting ego—'I can do better than that!' and my husband, Harry, said, 'Well, for goodness sakes, why don't you?

"Harry has a friend on his newspaper who gave me the name of his literary agent. The time to pay the school tuition was breathing down my neck and the wolf had got its paw inside the door," Marion recalls. "I wrote the first fifty pages of *Regency Gold*, plus the plot, and sent it to the agent. She sent it to Fawcett who bought it on the spot and the advance was what I owed St. Ann's School down to the last penny."

Since then, fifteen contracts from four different publishers have come from all over. She's also published in Britain, all under her maiden name, Marion Chesney, and in Italy and Germany.

"I am no longer so snooty about American writers and have a great admiration for them," she confesses. "I think I am very lucky not to have to worry about baby sitters and be able to work at home. And that gratitude, plus a great deal of pleasure in my work, keeps me glued to the typewriter."

Regency novel-writing comes easily for Marion. She knows the scenes and dialogue she writes because older members of her family have similar speech patterns. She can write a Regency romance in about three months, and she generally does. "The English Regency (1811–1819) captures my imagination with the colorfulness of the age. It was an age of practical jokers, of outrageous snobbery, of beautiful clothes for both men and women, and of great entertainment among the rich. Oddly, enough, Regency women were no more chaste than the women of other periods. We make them virgins because that's what our readers want."

Marion's position in the Regency novel world is a lofty one these days. Her books receive the best reviews both in America and England. She's praised for "her high-spirited romance, and some genuinely comic scenes." (So saith the *London Daily Express* in a review of *My Dear Duchess* and *Henrietta*.)

Scrupulous accuracy is probably her most frequent praise. Her bookshelves overflow with Regency reference books. "For my novel *Quadrille*, which takes place on the eve of the battle of Waterloo and revolves around four couples who meet at the Duchess of Richmond's ball, I read four detailed histories of the battle of Waterloo," says Marion. "I was interested in slang, small talk, turns of phrase, and the clothes. I don't believe readers want a history lesson. For the Duchess's ball, I concentrated on the type of silk hangings, the chandeliers, the sort of flowers, what they had for supper, the dresses they wore—that sort of thing.

"I am concerned with the humor of the period. The Regency period was a time for quite horrible puns. People would polish up their puns over and over, as if going into show business. It was the beginning of snobbery in British society, the age of elegance, of dandys, when women wore less clothes than ever before or since. In the middle of winter they'd wear a muslin gown, a scant petticoat, stockings rolled up at the knee, and they would dampen their dresses to cling to the body. Women were expected then to be very feminine and useless. The men were very masculine. Which means the men can come and take the heroine away from it all!" concludes Marion. She gives a ravishing smile that would have broken the heart of even "Prinnie" in Regency England.

Currently, Marion is taking her first step away from her Regency genre. She's starting a four-book family saga under the name of Charlotte Ward. Husband Harry, too, "has taken up the pen," says Marion proudly. "He's just had two spy stories published, *Fools Gamble* and *The Peacock*, under the name of Scott Gibbons. Harry should know about spies!" she adds knowingly.

Being so thoroughly Regency, Marion Chesney would naturally suggest a recipe pertaining to her historical period. But, with her busy writing schedule, Harry, and son, Charlie, to look after, and the usual routine that comes with living in a brownstone apartment, she doesn't have time to utilize all of her rare Regency cookbooks. "My idea of a favorite menu would be roast quail with a raisin sauce. I don't know if I'd serve Madeira or port, as they did then. (It seems the British didn't trust the burgundies; they thought them too weak.) As it was, the

London wine merchants fortified the French wines with brandy. It was also considered correct etiquette to put a little bit of every food—cauliflower, cold meats, fruits, etc., on their plates, and then fill up their forks with as many different foods. As one Captain Granow said, and he wrote his recollection of life during the Regency period, 'We did our compoundings between our jaws.' I'd close my Regency meal with a dessert, one of the most frequently mentioned desserts of the time—Syllabub."

SYLLABUB

To a quart of rich cream, put a quart of white wine, the juice of two lemons with the rind of one grated and sweeten to taste. Whip it up well and take off the froth as it rises, put it upon a hair sieve and let it stand in a cool place until the next day. Then half fill the dessert glasses with the scum and heap up the froth as high as possible. The bottom will look clear and it will keep several days.

Virginia Coffman

*"Personality is everything," he re-
minded her. "Looks are unimpor-
tant. In the movies, it is pantomime,
of course, and there must be grace.
But you will have that. Indeed, I
believe you have it now."*

*When he took her home to the
hotel, he kissed Eden's hand with a
sincerity that made her think he had
truly enjoyed himself tonight. Several men and women in evening
clothes turned to stare at them. Andre
ignored them all. Then he kissed the
palm of her hand and walked rapidly
away under the arches.*

—Pacific Cavalcade

Someone once asked Virginia Coffman how long it took her
to research her first book. "It took me thirty years to research,"
she replies. "That's all I was doing in my youth and young
womanhood; constantly reading, because history is something I
love.

"I care more about background in my books than anything
else," she says, smiling warmly at the mere thought of it. Indeed,
Virginia is an expert on various periods of history.

"I know the French Revolution so well, and Ancient Rome. If
I were to visit Rome in that time and place tomorrow I'd know
exactly where to go and what to do. I'm crazy about it, have been
ever since I saw the silent movie, *Ben Hur*," she says. "That
changed my life. I saw the movie on October 16, 1927. I was a

little kid then, and when I saw it, I knew what I wanted to do in my life—I wanted to write historical novels."

Virginia fulfilled her burning childhood ambition, though not without a struggle and her share of rejection slips. But determination has its rewards. And now, when most women are counting grandchildren, this vivacious lady is toting up successful novels. If the count is correct, there are more than sixty-five published in all, including paperbacks and nineteen hardcover novels, with foreign sales in England and throughout Europe. Her novels have sold over seven million copies; her first published novel, *Moura*, has been reprinted and reissued six times.

Virginia's blue eyes widen when she discusses her enjoyment in giving a novel an unconventional twist. Take *Moura*, for example. In this story, she took three ingredients of a typical nineteenth century Gothic—an evil uncle, equally wicked housekeeper and innocent niece—and surprised readers with a shocking plot turn. "I made the wicked uncle the hero, the villainous housekeeper the heroine, and the sweetest-girl-who-ever-lived the monster. And nobody has ever guessed the solution until the end. It's always been such a shock," she says with pride.

Reminiscing on her career, Virginia recalls it took her nearly twenty-five years of writing before she ever sold anything. She was in her forties and was the secretary to a Reno real estate agent when *Moura*, the product of nine years of on-again, off-again work, was published in 1959. But like most successful authors, she had begun writing seriously years before, after graduating from the University of California at Berkeley in 1938.

For twelve years (beginning in 1944), she worked in Hollywood, first as a secretary and writer for David Selznick, then as a publicist for Monogram, a brief stint with Howard Hughes at RKO, and eventually as an editor of sorts for Hal Roach. "I started out as a secretary and sneaked in the back door as a writer," as she laughingly puts it. "Eventually I was polishing or editing scripts, which really meant I was writing the whole thing, but not getting any credit for it."

It was in 1965 that Virginia turned full-time writer. "That was when I got mad at the publishers who were rejecting my manuscripts," she recalls. She resorted to a last-ditch attempt to get her work printed. On the same day, she sent three different manuscripts to three different paperback publishers. Within ten days she was notified by mail and three $1,500 checks that all three books had been accepted. "That was the real beginning, and it was in paperback," she says.

Life today is a far cry from Virginia's earlier years as a struggling writer. Independently single and glad of it, the exuberant lady admits she has little time for a social life, preferring to spend an average of sixty hours a week writing for her pleasure and her living.

The assertive, outgoing author claims no quirks—no unusual or scintillating atmosphere is needed to get her creative juices flowing. "I get up around 7:30, have breakfast and write longhand on a yellow legal pad until I have five good pages," she confides. She frequently writes while casting sidelong glances at her favorite television serials: "One Life to Live," "General Hospital," and "Edge of Night." By the time she's finished, it may be four o'clock; sometimes it's 10 P.M.

Where does she get the discipline to write every day? "It's hard. You have to have that burning ambition. And of course it helps to have contracts. Then you have to do it."

Another key to her success, she says, has been a worldly, stimulating life. Her socially prominent family had a nodding acquaintance with men like Herbert Hoover and Douglas MacArthur, among others, and the family owned property in Hawaii when most people weren't even sure where Hawaii was.

Her father, a corporate executive, was as egotistical and domineering as he was charming, and Virginia says she never really gave up trying to impress him. Not surprisingly, in more than one of her books he is recreated as one of the characters, sometimes as the villain, other times as the hero. Daddy's pale blue eyes gaze piercingly out of a picture which the author displays prominently in her living room. He died eleven years ago, but the ghost of William Coffman still walks one step behind his daughter.

Although Virginia never married, there is nothing of the spinster image about her. "It is my personal opinion that single people have more fun," she says, though she doesn't deny having been in love at various times in her life. In one romance, at least, the object of her affection was a combination "Don Juan, mother's boy, and gigolo." She capitalized on the broken romance and put the character in her novel *Fire Dawn*.

"Possibly I defend being single too much, but I truly believe many people marry because they're supposed to. I always knew I wasn't going to marry. Thirty or forty years ago that was rare. People would ask, 'Oh, you're such a *nice* girl. Why aren't you married?' As though the reward for being nice was marriage," she comments wearily.

Born in San Francisco on July 30, 1914, author Coffman displays many traits of the Leo personality: strength, courage, fire, an active imagination and interest in a variety of subjects. The self-assured woman is not afraid to defy convention, to "do her own thing." Despite her years, she is in tune with the times, as are her novels. When you tell her she looks twenty years younger than her age, she assures you she feels thirty years younger.

Virginia loves to travel and does so almost exclusively by ship. "I believe in going first-class all the way," she admits pleasantly. Travel also seems to nourish Virginia's imagination and satisfies her appetite for history *and* the macabre. "In Paris, people will say, 'Don't you see the magic beauty of it?' And I say, yes, of course I love it. But then I tell them, that's where they cut off the head of so-and-so, and this is the place where so-and-so was stabbed! In other words, to me it's all bloody and horrifying and dramatic. It's the drama that intrigues me. That's the magic."

You might expect that someone with as much vitality as Virginia would have a recipe for an energy booster. She has, and she shares it with us. She calls the recipe a healthy pick-me-up for those 11:00 A.M. blues.

11:00 A.M. BLUES BREAKER
Save the half-cup of water used to pressure-cook vegetables

(the more vegetables cooked the better). Add slices of fresh mushrooms. Next day, heat and add seasoning and a dash of milk or sour cream.

It's a vitamin-loaded drink and hardly any calories, she assures us.

Susannah Collins

*His lips were caressing hers, whis-
pering her name as though it were
the sound of a breeze rustling
through the palm fronds. Her fingers flitted through his thick gold-
en mane and across his strong
shoulders, grasping his massive back
as though he were a verdant cliff
jutting out to the sky and she was in
danger of falling, plunging like a
waterfall from its dizzying heights.*

—*Destiny's Spell*

You may know Susan Ellen Gross by the name of Susannah
Collins, for that is the pen-name she used for the Second Chance
at Love series. She's quite an unusual lady.

On Susan's sixteenth birthday she made a list of the things she
wanted to accomplish in her life. "I wanted to write a novel,
make a film, sing on the stage of the Hollywood Bowl and make
love at the top of the Eiffel Tower in Paris. I've done the first
three, and although I have had some *wonderful* love affairs in
Paris, no one has yet been daring enough for the top of the Eiffel
Tower! But who knows?"

This is one author who lives out her fantasies before writing
them. "I filled diaries as a child, scribbled anguished poems on
napkins in restaurants, dashed off ten-page letters to friends. No
matter how jumbled my emotions were, once they were written
down, they weren't nearly so painful. Writing was an early,
unconscious drive, perhaps."

At the age of twenty, she began her first novel, an autobiographical work about her ill-fated love for a bull-fighter in Mexico, where she was going to school. "I was too young and too close to the subject to finish it. Too many tears spilled over the typewriter. Twelve years went by before I finally published the story. The book was not about the bull-fighter, but I still think about him. The Eiffel Tower, by coincidence, was also on *his* list!"

Susan is a devotee of the high life, and a daring writer. She was born under a popular sign of romantic authors—Sagittarius, the archer, on December 12, 1944. The archer more than typifies her personality. Not only does she seem destined to travel the rest of her life, in one way or another, but she loves horses. Her steed is kept in a stable behind her house, along with a German shepherd. When she's not roaming the world, she and her animals amble around the hills of Burbank, California, her neighborhood for many years, In her contemporary novels, horse lore is a favorite subject matter.

Horses have always been her favorite hobby, after writing novels. "If I ever find a man as handsome, well-mannered, and exciting to be with as my horse," teases Susan, with a devilish twinkle in her stunning brown eyes, "I might marry him. But I would never give up the horse in exchange."

Susan once considered art for a career, but professors advised her to give up. "They said I had no talent. I was so discouraged that I threw away my paint brushes. Years later, when I was working as a secretary to a TV game show producer, I noticed that the cartoonist did mediocre work. I asked for a chance to try my hand and my boss gave me an assignment to turn in the next morning. I stayed up all night. Bleary-eyed and full of trepidation, I laid my cartoon drawings on the producer's desk the next morning. He immediately fired me as his secretary, and sat me down at the drawing board. Today I'm a graphic designer for CBS, my regular job."

This author's first indication that she might be able to write was a horrible personal experience. "They say you can look back after a number of years and laugh," sighed Susan, "but after twelve years I still cringe when I remember. I was madly in love with a young film maker," she recalls, "and he was taking a class in screen writing. He used to skip classes a lot and would send me to take notes for him. I also cleaned his apartment.

"We both worked together on the script he had to turn in, but I ended up doing all the work while he slept. One night while I was typing, and he was asleep, the telephone rang and I answered it. It was his old girlfriend. He took the phone in the other room. A few minutes later he asked me if I'd finished the script. I had, and was just doing some revisions. He told me to leave the script on the table and go home. His ex-girlfriend was coming over and he didn't want her to find me there.

"That was a bad time in my life," Susan confides, shaking her head. "But—his professor was so impressed by my script that he took it to a TV producer. Of course, it did not have my name on it, but just the same it gave me the confidence to do some more screenplays and eventually a novel.

"There is a good moral in that story," she adds philosophically. "No matter how bleak things look at the moment, I always believe something good will come of it."

Today, Susan amuses herself with her writing, and there is nothing, in her opinion, more wonderfully amusing than romance. If she's not in the midst of a real romance, she will be reading or writing one. And if her own love affairs don't always turn out the way she wants, she can at least write about them so that all the strings tie up neatly at the end of the traumas.

She insists she still has fantasies to live out on paper. "That's partly what's so much fun about writing. It is especially true of my historical romances. What more exciting escape could there be than to whisk yourself into another era? But where fantasy becomes the most inspiring is when I'm writing love scenes. I just adore my passionate scene on a tropical beach in my contemporary romance, *Destiny's Spell.* It's something I've always imagined doing, like the Eiffel Tower. Well, maybe some day!"

Susan believes that there is a psychic power in all of us—some more than others are able to channel it. She is one of them. She believes that in many cases we are catching some sort of message, though she's not sure how it's transmitted.

"A few years ago," recalls Susan, "I became intrigued with the

75

idea of hypnotic regression, looking for former lives we might have lived. Several psychics had told me that I had been reincarnated many times. But I wasn't convinced. A friend of mine knew a psychologist who was conducting legitimate experiments and we decided to attend.

"I'm an excellent hypnotic subject, and went easily into the trance. I saw myself on a pathway that wound around some rock overlooking a turbulent sea, surf crashing up against jagged black rocks. There was a castle behind me. A handsome man I somehow knew was my lover was standing with me. We were about to kiss. He was dressed in a black velvet doublet with billowy sleeves slashed that revealed gold cloth. I described this in detail to the psychologist and he asked me what year it was. I told him 1492. More things occurred and frightened me. The psychologist became alarmed and took me out of the regression before it went any farther.

"That weekend I went to the UCLA library and began to put the pieces together for myself. It turned out that 1492 was the beginning of the Spanish Inquisition, the year the Jews were exiled from Spain. I still do not know if what I saw actually happened to me in a previous life or not. But there were moments when I recognized castles and places, and after a year of more research I began writing *The Midnight Fury.*"

As author Susannah Collins, for the Second Chance at Love line, her heroines in these stories experience love for the second time around. It's not surprising that she's attracting a wide audience of readers with these more realistic heroines. And don't even be surprised to find one of her heroines in a romantic encounter atop the Eiffel Tower. It's in the stars, so they say!

Susan prefers eating in a French restaurant with a romantic male companion to *ever* cooking meals at home! So, no personal recipes!

Janet Dailey

*His mouth moved onto her lips in
an unhurried and sensuous explora-
tion, warm and without pressure. It
teased her for a response, lightly
brushing her lips, going away and
coming back until her lips parted to
invite the kind of deep kiss that had
so thrilled her once before. The taste
of him filled her mouth.*

—This Calder Range

Ever since the 1976 publication of her first romantic novel,
Janet Dailey has gone on to become America's best-selling
female author. With more than sixty titles, and eighty million
copies sold, Janet has created her own romance industry.
Masterminded by her husband Bill Dailey, and gifted with an
amazing talent for prodigious writing, she has accomplished an
incredible record in the history of the paperback industry.

Janet didn't begin writing romances until she was thirty-one,
traveling with her husband in a 34-foot Silver Streak trailer
across the United States.

"It was while we were on the road that I finally found time to
catch up on my reading. I began buying Harlequin Romances
because they gave me a positive feeling when I was done with
them. I felt a complete identification with the books and knew
there was a natural link. Then I kept coming up with ideas for
plots until I was convinced I could write them," she says.

Janet had always dreamed of being an author. She began

77

writing in the fifth grade and decided there and then that she was going to be a novelist when she grew up—"not a *writer*, but a novelist." (Despite the urgings of her high school teachers, she did not go on to college after she graduated, because a college education could not guarantee that she would be a novelist; instead she went to secretarial school.)

Then in 1974, she began to have an idea of *what* to write about. "I began to talk nonstop until my husband Bill, who has no patience with words that aren't backed by action, finally said, 'Okay, then get off your duff and do it.'

"I stayed at the typewriter for six months and when the first story, *No Quarter Asked,* was finished, I showed it to Bill and asked him what to do next. His advice: 'Send it to Harlequin. If you're going to get turned down by somebody, it ought to be by the best and the biggest.'

"Ignorance is truly bliss," recalls Janet. "I didn't know that the first work of an unpublished author usually ends up in the slush pile. But my story was accepted without revisions."

Janet admits she's a lucky person. "I was in the right place at the right time with the right product. Harlequin had decided that they wanted to test the market and try the work of an American author who used American backgrounds and settings. Until I arrived on the scene, they had only bought books with foreign backgrounds."

It took three months before Janet finally received news of that first sale and a $5,000 check in the mail, but when it happened, she immediately sat down at the typewriter and wrote another one, and then another, and another. Twelve books appeared in 1976. It was Bill Dailey's idea to set a book in each of the fifty states, an achievement which got her nominated for an entry into the *Guinness Book of World Records.*

The Dailey "collaboration" originally began when she moved to Omaha, shortly after her graduation from high school, to live with her oldest sister Shirley. "As I was coming back from secretarial school one night, Bill was coming out of a coffee shop," says Janet of their first meeting. "He said, 'Hi.' A few days later I ran into him again and he told me his secretary had quit and if I wanted a job I could come and apply, and I did and I got it. It was attraction at first sight."

She fell in love with the boss, and the boss fell in love with her. "He used to call me Sam. At first I couldn't find out why, but apparently he decided that if he thought of me as one of the fellas he could manage not to fall in love with me. It didn't work. I married the boss!" she says.

Bill, a rangy, sandy-haired, Western-type man, was fifteen years senior to her eighteen years, the father of two children, and separated from his wife. He was in land development and just beginning to build up his fast-growing construction business when Janet became his secretary. Janet says he's a "typical Harlequin hero. He's a self-made man (who only had a fifth-grade education), and he thinks so fast he's always five steps ahead of everyone else. He knows exactly where he's going, and he says what he thinks. He doesn't pull any punches. It's impossible to keep up with him sometimes," she says softly. "He's the most intelligent and dynamic man I've ever met."

After living together for two years, they married on January 27th. The year was around 1964 or 1965. Janet and Bill aren't sure of the date—for a very sentimental and perhaps, practical reason. "Neither Bill nor I can remember the year we were married," Janet explains, "We don't regard marriage as an endurance contest or a marathon, so we won't look at our marriage license to find out the exact dating. The minister who married us advised us to put the license away and forget that we had it. We're together because we love each other—not because of some piece of paper."

Their business relationship was as successful as their romance. For more than twelve years they worked fourteen hours a day, seven days a week, with Janet acting as right-hand assistant and office manager, while Bill was the field planner who took the company from construction to real estate to oil speculation; the couple eventually had a work force of two hundred employees.

On one of their business trips with Bill as pilot of a light plane, an air drama took place which changed their lives. "We

79

were flying from Omaha to Delaware when we ran out of fuel. There wasn't any place we could glide to," says Janet. "We finally found a strip of land. There was a crosswind and Bill couldn't correct it, so we cartwheeled wing-tip to wing-tip. It was miraculous. We survived and didn't get a bruise. But the narrow escape did make us think seriously about our lives. It was shortly after the accident that we decided to retire."

Bill's goal had always been to retire at forty-five and the time was right. In 1974, they sold everything—their construction business, investments, house, and most of their personal possessions. All they kept were a few things that would fit into the trailer. Financially secure, the idea was to travel and enjoy life.

With their comfy trailer hooked to a fancy high-powered car, they headed west, to Texas. The next year it was east, with Florida their winter destination. But Janet's writing career shortened their leisurely retirement. "At first, it surprised the hell out of me," recalls Bill Dailey. "But after I considered all the time and work she'd contributed to my businesses, it seemed only right that turnabout was fair play, so I became her researcher-manager. After all, Janet worked for me for more than twelve years. It seemed fitting that I should work for her so she could attain the success in her field that I had enjoyed in mine. And as a boss, Janet isn't bad—plus, you sure as hell can't beat the fringe benefits. So, in addition to being married to a romance writer, I work for one, too!"

Bill and Janet and their two-and-a-half pound Yorkshire terrier began moving from state to state in their trailer to research and write her books for Harlequin Romances. The method Janet developed for her writing is to get up every morning at four o'clock when she's working on a book. "Bill says it's called the crack of dawn because you have to be cracked to get up at that hour," chuckles Janet. "I like it because there is nothing to keep me from going straight to the typewriter—no beds to make, no breakfast to cook, no makeup to put on—not even the dog wants to go for a walk at that hour! By the time everyone else is up, I'm so into the book that nothing can interrupt me for long. I use a typewriter and write one draft.

Being a secretary for so many years has made the typewriter keys extensions of my fingers. Longhand had never worked for me, because I can't write as fast as I think so I tend to worry over every word, like a dog with a bone."

Self-discipline was one of the hardest things for her to learn. "Once I start a book I keep very regular hours. On a light romance, I work eight straight days from four in the morning until five in the afternoon (or however long—or short—it takes me to do twenty-five manuscript pages), and the book is finished. On a major novel, I work six days a week for thirty to forty-five days doing fifteen pages a day—four A.M. until roughly two P.M. The research and details are Bill's responsibilities: the layout of the area, and streets, locations of public buildings, even the decor of hotels and restaurants. If we describe a real restaurant, and the table at which the hero and heroine dine has a blue tablecloth, you can be certain that the tablecloth is blue."

When Janet is writing, Bill takes care of everything. She doesn't cook to begin with, which is one reason they eat out a lot. "When I'm at the typewriter all day, Bill brings my food and coffee," says Janet. "He proofs my rough drafts, arranges for the finished typing, fields phone calls, handles my publishers and speaking tours, and lets me know I'm loved and appreciated. He's my right arm."

Janet's appreciation of a strong, older man might very well be partially explained because of her father, who died when she was five. Janet was the youngest of four daughters. "My recollection of my father is minimal—mainly what my sisters and mother told me about him. My mother remarried when I was thirteen. By then, all my sisters were married or gone, leaving me the only one home. My stepdad is really the only father I can remember. He made my mother very happy, and I'm glad about that."

The remarriage brought about a change in Janet's life. They moved from Early, Iowa, population 500, to the big town of Independence, Iowa, population 4,000. "It was quite an adjustment—more exciting than traumatic," says Janet. "I graduated from high school there, was a cheerleader, editor of the school newspaper and yearbook, and was in any other organization there was to join.''

Growing up in Early, Iowa, living there for her first thirteen years, left an indelible impression on Janet. She loves small towns and is especially sensitive to day-by-day existence. "Both my parents came from big families, so I grew up literally surrounded by family.'' She readily admits that she basks in the remembered warmth of that early social life and emotional security.

The dark-eyed 5'3" brunette was born on May 21, 1944 in Storm Lake, Iowa. "I was born on the cusp between Gemini and Taurus,'' she reveals. "Most astrologers disagree about which sign I'm under, so if I read the daily horoscopes, I generally read both signs and pick the one that sounds the most exciting.''

In 1979 the Daileys entered a new, expanded writing phase. Janet switched publishers, leaving Harlequin to sign a multi-million dollar contract with Pocket Books. She wrote four long novels and then began the Calder Sky Series. She is continuing to write short romances for Silhouette Books. When Janet's not writing, she's busy in her garden or putting up jams and jellies, and enjoys being surrounded by her parents and sisters. Bill's two grown children have made them grandparents.

The Silver Streak trailer has now become their second home and is parked next to their fifteen-room house on Lake Taneycomo, outside of Branston, Missouri. Bill is planning to build a giant theme park there, and many of the amusement rides will be named after Janet's books. "Imagine riding *Touch the Wind?*" asks Janet.

Janet is also acquiring a reputation in the country music industry. Not only is she trying her hand at lyricwriting, but Grammy nominee Johnny Mullins wrote a song appropriately entitled "Janet," because he enjoys her books. It is on the flipside of Stan Hitchcock's record, "She Sings Amazin' Grace.'' Other Dailey enterprises include plans for a series of movies based on Janet's books, with the script calling for Janet to be the hostess of each segment, in similar fashion to Loretta Young's show in the early days of television. She has also written a Silhouette screenplay and she's seen on television as spokeswoman for the Silhouette Romances. And The Daileys' Ramblin' Productions are keeping Bill even busier producing new television and music properties, opening television stations, etc.

Through it all, the Daileys remain as romantic as any of the couples in her best-selling books. Bill has come up with a new creation for his lady love. "I've built a massive swimming pool at our house, and I'm having tiles made to go around the edge which will be ceramic reproductions of all of Janet's book covers," he says with pride and love in his eyes. "With her writing speed, I may have an acre of tiles around my pool before I'm finished."

A favorite recipe? "I'm not much of a cook," Janet confesses. "When they were passing out cooking skills, I thought they said 'book' and went back for a second helping. So what recipes I do have are the foolproof, any-simpleton-can do-it kind. Here is an appetizer I love to fix—especially when we're in Texas where we can get our hands on some fresh Ruby Red Texas grapefruit. It's scrumptious, I promise."

BROILED GRAPEFRUIT FOR TWO

1 tb. granulated sugar
1 tb. brown sugar
2 tbs. Liquore Galliano
1 grapefruit

Mix together the brown sugar and granulated sugar. Cut in half and sprinkle a tablespoon of the mixed sugar on top of a grapefruit half. Pour a tablespoon of Galliano over the grapefruit half. Repeat procedure for second grapefruit half. If possible, allow the grapefruit halves to marinate in this for a couple of hours (or overnight if you want to prepare it in advance). Then place the grapefruit halves in a shallow broiling pan and broil until they begin to turn brown.

Celeste De Blaisis

"Oh, you are beautiful," she whispered. She knelt over him, smoothing the sleek hard lines, tracing the sinews of shoulder and rib cage and flat belly while his hands played with her breast. She pulled gently at the fur on his chest, and leaned over to kiss the scar on his thigh, moving her mouth upward over his flesh until he groaned, "You take me, Sara, you take me."

—*The Tiger's Woman*

Sultry, green-eyed Celeste de Blaisis has the charm and mysterious type of beauty that one associates with an Egyptian princess. Actually, she is half Italian, has no Egyptian ancestry, and spent most of her life on a ranch in Victorville, California. "Any attempt to define myself without giving some image of the ranch is an impossibility; it has shaped so much of me," she says with a warm smile.

Imagine a childhood spent on a ranch of some 2,000 acres where a child has "the freedom to run wild in the country, to build endless tree houses in the forest, to organize armies and fight imaginary wars, or to adopt alter egos such an Indian princess, who spoke all Indian dialects." This was Celeste's youthful paradise. The ranch, on the high Mojave desert, is surrounded by bushes and trees and the multicolored sand and shadows of the desert, while the heart of the ranch is green forest and pastures, watered by the north-flowing Mojave River.

Free to roam where she would, along with her brother, David, and their cousins, it is understandable that the bright child's imagination also took flight. After spinning off yarns throughout her early childhood, Celeste began her first novel in the seventh grade. Her classmates, to whom she submitted the chapters for perusal, gave the young author her "first taste of the power that comes from creating and sharing a fictional world."

A Taurean sun sign (May 8, 1946), power is essential to her being and her style of writing today. In her last years of a Catholic elementary school, she decided to extend that power by writing plays for history classes. As playwright, she also claimed the privilege of playing whichever character she preferred, inevitably the damsel in distress, which was somewhat awkward for the other players since she was already five-foot-nine and taller than most of the "leading men."

After a brief interest in medicine while in public high school, Celeste reconsidered the goal of a career in medicine, particularly when she learned that such a career would entail many years of biochemistry, a subject which, to her, was akin to "a lecture by Merlin the magician." The desire to be a writer finally surfaced with new urgency. She would be a writer, a poet, to be exact. An English teacher in high school encouraged her, and she went on to major in English in college.

Within a few weeks of arriving in Maine, for her freshman year at Wellesley, she became claustrophobic and it seemed to her that the people were "as hemmed in as the landscape." The realization then hit her that she was "addicted to space and openness in land and people." It was off to Oregon State for a year and finally to Pomona College in Claremont, California, for her junior and senior years.

While taking a special writing course at Pomona, Celeste arrived at the conclusion that, "One can be taught techniques and guidelines, but I don't think anyone can be taught to be a writer. The urge and the ability to write are either there, or they are not."

Graduated cum laude in 1968 with a Bachelor's degree in English, the enthusiastic young woman embarked on a career as a script reader, later to be a screen writer, journalist, and possibly a teacher on the side. Strangely, she began to find it an effort to get up in the morning or to go anywhere. A doctor's diagnosis was frightening: she had lupus, a disease which can be controlled with modern drugs if caught in time, but if it becomes systemic and acute, it is often fatal in disfiguring, crippling stages. And horrifyingly, to Celeste, was the fact that to lupus patients, the sun is deadly, acting as a trigger for the disease.

Celeste's first reaction, understandably, was terror. "I felt like a prisoner," she recalls. "All my freedom to be outdoors in the daylight was gone. And it seemed possible, and on the worst days probable, that my life was going to be very much shorter than I had planned." Yet she was stout-hearted, overcame her despondency, and accepted her handicap as a challenge.

She was determined to make the most of her life, to realize her potential in an area that would be of her own choosing. "The goals and roles other people thought I ought to have became insignificant. I took part-time secretarial and clerking jobs and traveled when I could. I painted and I wrote." Celeste developed a sense of life's immediacy, an outlook that she believes her parents always had, and which perhaps came from coping with the unforeseeable ups and downs of farm life. "Though there are still problems, I have lost much of my fear of the disease, but I will never lose the sense of time being precious and essential to the task of defining one's self in one's own terms," she says philosophically.

Celeste is grateful to her parents for the adventures they enabled her to have abroad, "among the loveliest of the many gifts they gave my brother and me," she says, her dark green eyes widening with fond reminiscences. "Born in this country of immigrant parents, my father is European in ways even he himself does not understand," she explains. "He has a sense of the world as a vast, continuous treasure house of man's history. And my mother's view is identical." In 1970, Celeste spent six months in the British Isles, developing a wild love for Scotland. Her brother David, meanwhile, went to school in Florence and became, as Celeste says, "the complete Italian."

"Though my parents could ill afford it, they helped give us both time to savor those different cultures," she says warmly.

There is a sadness in her green eyes when she continues. "They were wise in their knowledge that the realization of a dream should not be put off. Shortly after David returned home, he found that he was suffering from a rare and fast-growing form of cancer. He fought an incredible battle for two years. His laughter, wit, courage, and dignity never failed; only his body could not bear the burden." David died two years later in September, 1973, at the age of twenty-five.

Celeste credits David with her renewed interest in prose. During the last years of his life, her poetry had grown more and more truncated, and obsessed with death. "I wanted to escape," she says. Her escape was into writing a mystery, an exercise in creating a world where she could control the destiny of the characters. She found that poetry and mysteries had a pleasing similarity in one respect. "They both demand that all elements, even the seemingly insignificant, fit precisely together." And when the world seemed especially grim and unacceptable to her, there was, at least, her work to be done, there was her story, *The Night Child.* A week before David died, she finished the manuscript and sent it to her agent. When told of it, David answered her that it would be a success. And it was.

Celeste often writes with the stereo or television on in the background, but she hates interruptions by people because they demand a response and this breaks her thought continuity. "It has taken some time," she confides, "but I have trained friends and family to observe my working hours despite the fact that I work in my apartment rather than in an office." In fact, her family is now used to the signs of warning or welcoming that she posts. Her best writing times, she says, are the mornings and evenings—late afternoon is the worst. Presently, she is immersed in a new novel which takes place in England in the early 1800s and progresses to Maryland. "Historical novels intrigue me because while circumstances might change somewhat, the basic emotions of human beings remain the same through the ages," she says.

Success has changed Celeste's life in major ways, she says, "I am able to pay my rent on time and to travel more than I did before," she grins. "Most important, I am able to make my living doing what I most love. When the writing is going badly," she admits, "I think of all the other jobs I might be doing, but when it is going well, there is nothing else that gives the same energy and excitement. I laugh and weep with my characters; I believe in them absolutely. When it all works, the joy is boundless," she exclaims.

Celeste's favorite recipes, Kuo Teh—Pot Stickers, is actually a Chinese legend. Once upon a time, a chef burned an Emperor's dumplings, but the Emperor loved them, and thus developed this delicious Oriental treat.

KUO TEH—POT STICKERS
It's easier to buy pot sticker wrappers in the deli section of your market than to make the thin dough ovals.
Filling:
1 lb. ground pork (part ground veal if you wish)
1 pkg. (10 oz.) frozen chopped spinach
1 tbsp. light soy sauce
1 tbsp. sherry
1 tbsp. sesame oil
1 tsp. salt (use a little more if you like a salty taste—I don't)
3 tbsp. minced green onions
3 tbsp. minced fresh ginger
3 tbsp. minced parsley (may use cilantro if you wish—
   I don't like the taste)
Thaw the spinach a little and squeeze out liquid, but leave some liquid with the vegetable. Mix with rest of above.

Put about 1 tbsp. of filling in center of each pot sticker wrapper and fold dough over filling, pinching together just the top to make a half-circle. Then on side nearest you, make 2 or 3 pleats on each side and pinch them to meet opposite side to seal. May use a little water to make stick.

Heat 2 tbsp. of oil in a 12″ heavy skillet over medium-high heat (nonstick finish is helpful). Lightly brown Pot Stickers until golden on bottom, pour 1 cup water into skillet, cover immediately. Cook over medium heat until most of the liquid is absorbed. Uncover and continue cooking until liquid is completely absorbed and Pot Stickers are golden brown on bottom.

Serve with any Oriental dip you like—Hoisin sauce, sweet and sour, oyster sauce, or soy sauce with a little white vinegar added to taste.

Jude Deveraux

Gavin felt more than saw her presence. He turned slowly, his breath held. Her hair looked darker in the candlelight. The dark mink emphasized the rich creaminess of her skin. He could not speak. She stared at him, then slowly untied her robe and it glided languidly over her smooth skin, falling to her feet.

—The Velvet Promise

At first glance, blonde, blue-eyed, petite Jude Deveraux looks like she might be the all-American, girl-next-door. She certainly fits all the necessary requirements. But she's also a very successful writer with several published historical novels to her credit.

"I never wrote anything other than school assignments before I wrote my first novel. I loved the Kathleen Woodiwiss books but they just didn't come out often enough. I wrote *The Enchanted Land* because I couldn't find a book that I wanted to read," confesses Deveraux. "I wanted a heroine with a mind of her own, and one who had a decided purpose in life, other than being raped. I was *sick* of a sea captain who looked wantonly through spy glasses in search of a nude nymphet on a beach, whom he would alternately kidnap and rape until she admitted she loved him. Personally, I wouldn't want a kidnapper and rapist in my house. I'm the old-fashioned type. I like my heroine to love one man and sleep with one man—some exciting near

91

misses maybe—but no rapes or other lovers. I think there's a little Barbara Cartland in me somewhere," she adds wistfully.

Jude Gilliam White (she had always liked the name Deveraux and chose it as a pen-name) was born in Fairdale, Kentucky. "A place where women are taught their only role in life is cleaning house and bearing children," she said with a sigh. But Jude dispelled that myth personally by studying art and weaving at Murray State University (class of '70), where she met her second husband, Claude. Soon after they were married, they moved to Santa Fe, New Mexico, where her husband started a construction business. "Those were such rough years financially that we barely survived," recalls Jude. "We hardly had enough to eat and had to give up eating meat for a while."

She did find her first teaching job in an elementary school, and that "eased the financial burden somewhat." Slowly her husband's business began to prosper. Life went along smoothly in Santa Fe, and they eventually moved into a comfortable adobe house outside the city. "But at the age of twenty-nine, a strange depression set in over me," she says wistfully. "I began to lose my confidence. I felt that nothing *wonderful* was going to happen to me." An obsession to become an author grew.

Her husband managed to persuade her to mail forty pages of her manuscript, *The Enchanted Land,* to a publisher. She selected Avon Books, "because of the romantic covers." Four weeks later word arrived from Nancy Coffey, then Kathleen Woodiwiss's editor, that a contract was being offered.

Deveraux's book was set in the Bluegrass splendors of nineteenth-century Kentucky, a setting she knew well. The heroine, Morgan Wakefield, endured life as a Spaniard's captive and a land baron's wife, for always "she held in her heart the beloved caress of the man who defied a continent's dangers to possess her." This book's dedication was "To Claude—who gave me the time to write." Eventually, he would take the role of her husband-manager as her fame spread.

Jude's second novel was even more of a challenge. "It's a romantic adventure of medieval times with a thirteenth-century hero named Ranulf, and a beautiful heroine with the romantic name of Lyonese. I titled that book *The Black Lyon.*"

Then the world of publishing really opened up to Jude. She flew to New York for the first time, and spent a whirlwind two-day visit, and signed a contract for six books with Richard Gallen. "Before this trip," she says with a shy smile, "I had never been anywhere or done much of anything. I always felt like Agatha Christie's Miss Marple."

On a recent trip to Colorado with Claude, she did have something scary and unusual happen to her. She experienced a psychic happening and heard the voices of the coal miners who used to live and work there. "Even their names came to me," she says, still amazed. "I think I will be able to write books that will make their history and their memories proud." The wheels of the storyteller were turning in her imagination as she spoke.

Contrary to what her readers may think, "I don't live out my fantasies on paper. I, as an individual, feel very detached from my characters. But I let them take over. They just seem to pop into my head and *scream* at me until I let them come alive on paper. Sometimes I'm appalled at what they do. Sometimes I yell at them to try trusting each other. Since I'm one of those writers who never really knows what the outcome of my story will be," she confesses, "I can get very scared when the hero and heroine are in tight corners."

A prolific writer these days, Jude averages between 3,500 and 4,500 words a day, writing longhand in pencil. "My husband often makes me stop writing or I'd write sixteen hours a day and exhaust myself. My mind never stops thinking. I even plot my novels in the shower," she confides.

True to her Virgo sign—she was born September 20, 1947—Jude is persevering, methodical and hard-working, striving for sheer perfection in her creative endeavors. "My personal goal is to improve my writing with each book and to some day write a story the caliber of Susan Howatch's novels. My material goal is to have a separate writing studio, something large and beautiful, dug into the side of a hill so it's sound-proof."

Because of the long hours she devotes to writing, Claude suggested that she start exercising. "Sitting behind a desk for hours is extremely tiring," she admits. "I needed to limber up and develop muscle tone. So I joined a health spa, and decided to pump iron," Jude reveals proudly. "It wasn't easy at first, doing deep-knee bends with a heavy barbell over my shoulders. But," she grins, "after six months, I was hooked. Now it's an addictive form of exercise." She can now bench press sixty pounds, and dead lift (pulling a weight off the floor and up to the hips in one continuous motion) 135 pounds. "It's difficult for me to keep my weight under 104 pounds (she's five feet tall). With bodybuilding, I have lost two inches off my thighs and added a half-inch to my chest. My husband *does* think of good ideas for me." Her eyes brighten when she talks of handsome silver-haired Claude.

Now that success has arrived, she finds that her life is simpler. "Success has changed the way I feel about myself," she says with a satisfying sigh. "I respect myself more and look ahead to see a comfortable future where I don't panic everytime a bill arrives in the mail." She then revealed her most remarkable personal achievement. "I have peacefulness every day."

As for the future? I have a gorgeous, sexy husband and an exciting career. My life is so happy it frightens me sometimes."

Her favorite recipe follows. Jude makes about ten batches of this every Christmas and people rave about it. She uses hot sausage rather than the plain kind.

SAUSAGE CAKE

1 lb. pork sausage
1½ cups firmly packed brown sugar
1½ cups sugar
2 eggs, lightly beaten
3 cups sifted flour
1 tsp. ginger
1 tsp. baking powder
1 tsp. pumpkin pie spice
1 tsp. baking soda
1 cup cold strong coffee
1 cup raisins
1 cup chopped walnuts

In mixing bowl, combine meat and sugars and stir until mixture is well blended. Add eggs and beat well. Onto a piece of waxed paper, sift flour, ginger, baking powder, and pumpkin pie spice. Stir baking soda into coffee. Add flour mixture and coffee alternately to meat mixture, beating well after each addition. Pour boiling water over raisins and let stand 5 minutes; drain well and dry raisins in cloth. Fold raisins and walnuts into cake batter. Turn batter into well-greased and floured mini-Bundt pan. Bake 1½ hours at 350 degrees or until done. Cool 15 minutes in pan before turning out.

Joan Dial

She felt Kamakani's strength, his masculinity, the comfort of his arms, and a sensual promise deep inside her that was in tune with all the elements—the sea, the earth, the air, and the fire . . .
"Iona! See the might of the great fire-god, feel her power," he cried. Then his mouth came down over hers, consuming, devouring, and Anne parted her lips and yielded her mouth, pressing her body close to his, as demanding and wanton as the unrelenting flow of lava; and she was Iona and the molten flow was from her own loins.

—Waters of Eden

The room is filled with soft music and suffused with the aroma of fresh-cut flowers. Scented candles cast glimmering shadows on the wall. A breeze wafts in from the ocean, delicately ruffling silk curtains and heightening the romantic ambience.

What have we here? A setting from a romantic novel? Perhaps. It is also the real-life work-study of author Joan Dial, specifically designed for inspiration to write romance. And write romance she does! Prolifically. Successfully. Joan can boast of having written fifteen novels in the last five years. Or is it seventeen? It's hard to keep pace.

Currently, she is excited about three new novels, including a long saga set in this century and a contemporary suspense set in northern Ireland. "If I bog down with one, I go to another," she says with a smile, "and have never suffered 'writer's block,' if there is such a thing."

Since writing her first novel, *Susanna,* in 1977, Joan keeps spinning her wonderful, well-researched tales. Because she writes for different publishers, the charming, blue-eyed blonde often uses pseudonyms. Remembering her pen-names is almost as complicated as keeping track of her book titles. Including Joan Dial, the tally thus far goes: Amanda York, Katherine Kent and Alexandra Devon.

Where did this insatiable desire to write germinate? With a splendid English accent, the soft-spoken author traces her literary propensity to a childhood spent in Liverpool, England, amidst stimulating people. Her gift for storytelling was evinced at the tender age of six when the bright youngster would dash off twenty-page "books" for her school chums. "The heroine of these stories was a plucky, imaginative little girl who had hair-raising adventures with Nazi spies, crooks, and haunted houses," she recalls.

"Growing up in England, I was surrounded by wonderfully diverse characters." People from all walks of life were attracted to her childhood home by the author's mother, who loved to surround herself with "aristocrats, radicals, poets, dreamers, beggars, and thieves." Eavesdropping on interesting adult conversations prompted the precocious child to speculate on the lives of these colorful people and to concoct stories of her own. "This and rather sophisticated reading tastes and habits gave me an early desire to explore and understand the bonds that unite human beings and the forces that divide them," she says.

One can imagine a youngster's flights of fancy upon arriving home one day to find an entire gypsy caravan camped around the house. "Mother supplied the whole tribe with tea and sandwiches," Joan remembers fondly. "In return, they told our fortunes. Mine was that my life would be tremendously exciting; I was for 'two countries' (how true!) and a tragic love affair. . . ." An enigmatic smile comes across her pretty face. "But perhaps we won't go into all of that," she adds softly, leaving us to wonder.

"I consider myself fortunate that my wake is littered with such fascinating, real-life characters," she declares. Creative artist that she is, she has adroitly "reshaped, combined, dissected and molded" these characters to play their parts in her heart-pounding romance-adventure stories. "Character is the critical factor in any story—short or long. How many people remember plots from the books they have read? But fascinating characters live on forever," she goes on.

What does she aim for in her novels? "To explore love as well as lust, to write a rattling good adventure, and to reveal to the reader how absolutely fascinating our history is," she replies. "I spend more time researching than writing, then discard everything but the perfectly cogent detail," she explains. "I hope when the reader finishes one of my books she will have been so caught up with my characters—their passions and drama—that only later will she realize how much she has learned about an earlier era."

Joan takes seriously her responsibility to the reader. A sign over her desk reads: Have I examined all aspects of the situation? If not, the reader wil not be satisfied.

In certain respects, Dial does not follow rules. "I don't believe in detailing a story outline, or preplanning a story," she says. "My belief is that good literature has to be a great deal like life itself. You might know where you want to go, but the experiences you encounter along the way, both good and bad, are what is of interest, in life as well as in a good book."

Her special technique is to write from the inside out. Sound bewildering? She hastens to explain, "My characters are born and come to life first. I must know them very, very well. Then I write a scene with two or three of them in conflict, or facing some decision, or in a terrible pickle. I usually start backwards— to find out how they got into such a mess. After that I move forward to the end," she says simply—as though it were all quite simple.

Like many another aspiring writer, Dial once decided to take a writing course. "That was a mistake!" She is emphatic about this. "I feel it set me back ten years. Someone should put together a course teaching writers how to market their wares. No one can teach you *how* to write; that is learned by experience." She leaves no room for argument here.

Tabulating her literary successes, it is hard to believe that this dedicated writer worked for many years in other fields. "I worked in so many different jobs it would be impossible to remember them all: secretary, editorial assistant, office worker —I hated all of them and wanted only to write," she admits. Her first literary sale was to a "confessions" magazine and Dial recalls its contents were such that she couldn't send home a copy to Mother.

Bolstered by this glimmer of success, she went on to write her first novel in 1977 when she was forty and her children were growing up. Thanks to her boundless energy, she was able to sandwich writing between household and family responsibilities. The novel was a success, and the rest, as they say, is history.

Though she writes regularly—"every weekday, most evenings, sometimes late at night"—weekends are reserved for husband, family, and friends. Possessed of many typical traits of the Scorpio personality (she was born on November 9, 1937), Joan is intensely loyal and dedicated to ties of family and love. Comfortable with success, she is even more comfortable with her close-knit family. Indeed, her biggest fans are her husband, Paul Dial, a supervisor at Hughes Aircraft; two college-aged sons, and a teen-aged daughter, who is so caught up in her mother's literary projects that she "reads the pages as they come off the typewriter."

To observe this loving wife and mother in her happy home setting, one can't help but note the sharp contrast with the lusty, dynamic, unforgettable characters who inhabit her adventurous novels. Nor does Joan live out her fantasies on paper. "If I did they would be unpublishable," she comments.

When complimented on her admirable figure, she is quick to credit her love for vigorous outdoor activity: swimming, surfing, hiking, and sailing. The sea is her favorite milieu—"on the beach or in the surf." She also travels extensively. Research for her books has taken her around the world and to all parts of the United States, the country she adopted and fell in love with after marriage to an American from Illinois.

Joan has taken success in stride. "When the money first started to come in large chunks I tried to live differently," she admits, "but I found I wasn't comfortable in a fancy house and fancy car. I prefer to live modestly, but travel first-class," she says.

Understandably, monetary rewards are gratifying to a writer. But Joan derives great satisfaction from the thought that she has entertained her readers, for she sincerely believes that "this is a writer's only function." If you enjoy her novels she would like to hear about it. "There's no question about it," she sums up, "a writer's task is a lonely one and reader mail is manna from heaven."

Though Joan admittedly hates to cook, she does have an enticing dessert recipe to share. She calls it Americanized English Trifle.

AMERICANIZED ENGLISH TRIFLE

This froth of a dessert looks best in a clear glass bowl, so that all layers are visible. It should be well chilled.

Quantities depend on number of servings desired—no need to measure anything!
You need:
Ladyfingers—or sponge cake, split with raspberry jam inside. If using cake, slightly stale is best.
Dry sherry or cream sherry
Fruit-flavored Jello
Fresh or canned fruit (strawberries and raspberries are particularly good)
Custard (make before assembling Trifle—can use a mix, or old-fashioned scalded milk/eggs/sugar in a double-boiler method—COOL)
Whipped cream
Chopped nuts, maraschino cherries, angelica, chocolate flakes, etc. for decoration.
Place layer of ladyfingers or sponge cake in bottom of dish, sprinkle with sherry. Pour (liquid) Jello over—allow to set.

101

Place layer of fruit next, then cooled custard. Thick layer of whipped cream goes on top, decorated with any or all of last item. Layers can, of course, be repeated. Chill thoroughly and serve in delicate stemmed glasses.

Bonnie Drake

There was a warmth and comfort in his embrace, pure pleasure in his kiss. At that moment, she would let him take her anywhere, as long as he was there. His kiss deepened and she followed, willingly, and passionately, his hunger a stimulant for her own. Her appetite had hardly peaked when he gently laid her back against the pillows, freeing his hands for new discovery.

—*The Ardent Protector*

Barbara Delinsky, better known to readers of romance novels by her pseudonyms Bonnie Drake and Billie Douglass, enjoys writing romances for three reasons. "First," she says matter-of-factly, "I write them well; second, there is a market for them, and third, it is as much of a pleasant sojourn for me to write them as for my readers to read them!" Occasionally, Barbara lives out her fantasies on paper. She derives gratification, she admits, in "creating characters—women, in particular—who are modern achievers yet manage to preserve and acknowledge their femininity and their need for love."

Brown-haired, hazel-eyed Barbara was born in Boston on August 9, 1945. Her birth sign, Leo, represents the romantic and entertaining section of the zodiac. True to her sign, she has the Leo's romantic nature and deep insight into other people, as well as the active imagination which is so essential in her craft.

Barbara was the second of three daughters born to a prominent Boston attorney. Her childhood was a happy one, despite her mother's death when she was eight. "My father," she recalls lovingly, "encouraged reading and attendance at the theater, as well as the standard of perfection in our studies toward which we all strived."

She mentions one particularly memorable instance when she was given an assignment in the sixth grade to write a descriptive paragraph about the sun. "After struggling for hours, an aunt suggested that I dictate my thoughts to her as they came, which I did. After recopying these 'thoughts,' I received an 'A' on the paper," she says, her face beaming.

Though Barbara used her writing skills thoughout college and graduate school (she received her M.A. in sociology from Boston College in 1969) she did not become aware of any particular talent until, through her then-chosen field of photography, she did occasional reporting for a local newspaper in the small town where she and her husband lived.

The slender, fair-complexioned author met her husband, Stephen R. Delinsky, when both were students at Tufts University. Barbara was a psychology major and her husband-to-be was the president of the student body. "We spent long afternoons in the library, talking before we ever began to date," she relates. They were married a year and a half later, during the summer following Barbara's graduation. Her husband is presently Chief of the Criminal Bureau of the Department of the Attorney General of the Commonwealth of Massachusetts.

Barbara recalls vividly their first apartment. "It was a fourth-floor walkup in Cambridge—a 'Barefoot in the Park' kind of place," she says. "He started law school; I went on for my Master's degree. Our son was born two and a half years later. Then we specifically spaced our children so that I would not have two in diapers at once, and so that my husband would not have to put two through college at once." At least, so they thought! Five years after the birth of their first child, Barbara gave birth to twins, two more boys. "We laughed at our well-laid plans," she says.

"Actually, it was as a mother, and in large part as a mother of twins, that I first thought of writing on *that* subject, its many frustrations as well as its rewards and joys. In reality, I was too busy living the life to write about it at the time. Even now with the twins six years old, I still feel too close to the experience to write objectively about it," she muses.

Through Barbara's work as editor of *Highlights,* the biannual bulletin of the Beth Israel Hospital Women's Auxiliary in Boston, she discovered a true writing strength, as she calls it. Suddenly besieged by requests for descriptive pieces and speeches, and finding that she could dash off a three-page speech in no time at all, she realized that much of her previous work experience had been misdirected. It was at that point that she conceived of her first novel, *The Passionate Touch,* and published as a Dell Ecstasy Romance in January, 1981. After that there was no stopping her. Now she writes at any and every time of the day, whenever she finds a free moment.

Where does she write? Mostly at home. "Either in the den, dining room, living room, kitchen, or family room" of their warm, comfortable Colonial-style house in Needham, a suburb about seventeen miles from downtown Boston. Barbara loves her home: "I have decorated the house with a contemporary flair—simple, warm and open," she says. Yet she is not above writing on occasion at the public library, in the car waiting to pick up a child, or in a doctor's or dentist's waiting room. In short, she admits, "I write wherever I happen to be when I have time."

Since fitness is an important adjunct for a writer, Barbara makes sure to keep her lithe body in tune with a mile-long swim every morning. Then, on weekends, she rides her ten-speed bicycle up to ten miles a day with her husband. Not easy feats when coupled with the energy required to take care of three energetic sons!

Asked for her favorite recipe, Barbara came up with a super one that her family can't resist.

CRABMEAT CREPES

Crepes

3 eggs	pinch of salt
½ cup cold water	½ cup flour
½ cup milk	

Blend all ingredients in blender for a minute. Refrigerate, covered for two hours or more. Heat a small skillet or frying pan with a drop of margarine. Spoon enough batter into pan to cover bottom when swirled. Cook until top is beginning to dry. Dump onto tin foil or wax paper. Stack, with foil or paper between each crepe.

Filling

½ cup chopped scallions
½ lb. mushrooms, sliced
½ lb. butter
5 tbsp. flour
2 tsp. salt

¼ tsp. white pepper
1¼ cups light cream
½ cup white wine (optional)
2 egg yolks
½ lb. crabmeat
½ lb. cooked shrimp

Saute the scallions and mushrooms in half the butter for 5 minutes. Blend in flour and salt and pepper, then gradually add the cream and wine, stirring steadily to boiling point. Cook over low heat 10 minutes. Beat the egg yolks in a bowl; slowly add the hot sauce, stirring steadily to prevent curdling.

Saute the crabmeat and shrimp in the remaining butter for 3 minutes. Place 3 tbsp. of the mixture on each of the crepes and roll up. Pour remaining sauce over them.

Makes 10–12 crepes.

Note on recipe: this meal can be prepared ahead of time. I have fixed it in the morning (even made the crepes the day before and refrigerated them) when guests were expected in the evening. My husband claims the dinner is even better the next day, when I reheat the whole thing in tin foil!

Julie Ellis

Caroline felt herself lifted onto a velvet plateau isolated from the world. She trembled at the touch of Victor's arms about her. His mouth on hers. His body demanding. She laid back across the sofa, matching passion with passion while the storm played a tumultuous symphony outside.

—The Hampton Women

Julie Ellis's plantation sagas have been acclaimed as some of the best and the heroines in her Hampton Series novels are described as unforgettable. "It's necessary, in my opinion, that the girl be quite beautiful," Julie explains. "I think it's what the reader expects. It's part of the fantasy. At the same time I really try to portray my women as independent and intelligent. And when the female lead is *not* a virgin, it's not of her own volition," adds Julie, with a twinkle in her green eyes.

"I'm big on research and big on authenticity, so what if I do wear a size three shoe! Even though I'm a native of Columbus, Georgia, I felt I had to make the trip to Atlanta three times during the research of the Hampton Series, to talk to Georgia historians. These books have been a labor of love," declares the 5'1" strawberry blonde. "Fortunately, I'm a compulsive researcher. I'm so furious when I read a novel where the writer has been careless—like one recent novel set in the nineteenth century where the writer talked about a carpetbag with a zipper." (The Goodrich Company created the trade name *zipper* in 1928.)

Another passion that engages Julie Ellis is women's liberation. "I'm proud that I wrote the first book on woman's lib after Betty Friedan," explains Julie, who wrote many other types of books before settling on the historical romance genre. "It was titled *The Revolt of the Second Sex* and came out a few years after Friedan's. I used the pseudonym Richard Marvin, and it sold very well in campus bookshops throughout the country and received excellent reviews. I researched the subject for two and a half weeks, interviewed and researched by day, typed by night, and prayed the neighbors wouldn't complain that I worked till 3 A.M. I was asked to lecture after that, but I didn't feel qualified to *talk* on the subject. Maybe I missed a golden opportunity."

An Aquarian on the cusp of Pisces, Julie was born on February 21, 1933, and has made the most of the characteristics of her cusp position. She is quite content combining her intellectual individuality (Aquarius) and her sympathetic, intuitive qualities (Pisces). The two traits help her form believable, lifelike characters. Whenever reference is made to her strong heroines, she adds this comment, "Damned gutsy feminists . . . independent women."

A veritable creative dynamo, Julie, in the past two decades, has sometimes written two or three books a month, using various pen names. "I'm happy to have my own name back, after writing 146 books under eight different names. When I started writing in the 1960s, publishers always wanted a certain name for a certain category of books. They said it was upsetting to a reader who expects a Gothic novel to find it's contemporary. That rule has changed considerably in the past years, and fewer pseudonyms are being used, I'm happy to say."

It was after the publication of book number 149 that Julie Ellis screamed "Stop!" She wanted to step off the literary treadmill and find out if she could write longer books, hardcover books and stories based on scrupulous historical research. "A book that would take a year to write." That was the schedule she gave herself and everything she planned for has come true. The Hampton Series has been published in hard cover and paperback, and has sold more than one million copies.

Before becoming a novelist, Julie was active as an off-Broadway actress and playwright. "The theatre was real love, despite all the headaches," she recalls. "It was after the birth of my daughter, Susie, that I decided to write novels. Acting had become an exhausting effort. I was taking care of an infant, and coproducing and writing plays. At first I thought to myself, How can I survive without theater? But I did. In my estimation, writing novels is far more lucrative and it's certainly easier to sell a book than a play. In novels you're in control," she adds. "You avoid the problem of pleasing the director and the cast. You take all the bows and falls, and you're not at the mercy of temperaments, at least not real ones."

One of the most pleasant memories of her writing career was an acquaintance with Gloria Swanson. "I was just seventeen when I walked into Swanson's sumptuous Fifth Avenue apartment to work on a children's song album with her. My mother told all our neighbors back home in Georgia. They kept calling and asking, 'What's it like being around a Big Star?' I just said she was down to earth. They didn't know what I meant. How could I tell them that one day I walked into the apartment and found Gloria Swanson scrubbing the bathroom floor on her hands and knees! 'Gloria, what are you doing?' I asked, horrified. Her Swanson-like answer was—'The butler and maid have the flu and this has to get done.' Gloria also started me eating healthier foods and for that I'm very grateful. People rarely guess my age," adds young Julie whose children are now college age.

Today Julie is a widow, but while her husband was alive and she was raising her children, she led a leisurely life, traveling with her family around the world. For one year she lived in the Valais section of Switzerland, in the midst of the famous white wine region. "My typewriter was poised on the terrace and I had the most spectacular view in the world. I can write in the most gorgeous places or I can write on planes, trains, and in restaurants. I never dry up, the constant flow of ideas comes from above, I guess." She says she is unable to explain the mystery of her prolific writing. An unyielding drive and an inexhaustible supply of talent are deeply interwoven in this unique author who claims to "have enough plots to keep me busy for the next twenty years."

In between books, she does find time to date eligible New York bachelors. "If he's late and I'm waiting, I'll pull out my notebook and start writing. But if he's late too often, I don't see him again!" she says emphatically, sounding very much like one of her "liberated heroines."

Cooking has never been one of her hobbies. But she has an incurable passion for Southern Pecan Pie. "All I can reveal of its secrets are—use a lot of pecans."

Zabrina Faire

Seeing his face in the glow of the firelight, she thought it looked murderous. Terror thrilled through her and again she strove to escape him, only to be caught and pressed against the bed, held easily with one strong hand while, with the other, he divested himself of his own garment then, falling upon her, he pinioned her beneath him.

—*The Chadbourne Luck*

Despite the uninspiring din of heavy traffic and noisy children from a nearby school, Florence Stevenson—better known as Zabrina Faire or Lucia Curzon to her Regency readers—somehow manages to escape the reality of her Manhattan apartment. Deep in thought, she drifts off to a world of romance and mystery and, occasionally, the occult. Working in her bedroom-study (she lives in a two-room apartment), the six-foot-tall brunette loses herself in the wanderings of her imagination during her afternoon and evening writing hours.

"I'm one of the few romantic authors, aside from Barbara Michaels, who has a preference for ghosts and other things that go bump in the night," she says, smiling. "I like to stay at haunted inns in the summer—even if I fail to meet the spectres. I have a half belief in ghosts, mainly because I'm psychic and mediumstic, and I have picked up other world entities for sorrowing friends," she explains, sounding as knowledgeable as some of her psychic Regency heroines.

111

Born November 18, she considers herself a Scorpio through and through—the sign of intensity and secretiveness—with four planets in the sign, the sun, moon, Mercury, and Jupiter. She also possesses a keen perception and a strong sense of precognition. "Jeanne Dixon was not the only one to know about John F. Kennedy's death before it happened," she remarks. "I felt so strongly about this tragedy, I wanted to call the FBI to warn him. The feeling was like a bolt from the blue," she says, recalling the frightening experience. "Even as a child, I periodically had flashes into the future. No wonder I'm a believer in the supernatural and so interested in the occult!"

Zabrina, as she doesn't mind being called, was raised in Los Angeles, California, and educated at the Elementary Training School at UCLA, where she and her classmates built radios and gliders, with no special attention to grammar or math. "My lack of a background in both has bothered me all my life," she confides. "I seem to have a penchant for putting commas everywhere and never making paragraphs." From there she went on to the Dominican Convent of San Rafael, at the insistence of her very Catholic parents (she was an only child) and then Santa Monica City College, returning to UCLA for her M.S. in drama.

"I had wanted to be a writer from the time I was a child," she reminisces. Her early years had been lonely and unhappy. Reading was her only escape. "I always thought I would write novels, and picked out a pseudonym—Shahrane Nahvarre—because I intended to write about tigers and India. I was about fourteen at the time," she recalls and laughs heartily. "Later, I decided to become an actress and went to a top playwriting school, the Yale Drama School, as an acting major."

Soon after the completion of her studies, she auditioned for and won all sorts of character roles in summer stock in California theaters. She returned to Los Angeles and accepted an understudy role in a play called *Dipper Over Gimbels*, which was short lived. "It was my exposure to playwriting, however, that encouraged me to write my first professional effort—a play called *Pleasure Dome*. It created a stir of interest but nothing more," she comments regretfully. But my third play, *The Door*

Between (about John Keats), and my seventh script, *Child's Play,* were produced at the Theatre Americana."

There was no romantic interest in her own life, so pulling up stakes and moving to New York was just another stage in her career. She eventually found work as an editorial assistant on *Mademoiselle* but was later fired. "They said I was more interested in extracurricular activities, such as playwriting, than I was in *Mademoiselle.* How right they were!"

Zabrina does have a "mad passion for opera." Her columns have appeared in the *Metropolitan Opera Program.* "I am indulging in this love now by reviewing operas for a small New York newspaper. And many of my holidays are spent in Europe, visiting the great opera houses and festivals. I could have been a concert pianist, if I had liked to practice," Zabrina remarks and sighs. "But when I turned my attention to writing, I forgot all about music, except as a passion. I guess I felt that one couldn't say enough with the piano, limited by the keyboard. And there was so much I wanted to say."

Zabrina Faire's Gothic writing began with a story called *Ophelia.* An intriguing tale written from a cat's point of view; the heroine, who at the start of the story is a cat, falls into a wishing well and becomes a woman with a cat's memories intact. "I took it around to publishers and on the fifth attempt, it fell into the right slush pile. An editor at New American Library picked it up and liked it. It was published in 1968 and *voilà!* I was on my way. And here I am, some forty books later."

But it wasn't until 1979, and many Gothics later, that Zabrina was asked by her agent to try her hand at writing Regency romances. "At first I said no. But then I went home and thought—why not? I love to read them. Georgette Heyer was always one of my favorite authors, along with Edgar Allen Poe."

Her first effort, *Lady Blue,* in 1979 was bought by Warner Books, and has been reprinted several times. "It was another form of expression for me. I didn't want to be a carbon copy of Georgette Heyer. I couldn't write about balls, Bath, and teas alone. I wanted to explore the fascinating historical happenings of the period. For instance, Lord Elgin finding the famous

113

Elgin Marbles, now in the British Museum, which inspired Keats and Byron, and so many other artists of the era. Also," she smiles, "I like to add a little mystery and supernatural whenever possible." *Pretender to Love* takes place mainly in Cornwall and has a touch of witchcraft.

Besides the Warner Regency Romances, she also writes Regencies for the Second Chance at Love series, published by Jove. As Lucia Curzon, she wrote their first Regency offering, *The Chadbourne Luck,* which varies from the usual formula.

"For this line," she explains, "the plots must involve the heroine's experience with a second chance at love. Usually, the previous relationship or marriage has ended (she can be a divorcee or a widow) and in the novel she will succeed in finding all the happiness she missed or lost before. In these Regency novels, sex can stop before intercourse, since the lack of birth control devices in that day and time creates an element of worry not all that present in contemporary romances. But my plot situations circumvent this problem!" she adds, with a twinkle in her eye.

"I would like to write historical novels, but I'm afraid everyone beat me to the punch. I did publish two, *Julie* and *The Golden Galatea,* under my real name, Florence Stevenson. But I just wasn't aware soon enough to get into that genre," she says regretfully.

"They say your first novel is always autobiographical. I had a really mixed-up childhood. I was all by myself in a large house which looked like it had been drawn by Charles Addams! Having one's imagination flourish in these narrow and lonely confines, why, it's no wonder I liked romance and horror!" she explains.

"I've been reading horror stories since I was eight and I'm still passionately addicted to them. I don't believe in ghosts actually floating around, but I do believe certain elements of black magic exist and I think it's dangerous. It frightens me a little, but not when I'm reading or writing ghost stories."

Zabrina has not the same luck with love in her own life as her heroines have had in her novels. "A good man is hard to find," she sighs. Someday she hopes to have her personal life exactly the way she wants, and all the elements she needs—writing, love, happiness.

Zabrina's most frequent fare these days is what she calls a pine-float (a glass of water and a toothpick). "I'm on an *extreme* diet," she admits. Other than that, steak rare, salted, peppered, and soaked in French dressing and "stuck with garlic" is her choice for a savory dish.

Barbara Faith

Before she could prevent it Lad pulled her into his arms and kissed her, his lips hard and strong, his body against hers demanding that she yield, trying to force her lips apart, resisting the push of her hands against his shoulders. "I want you, Merrie. And I'll take you on any terms I can get you. Remember that."

—*The Sun Dancers*

Like that old radio program, "Helen Trent," life for novelist Barbara Faith really began at age thirty-five. "When I reached thirty-five I completely turned my life around," exclaims the tall, blue-eyed blonde. "I'd been working at the same job—broadcasting—for ten years. I was single. My relatives were always introducing me as, 'This is my niece-Barbara-she-never-married,' like it was a part of my name! I quit my job."

Barbara's father flew in from Tennessee for the sole purpose of telling her that she was "out of her gourd to give up a job where she would get a lovely pension when she was sixty-five." With dire predictions hanging over her head, she packed typewriter, books, blue jeans, and herself in her ancient car and headed from Miami Beach to Mexico.

"I ended up in a charming colonial town named San Miguel de Allende. I rented a small two-story (with roof garden) apartment for $50 a month. I shopped in the outdoor market, I took some writing courses, I wrote another bad novel, I learned a language, and—thank the lord—I met my husband," she says. "Alfonso was a bullfighter. The minute somebody said, 'Barbara, I would like you to meet Alfonso," I knew. Boy, oh boy, I really knew that this was *it*." They were married in Tampiaco, Mexico, in 1970.

Then Barbara began to write at a furious pace. "I really worked at what I wanted to do now. And I listened to people. I looked around me. I tried to absorb a different culture. All I knew about Mexico was that a terrible fellow by the name of Santa Ana had done away with some of our favorite folk heroes. Now I found myself married to a Mexican and living in Mexico. He'd been a bullfighter for sixteen years so most of our friends were in, or had been in, that profession. And if I wanted to truly be a part of my new husband, and his country, I had to learn a whole lot of new things," she says wisely.

Soon she was beginning to write about Mexico—as she began to *feel* Mexico. *The Moon-Kissed* evolved out of seeing the Folklorico Ballet. "There was a dance of the Revolution and when the women came out with rifles and bandoliers I wanted to know what they had to do with the Revolution and my husband told me they were 'soldaderas'—women who followed their men all through the Revolution years. So, Sarah Finch, a Texas girl, was born in my imagination. She got caught up in the Revolution by the forces of Pancho Villa, and fell madly in love with a Mexican!" recalls Barbara. "*The Sun Dancers* is about a lady bullfighter. I would never have been able to have written the book if I hadn't gone with my husband to hundreds of bullfights."

Stories by Barbara appeared with regularity in magazines long before she became a novelist. "I began writing in 1966 when I took a course at Miami-Dade Junior College. I worked at the broadcasting company during the day, attended the class two nights a week, wrote a rather bad novel the first term, and one short story, which I immediately sold to *Alfred Hitchcock* magazine for the great sum of $116. And that made me believe writing was a snap!" she laughs. "Then it took four years before

I finally sold another short story—this time to *Mademoiselle*."
More stories appeared in smaller magazines.

Barbara and her husband are now living in Chula Vista,
California. Alfonso works for Mexican Customs and, according
to Barbara, "He works *a different shift every day,* seven days a
week. One morning I can be at the typewriter at eight. The next
day, when he leaves for work at four P.M., I may not hit my work
till after he leaves. It's not the way I would prefer to write, but I
have to do the best I can. When I'm into a book, I work at least
five hours a day, seven days a week."

Barbara was born in Cleveland, Ohio, on January 19, on the
cusp of Capricorn and Aquarius. High goals, determination,
and patience are the essential qualities of her earth sign, while
diplomacy and tolerance, and a quotum of originality manifest
in her air sign. It's not surprising that she would collect books
and seashells simultaneously, and be constantly traveling to
meet and talk to new friends.

No one in her husband's family speaks English, nor do many
of their friends. "I simply had to plunge in and do the best I
could," she admits. "My verbs are *dreadful,* but I just carry on
because I think communication—not perfection—is what's
important."

Barbara and her husband enjoy renting a car when they travel
and staying off the main highways. This is how she picks up her
best background research. "We'll probably end up in the
poorhouse, but we do love to travel. We picnic along the road,
chat with the people, just take our time. We now know all of
Mexico, most of Spain, and have driven through Germany,
Austria, Switzerland, Italy, France, and Portugal. Fortunately,
we can pay our dentist bills and travel," she says with a smile.
"And I guess I have more of a feeling of self-confidence these
days. I feel good about myself, happy about what I do. The
gratification of doing what I like cannot be described. Maybe it
was because everyone predicted I'd end up an unhappy old maid
and I certainly didn't!"

A friend gave a *despida* (shower) for Barbara before her
marriage, and asked everyone to bring a recipe. "My favorite

119

was: Cut up some garlic and onion and saute both in butter. Then open the refrigerator door and look around. Tired noodles? Old rice? Tuna? Ham? Okay; throw it in on top of the onions and garlic, cover and simmer while the wine is chilling. *Voilà*! A pretty decent meal!"

Patricia Gallagher

There was some initial violence, almost ravishment, and she gloried in it, her passion and desire pacing his. Then exquisite tenderness and artistry, prolonged and repeated paroxysms of ecstasy that transported her to another plane, unreached since their last intimacy. Only his consummate skill could fathom the true depths of her sensuality, evoke the ultimate sensations. And Devon knew, as she had always known, that for her, love made all the difference. Love created the perfect union. Without it, she could not commit herself totally to any man—husband or not.

—No Greater Love

"My women have spirit. They will take nothing from a man—even in those days when they were supposed to," Patricia Gallagher explains.

"That's the type of woman I admire. And that's the type of woman I am," she says, leaning across her coffee cup in emphasis of her point, her brown eyes glowing.

"I can't stand a weak-kneed sister . . . a woman has to be capable of something besides having a man," she continues, her voice impassioned.

Patricia's own life revolves entirely around these exquisitely lovely, proud-spirited heroines and irresistible male rogues. She controls their moods, motivates their accomplishments and—of course—manipulates their romantic involvements. She is even

121

responsible for their psychological well-being. And she has every right—she creates them.

Writing romantic novels successfully certainly has its ups and downs! But for the woman talking and gesturing animatedly with her smooth, small hands—success is worth it.

The author of nine historical novels, Patricia is the kind of Texas-born lady John Wayne used to carry off with him into the sunset. She's lovely, and spunky, especially when the subject turns to women.

"My novels *always* center around women," declares Gallagher who tours yearly for her books and speaks before dozens of college and civic groups. (Her accurately researched books are used by several college instructors of American literature.) "For years, we were second-class citizens. We owe so much to the women in our history, and I try to work that into a novel when the plot calls for it."

How does she imbue her stories with historical atmosphere that make her books so outstanding? "I research my novels thoroughly, about thirty months," she says with pride. A lifelong book lover, she estimates reading 200 books in preparation for most of her novels. In her newly purchased (thanks to lucrative royalties), rambling native stone house in the foothills of San Antonio, Texas, she maintains an extensive library. "It's a wonderful house," she says with pride. "And the library is the best you ever saw." More than 1,500 books are in the attic alone, stacked all over everything, mostly about Texas history. "There's always some history professor who will call you down if you make a mistake," she comments.

Patricia Gallagher's novels are decidedly sensuous, but she doesn't advocate or resort to the use of filthy language or brutal sex.

"We've all heard that women have rape fantasies? Nonsense!" she disagrees. "Women want tenderness and love. They are as sexual as any man, but they do not like being treated as sex objects. Not that there aren't any explicit sex scenes in my novels," she adds. "You have to write more than blank sex. It must be juicy. You have to give your reader a little satisfaction. But I know when to stop," she says. "I don't like brutal sex. And

122

I don't think any woman does. Women are finding out in real life, as well as novels, that they don't have to settle for being treated in a cheap way. They can be selective," she argues.

Of course, her heroines usually get the man, too—making for a happy ending. "Sometimes I don't think a happy ending is realistic . . . but this is escapist reading and that's what women want," she explains. "And ninety percent of my readers are women."

Patricia's writing career began as a result of her husband's time-consuming job; he was a television engineer and she found herself alone quite a bit. "I had to keep busy," she points out, "and so I decided to devote my time to writing." Her son had just entered school and that left her in her small white frame house with many empty hours.

Seven years of determined effort led her to sell her first novel (she completed seven novels which didn't sell), but Gallagher was never the kind of female easily vanquished. She did have the courage of her convictions, just like her fictitious heroines. And in 1961, *The Sons and the Daughters* was published, after thirteen rejections.

Texas-born, and a San Antonio resident since she was nine, Patricia used to walk three miles each way to check out library books during her childhood. She didn't have many at home then. "My family was not what you would call affluent."

As a teenager she wrote for school newspapers and turned out synopses of novels for fellow high school students who couldn't be bothered to read them.

Does she consider writing an easy profession? "No, no!" she exclaims emphatically. "It's a life filled with long, tedious hours of dedication and many disappointments. Perseverance plays a tremendous part. If you think your story is good, what Aunt Suzy says doesn't mean a hoot. Stick to it!" she advises all fledgling romance writers.

She herself diligently applied herself to this highly competitive romantic world of fiction shortly after her husband's death, partially for extra money, partially for therapy. She highly recommends the calling to all widows and lonely people in general as a comforting hobby. She thinks tracing one's family tree can be highly rewarding and could even turn into a novel. "A lot of people, in my opinion, have it in their systems to do a piece for *Reader's Digest* and they pay a *lot* of money. You need talent and imagination, you can develop a technique.

"I was a housewife and mother for years. My son was grown and my husband had died. I had to find something meaningful in my life," she explains. "Since that time, I'm always in the middle of writing a book."

Being a strong-willed, proud and confident woman, Patricia Gallagher epitomizes her Leo sign (August 18) with a never-say-die attitude. Her enviable characteristics are clearly expressed in the heroines she so vividly brings alive.

Her gratitude to the early feminists who shine so brightly in *Castles in the Air*, the women who endured ridicule and rejection, will never end. "We owe *everything* to those women," the slender, 5'5" author asserts. "We've come a long way, baby, but they certainly started it for us."

Patricia's favorite food is Barbecue, Texas style. Also Mexican food, for which San Antonio is famous. Her number one dessert for any time of the year is Southern fruit cake soaked in apricot brandy.

Dorothy Garlock

The first gentle touch of his lips awakened a bittersweet ache of passion. Glowing waves of pleasure spread like quickfire through her body. They were two beings blended together in a whirling tide.

—*This Loving Land*

"I'm younger than Barbara Cartland . . . but older than Brooke Shields," says perky Dorothy Garlock. "I tell everyone that I'm somewhere in between. I have bumps in all the wrong places, but my grandchildren love me, regardless!"

Readers know Dorothy as a historical novelist, writing under her own name, and category contemporary romance readers follow her titles when she writes as Dorothy Phillips and Johanna Phillips.

"What is on the outside of me does not even remotely resemble what is on the inside, where I'm young, beautiful, and as romantic as any of the heroines in my novels," she says with enthusiasm. "At this time in my life when I should be concerned with high-blood pressure and shuffleboard, I find myself somewhat an oddity. I've been writing since 1976 and I've sold seven books. It only proves to me that the body starts downhill long before the brain!"

Dorothy's husband retired from the oil business in 1975 and

wanted to travel around the United States with her. So she resigned her position as a reporter-columnist for a small newspaper in Iowa, and went traipsing along. "We toured the United States and Mexico, from the Canadian border to Merida in the Yucatan. It was enjoyable, but even all icing and no cake can be too much after awhile," she cautions.

"I didn't start writing because I thought I could write a better novel than what I was reading. I was plain bored! While cruising down the highways I began to daydream about making up my own stories. When I created my heroes I was furnishing my own entertainment. At any rate, I didn't have the slightest idea of how to get a manuscript published, or even in what form to present it. I gave my first story to my daughter and her friends to read and started another," explains Dorothy. "It was fun. I manipulated my characters into *all sorts* of situations. It was a little like playing God—and I loved it!"

All it took, she claims, was a few pats on the back and she was hooked. "I made a beeline to the public library to find the correct way of going about this exciting new venture. It did occur to me that if my friends didn't like my story, if they thought it was rotten, they wouldn't say so. I pushed the thought aside and blundered ahead," she says with zest.

The next year she sent two contemporary stories back and forth to publishers while she worked on a historical novel set in the Ohio Valley during the 1880s. "One advantage in living in a small town like Clear Lake, Iowa, is knowing the librarian," Dorothy recalls. "She allowed me to place my manscripts on loan in the library and checked it out for public reading. I wanted the opinion of readers who didn't know me. The answers to the questionnaire I attached to the manuscript gave me the encouragement to enter it in the National Writers Club contest for unpublished writers. I didn't place in the contest, but I did get a good enough rating that an agent took me on as a client and sold my *Love and Cherish* to the Richard Gallen company. It was published through Zebra and the first printing sold out. That was the beginning of my new career."

Dorothy Garlock was born on June 22 in Grand Saline,

Texas. Like most Cancerians, she enjoys her home life and at the same time likes to travel, too. Governed by the moon, her imagination has taken her in many directions throughout her life.

"My father was an engineer in the salt mine in Grand Saline. My mother was what was known as a real Southern lady," says Dorothy. "She wore her corset every day of her life and insisted that her girls—I was the second of four girls and a boy—keep their legs crossed, their mouths shut and marry a 'nice' man who would take care of them. My mother's code of behavior was so strict that she once forbid me to associate with a girl whose brother had got a girl 'in trouble.' Later I realized how unfair it was that her judgment deprived me of a friend. I'm not blaming her. She merely passed along the standards that were instilled in her by her own parents. I'm thankful my values were changed by the time my own children arrived."

Dorothy's family moved to Oklahoma City, where she spent a happy childhood. Her first job was wrapping packages in a department store. "How I envied the girls working behind the perfume counter! To me they were sophistication personified. I advanced to cashier, then later to head cashier and a red fox jacket. After two years I met the man of my dreams, Herb Garlock. We married in Oklahoma City in 1946, and have two children and two grandsons."

Dorothy's education ran a complete gamut. She attended junior college night classes and on-the-job training programs. Her occupations included being the paymaster at an aircraft factory to owner-operator of an antique-gift shop. For fourteen years she worked on the local paper, *The Clear Lake Mirror-Reporter*, where she wrote editorials, social notes, obituaries, and had a weekly column, "My Two Cents' Worth."

The Garlocks operated a rollerskating rink in Oklahoma City for ten years before moving to his hometown of Clear Lake, Iowa. "At first I hated the cold Iowa weather. Our children loved everything. I loved only the library. But eventually I came to appreciate life in a small town. The clerks in the stores, my attorney, dentist, banker, doctor, garbage collector, and UPS delivery man all call me by my first name. That's the way it is in a small town, USA. We even have a Main Street."

Dorothy feels that she and Herb must have done "something right," because their children are happy well-adjusted adults. "At the time I was so busy hauling kids, going to PTA, being a 4-H leader, and working, that I wasn't aware of it." Daughter Lindy helps type her manuscripts, and daughter-in-law Jacky has a silkscreening business. She designs and makes T-shirts for each of Dorothy's books and they're a favorite gift to bookstore managers. As Dorothy says, "How lucky can I be?"

She is also fortunate to receive encouragement of all kinds from her sisters. "Betty loves the historicals, while Mary favors contemporary romance and the suave heroes who live in luxurious penthouses. Mary would like for me to name one of my 'wild' women in one of my stories after her, but somehow I can't visualize a whore named Mary!"

Dorothy writes and lives in a mobile home court in Clear Lake. "When the snowflakes begin to fall in Iowa, we lock our door and head south in our travel trailer, knowing our little nest will be taken care of and waiting for us when we return. The people in our mobile home court are fantastic. When my first book was published they blocked off the streets and gave me a surprise party, complete with a thirty-foot sign saying 'Dorothy, we're proud of you!'"

An extra bedroom in her Iowa mobile home serves as Dorothy's office. "It's nothing—a desk, bookshelves and a Smith Corona. I spend a lot of time in my little nook, because, my husband, bless him, does all our shopping and cooking chores, leaving me to do my *thing*."

Her only hobbies are reading and walking. "I walk five miles every day," says the shapely 5'4" brunette. "Several times during the spring and again in the fall my friends and I take a twenty-mile hike. Walking is a great time for thinking and sometimes I head back to the typewriter with a clearer vision of what I wanted to say."

For the past decade Herb Garlock has taken over their cooking chores, so Dorothy recommends his favorite recipe. "This Bar-B-Q Brisket makes a heavenly sandwich," she brags.

BAR-B-Q BRISKET

Wipe meat dry (5 to 6 lbs.) and with cut side down, sprinkle generously with liquid smoke, celery salt, onion salt, garlic salt. Let stand one hour. Turn and repeat. (This will tenderize the meat.) Refrigerate overnight.

Before cooking, sprinkle again with liquid smoke and Worchestershire. Cover with foil and bake 5 hours at 275 degrees. Uncover and pour on 6 ounces of barbecue sauce and bake one more hour. Cool before you slice the meat across the grain.

Herb's Barbecue Sauce

In medium sauce pan simmer:

1 14 oz. bottle catsup
1/2 cup chili sauce
1/3 cup wine vinegar
1/4 cup brown sugar
2 tbs. lemon juice
2 tbs. Worchestershire sauce
Makes 2-2/3 cups

2 tbs. prepared mustard
2 tbs. cooking oil
2 tbs. steak sauce
1 tbs. dry mustard
1 clove garlic chopped
salt and pepper

Roberta Gellis

"Each time I see you," he said, "you are more beautiful than the previous time."

"Don't say that," Magaera replied, pretending crossness, but she did not pull her hand from Philip's grasp. "It is impossible to maintain such a record."

"Not for you."

—*The Cornish Heiress*

One of the most esteemed authors of historical romances is medieval expert Roberta Gellis, who lives on Long Island, New York. Authors such as Kathleen Woodiwiss, Rosemary Rogers, Beatrice Small, and John Jakes have written her notes and paid tribute to her on television interviews. Since 1965 she has written fourteen historical romances, the most popular being her Roselynde Chronicles. She also has two pseudonyms: Priscilla Hamilton and Max Daniels.

The gray-haired petite author was born in Brooklyn, New York, on September 27, 1927, under the sign of Libra, also known as the Charmers Club. Librans have a great need to express themselves, especially with one other intimate, and they usually are the most charming and lovely women in the zodiac. They have a highly developed sense of beauty and thrive in artistic surroundings.

Roberta also thrives in an academic surrounding. Her mother was a Greek and Latin scholar and her father, a well-known chemist. Thus, her dual interests in science and historical literature came naturally. Between them, her parents enchanted Roberta as a child with Greek and Roman myths and fairytales in French.

"Not only was it the stories I heard as a child, but the freedom I enjoyed to read anything on the shelves of my parents' enormous library. When I was about nine my father gave me the tales of King Arthur to read in Middle English. By the time I was through, I couldn't spell in American English!"

Roberta is a warm, humorous, extremely talented and diversified individual: Earning a B.S. in Chemistry from Hunter College led to ten years of research work at Foster D. Snell, during which time she obtained her M.S. from Brooklyn Polytechnic Institute in Biochemistry. Thereafter she held a number of positions including science editor at McGraw-Hill Book Company, microbiologist at Hudson Laboratories, and freelance editor of scientific texts for Macmillan and other publishers. (She still does freelance scientific editing for Macmillan.) During this time her interest in knights in shining armor induced her to begin a course of study in medieval literature and led to an M.A. in that subject from New York University. When asked which period she likes the most, she admits, "I prefer the Arthurian romances."

She can read French and German, knows some Spanish, and enough Latin and Greek to pick out some inscriptions when researching medieval material.

"I write all the time," says Roberta. "I write historical romances in which I am as accurate as it is possible to be, which are not pap, are not fantastical. Real people live real lives—but in a time when people believed in honor and love. They didn't always live up to their ideals; the noble knights often belted their gentle ladies in the mouth, but they *wanted* to be noble and faithful—and, I forgot to mention, the 'gentle' ladies were not above belting back, if they were strong enough. There is a lovely real story about a 'gentle' lady Adela who, in an argument with her husband, got hold of his sword and chased him around the room with it, remembering to make him swear on the cross before she gave it back that he would not beat her."

Roberta has been married to husband Charles Gellis since 1946. They have one son who is attending graduate school for English Literature. "I also have a large and excessively lively Airedale dog. I manage to work in and around my ordinary duties as a housewife—but I am a *terrible* housewife," she confesses.

"It takes me all day to grind out 1,200 words, what with the normal interruptions of living and the need to consult sources and chase down references, so I write morning and afternoon. Usually by evening I'm too tired to see straight, so I quit. My husband helps by keeping me happy and stable. What influences my writing most, I think, was reading medieval literature and being enchanted by people who believe in honor and true love, although naturally, being human beings, they were as dishonorable and faithless then as people are now. The difference is that they had ideals, even if they did not live up to them; and when they did not live up to them, they knew they had done wrong and sometimes, tried to do better."

Roberta is not particularly interested in people inspecting their own bellybuttons and moaning about their psyches. "The latter," she says, "virtually eliminates the contemporary main line novel—which seem to be full of drug smuggling and law-enforcement officers who are not any better than the thieves. When you add that to my knowledge and interest in history, it is obvious that the historical novels must be my field. Also, with a mother and a husband who were both teachers and my experience as an assistant on the university level, pedagogy is in my soul, I think. I want to give information, but in an interesting manner. I also think much can be learned from history. Men and women have not changed much; we are still driven by the same motives—greed, fear, hate, and sometimes love."

Would she like to have lived in medieval times like her heroines in the Roselynde Chronicles? "Absolutely *not!*" she exclaims. "I know far too much about life in medieval times, about chilblains and filth and disease and fleas and lice to have any fantasies about living then. Actually, I'm very content with my personal life. I don't need to fantasize. I just love to tell

133

stories. I like the idea of bringing a time past to life—as much as that is possible—of bringing a real understanding, I hope, of the lives people led and, perhaps, injecting a sense of the *realities* of love and marriage, which are the same at any time in a monogamous situation."

Roberta is also something of a feminist. She says, "In medieval fiction I chose to present the exceptionally strong woman—and they did exist—rather than the more typical nonentity."

Despite being a born storyteller, she is a "stickler" for facts. Three trips to Europe in the 1960s included England, mainly for research and to get a feel for the land—the hills and rivers so adeptly depicted in many of her books. A major portion of research is provided at home from her vast library.

"Actually, I write everywhere and anywhere. I have two offices, but spend as much time at the dining room table as in either of them. I can write on the subway or in the car while my husband drives. The only inhibiting factor is the need I have for my research materials. If I am using a single source, like a medieval chronicle, I can take it along. However, sometimes I need ten or twenty books when I am dealing with a complex political situation or must consult many biographies of historical persons to obtain *their* views (as well as possible) of the historical events about which I write."

This is Roberta's recipe for a chicken dish. "Anything I can cook must take less than half an hour for preparation time, actually ten minutes is what I aim for."

CHICKEN A LA GELLIS

First prepare the following marinade:

One-quarter cup each of honey and sherry (I use a medium sweet sherry, but dry will also do)

Soy sauce

Water

Mix well (the honey tends to coagulate on the bottom, so be careful). Marinate a quartered chicken, or pieces if you prefer, in the above marinade for at least four hours, turning from time to time. If more convenient, the chicken can be marinated for as long as 24 hours in the refrigerator. Then simply bake at 350 degrees for 1 to 1½ hours. I bake the chicken right in the marinade, because that way if your guests are late or you are writing and forget to make dinner on time, it really doesn't matter; the chicken doesn't dry out. The worse that can happen is that it will fall apart like potted chicken. However, for those who prefer a very crisp skin, you can bake dry, basting every ten minutes or so with the marinade.

Jean Hager

Tiana heard her heart pounding and abruptly she sensed a change in him. One moment he was holding her cruelly, deriding her efforts to free herself, and the next she saw strange lights moving in the depths of his eyes. He stared at her for a long moment, while a frown flitted across his face and was gone. Then, with a muffled exclamation, he bent his head and covered her lips, his mouth moving slowly, parting her own.

—*The Portrait of Love*

When two paperback publishers decided to introduce ethnic heroes and heroines to romance readers, they found one writer, Jean Hager of Oklahoma, who could provide them with just the kind of stories they needed. This native Oklahoman, who is one-eighth Cherokee on her mother's side, knows the Southwest well, and characters dance in her head like so many braves at an Indian religious ceremony.

But that's not her only writing skill; she's also a popular contemporary romance writer of non-ethnic romances and romantic suspense. Children know of her popular mysteries, aimed at eight-to-twelve-year-olds. And last, but not least, she's just written a Regency romance under the pen name Marlaine Kyle, a melange of the names of her three children.

The tall, 5′8″, 135-pound brunette explains that, "I get my complexion from my mostly Irish father and my dark hair and eyes from our Cherokee ancestors." Along with her husband of almost thirty years, Kenneth Hager, Jean makes her home on a ranch in Oklahoma, about halfway between the two small towns where they both attended high school. "Our roots are very deep in this northeastern Oklahoma soil," declares Jean. "We wanted to raise our children in the country where they could have horses, dogs, and cattle and we have never regretted that decision, even though my husband has an hour's drive to work in Tulsa each day where he is an assistant administrator at St. Francis Hospital.

"He loves ranching on the weekends," Jean says fondly. "We raise beef cattle and my husband and my older son are partners in a hog-raising operation." The two Hager sons and one daughter are a rancher, an engineering student, and a junior high school teacher.

Country life is also very beneficial to Jean and her writing. "I have no close neighbors who run in and out for coffee or gossip," she observes with a smile. She also needs absolute quiet when she works. "My friends know that I write until late afternoon and won't call me on the telephone until then. I usually begin writing at about nine in the morning and write until I've done my daily quota of ten pages. Sometimes I'm through by one or so. Other days, when the writing is harder, I may not finish until after five."

Born June 2, in Illinois, the only period of her youth when she was not living in Oklahoma, Jean Hager is a typical Gemini with penetrating intelligence that can appear to leap to difficult—and *correct*—conclusions, without the tedious effort shown by slower minds.

In high school, Jean was a member of both the newspaper and yearbook staffs, but it was in college at Oklahoma State University that she began considering a writing career. "I took a creative writing class and one of my stories was published in the college newspaper," she recalls. "This encouraged me greatly—but then I married and had children and did not write for a number of years. After my children were all in school, I took a correspondence course in fiction writing and joined a writing group in Tulsa. Through the course and the already published writers in my group, I learned the basics of fiction writing, manuscript mechanics, marketing, etc. At first," she continues, "I tried a lot of different kinds of writing—articles were much easier to sell, and so most of my early sales were articles.

"I did sell a few short stories and some confession stories and eventually sold my first children's book, *The Whispering House*. The sale of that first book was certainly a high point in my writing career, as I look back on it. There is nothing quite like the excitement of selling the first one!" she declares. "After publishing two children's books, I began trying to write an adult novel. The first two adult novels I wrote didn't sell, but I managed to get an agent on the basis of the potential he saw in them."

Along with learning to write in those early years, Jean Hager went back to college and got a degree in English. She taught school for a few years, but writing was always her first love and, finally, in 1975, she decided to quit work and write full-time.

"About a year later, I sold my first adult novel. Of course, there were many difficulties and disappointments along the way," she admits. "I think there are some people who simply have to write, though, and evidently I am one of them because no matter how discouraged I got, I always returned to writing."

Every writer has to consider the current market when she decides what kind of book she will write.

"I write romances because I am a romantic at heart—I love a good love story with a happy boy-gets-girl ending—I cry at sentimental movies and when reading sentimental novels—I am more in love with my husband today than on the day we married. I think most women want love and romance in their lives—which probably is why romance novels sell so well."

Although Jean wouldn't change her life for any other, she has made this observation about herself and other romantic authors: "I 'live' my heroine's story as I am writing it. Otherwise the stories don't ring true."

Jean's life has never been rosier. Although she says, a little misty-eyed, "About ten years ago we built a new native stone ranch-style house. It seems awfully large now that our children are grown—but I'm hoping for grandchildren to help fill it up one of these days."

The greatest change that success has made in her life is that she can afford to travel much more than she could before she was a published writer. She's been to various parts of the Southwest, Hawaii, Mexico, and the Caribbean, but she dreams of visiting Egypt, the British Isles, Greece, and Israel. "It comes into the category of research, after all!" she smiles.

As for foods, Jean admits, "Sweets are my greatest temptation—and I'm afraid I am almost constantly on a diet as a result." Here's one of her favorite desserts:

STRAWBERRY-CHEESE PIE

1 16-oz. or 2 10-oz. frozen strawberries (sweetened and sliced)
3½ tbs. cornstarch
¾ cup sugar
1 3-oz. package of cream cheese
2 tbs. milk
Baked pie shell

Mix sugar and cornstarch. Add to thawed berries. Cook in a saucepan over medium heat, stirring constantly, until mixture thickens and is clear rather than cloudy. Cool. While strawberry mixture cools, soften cream cheese at room temperature. Mix softened cream cheese with 2 tbs. milk and spread in bottom of a baked 9-inch pie shell. Add cooled strawberry mixture. Refrigerate several hours. Before serving, spread on top sweetened whipped cream or Cool Whip.

Anne Hampson

She shuddered and tried to swing away but the grip on her wrist was tightened, and slowly, as if to torture her, Carl brought her protesting body close against his own. She twisted about in frantic resistance to the threat of his merciless mouth, but with his other hand he took a grip on her chin, jerking it up. "Do you think you can escape me this time? I ought not to have let you escape before." His head came down, his lips seeking her mouth.

—*Payment in Full*

Few romantic fiction authors have written as many popular contemporary books over the years as English-born Anne Hampson. She wrote one hundred books alone for Mills and Boone, the famous English publishing firm which still supplies Harlequin with many of its reprint rights. However, Mills and Boone once rejected a Hampson novel seventeen years before finally publishing her and making her world famous. Today, Anne writes for Silhouette Romances and she's ready to publish a longer novel, with more pages and complicated love affairs. Her fans aren't content with her usual 200-page romances these days.

When Anne Hampson grew up in pre-war England, her future looked dismal. Ahead of her was poverty and hard work. "If only a clairvoyant could have told me that I would eventually travel the world, live in exotic countries and write novels," she says and sighs, shaking her head. "Probably the prediction would have been so far from my reality that I never would have believed it!"

The pretty, young brown-haired, brown-eyed girl had only two ambitions when she was young and living in Lancastershire. "To teach and to write," Anne recalls. "But we were so poor that it seemed very unlikely I would ever realize even one of these ambitions. At the age of fourteen, I was working in the rag trade earning the equivalent of seventy-five cents a day, with no prospects of ever bettering myself. How I envied those children who could attend the grammar schools! I was so frustrated at not having an education. But I read a good deal and for a while went to the free evening school. But even that came to an end suddenly when I was told I would have to pay. There was no money for that. My mother was a widow and my brother was only eight at the time. I was forced to leave school and go out to work."

Anne married young and raised a son, Peter. But the marriage didn't last too many years and eventually she sought a divorce. "Those years were also rough ones," says Anne. "For a while I struggled trying to make a fortune running a cafe. But I decided I wasn't cut out to be my own boss, so I went back to work in the rag trade, this time at a sewing factory in Manchester. However, it was directly opposite the College of Education, for the training of teachers.

"I was envious of those 'mature' students and gave my prospects some deep thought. They seemed to be women just like myself, and on impulse—for that's part of my Sagittarian nature—I decided to go over to the college and see the principal. She was a Scotswoman whose first request was to look at my matriculation certificates, which, of course, didn't exist," recalls Anne. "But apparently I was the only applicant ever who'd had the cheek to apply for a place in the college without possessing the necessary qualifications, so this wonderful woman took me under her wing."

Those years were war years, and a time when there was a

serious shortage of teachers in England, the shortage being caused partly by young women entering the professions to spend a couple of years in the classrooms before leaving to get married. The education committee decided to experiment with the training of older women, those who, with grown-up families, would give at least ten years to the profession. "I was fortunate to have made a good impression. It was one of the great thrills of my life when I was accepted in the program. I went to a College of Adult Education to get the necessary qualifications."

But to do this, Anne endured another hardship. "I had to leave my job in the rag trade and work on a milk-round, starting at four in the morning in order to get finished by half-past eleven. I would then cycle five miles home, wash and change and grab a sandwich, then cycle another five miles to the college. It was a tough time for me, right through a hard winter, and I worked seven days a week on the milk-round. However," she says, and the memory still brings happiness to her eyes, "I entered the Teacher's Training College and spent the happiest three years of my life to date. We were all mature students and most of us had missed out when young. The comradeship was wonderful; the tutors were marvelous, fully understanding of our difficulties."

With one ambition—teaching—realized at last, Anne began to ponder her second dream—writing. Would it be possible? She now had some money and the leisure to do limited travel. Greece intrigued her, particularly Delphi. Her first manuscript, a story set in modern-day Greece, was accepted. "It was a Christmas present because the letter of acceptance arrived on the day school broke up for the holiday," she says.

"I had six more novels already written," says Anne. "They were done years earlier and never submitted. Seventeen years before, in a brief bout of confidence, I'd sent a story to Mills and Boone which they rejected. It was titled *The Hawk and the Dove,* and—ironically—they eventually published it and it became a bestseller. However, English publishing is different than in America. I must explain that at that time, Mills and

Boone were such a small firm that they could not afford to publish a new author's work until it had first been accepted for serialization. However," she says brightly, "to this day they've published ninety-seven more of my novels!"

After her first novel was published, Anne cut short her five years of teaching and set off to see the world.

"I travel a good deal in order to get first-hand knowledge of the settings I use," she explains. "Travel books are often out of date even before they're published. I have to get things right; I buy maps, take numerous pictures, make friends with the natives and go into their homes, if it's possible—and this leads my thought to fascinating plots."

Anne Hampson's favorite settings for her novels, both for Harlequin and Silhouette, are glamorous and scenic Hellenic backgrounds. "I adore Greece and the people, and most of my romantic novels are set there. I speak a smattering of Greek, and have traveled everywhere, including visiting twenty-six Greek islands."

Born on November 28, Anne's fire sign, known for boundless energy and courage, keeps burning. And like many other Sagittarian authors, she found success in the latter half of her life.

"I'm an idealist. And a romantic," she confides. "I doubt if I'll remarry, however. I'm usually in love with the current hero in my book," she says and smiles at her private joke.

Her new home in England is elegant and ancestral. "I now have a housekeeper and secretary to help me with my work. I'm thrilled to be able to afford such a beautiful estate. It's certainly different from the eleven years I spent in a twenty-one-foot trailer," she says.

"The money I make doesn't mean as much as I once thought. Working as I do for such long hours, I don't have much time to spend the money I make. Spending needs time and patience— I'm afraid I'm short on both. I've learned that gratification lies in the knowledge that thousands of women are going to derive enjoyment from what I write."

Anne Hampson's favorite dessert is delicious and—romantic.

144

BANANAS FLAMBÉ

2 medium-size bananas
the juice of one lemon
6 oz. of dry red wine
a pinch each of cinnamon, ground ginger, and ground nutmeg
2 tsp. of brown sugar
2 tsp. of grated orange peel
2 oz. of chopped or split almonds
4 oz. of rum
cream or ice cream
Serves 2.

Peel the bananas and pour the lemon juice over them. Place the ingredients 3 to 6 in a fairly deep, 10″ skillet and bring to a boil quickly. Reduce the heat to simmer and place the bananas in the liquid, curved face down. Allow to simmer for two to three minutes before turning the bananas over. Baste frequently while continuing to poach the bananas until they are soft. Add the almonds and raise the heat to a rapid boil, then add the rum. Tilt the skillet slightly near to the flame and flambé for a few seconds before serving. Place cream or ice cream to one side of the bananas and pour on the sauce from the skillet.

Virginia Lee Hart

Without warning, he closed his mouth over hers and kissed her soundly until there was not a part of her that did not tingle with it. Karalee wiped one hand vigorously across her mouth and twisted her face into an expression of disgust. But Patrick only smiled. "It will do you no good to wipe that kiss away, Karalee Nolan. You'll taste it when you climb into your bed tonight, as I will, and it will keep you from sleeping."

—So Wild a Rose

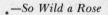

Virginia Lee Hart has a husband who is even *more* romantic than the heroes of her novels. She's married to Freddie Hart, the Country-Western singer, and he wrote "Easy Lovin'" just for her. If you watched the Academy of Country and Western awards on television, he swept up all the honors one year—except those which went to female performers. He also won several gold records and Song of the Year award from the Country Music Association. Sitting by his side during the ceremonies, was Virginia, his wife of twenty-three years, the mother of his two sons, and his romantic inspiration.

"Freddie is a strong supporter of my writing," says Virginia, a 5'7", auburn-haired beauty. "My first sale ever was to *True Romances.* When my check for $212 arrived in the mail, I was in a daze. Freddie was happier about that check than he was about all the royalty checks he had received over the years. We went out to celebrate that night and I paid."

147

Her next triumph, after selling dozens of stories in the romance field, was a sale to *Ellery Queen Mystery Magazine.* "My best friend and her husband had recently tried to establish their own business selling cosmetics. Their frustrations inspired me to write the mystery story, 'Red Letter Day.' It ended with my friend's husband murdering her because she wouldn't allow him to do a trial makeup on her! Of course, this didn't happen in real life, but it was a plot that begged to be written. I wrote it more to tease them than to make a sale."

Selling her first novel *So Wild a Rose,* became the big milestone of her writing life. She'd finally convinced herself that she could write short stories, but *books* were something else. When she received word that Pinnacle Books would buy her manuscript, she said, "I felt like a writer at last."

Writers abound in Virginia's family background. Her parents ran the Little Playhouse of Dramatic Arts—a school of drama and dance. "Mother wrote and directed a radio show and then a TV show, both of which I took part in from age seven," she reminisces. "Dad and Mother were in vaudeville. They were adagio dancers, and along with another man who did comedy, made up the Trendall Trio on the Orpheum Circuit."

Virginia remembers the vaudeville days as a busy period of her life. "Dad went on to do a single act—comedy and juggling. I taught tap, ballet, etc., for Mother. In my teens, I went on the road with a sort of medicine show circus, walking tight-rope. Later, I joined a line-up of dancers (The Rockettes on a minute scale). However, my first writing achievement was when my mother allowed me to write one of the scripts for the children's show she had on radio station KFUO in St. Louis. I was about twelve. I'm certain she did extensive rewriting, but my name was read on the air as sole writer and I burst with pride."

Today, the mother of Virginia Hart writes the *Fur'n Feathers* newspaper column, under the name of Virginia Trendall. (Both Virginias are champions for animal rights.) Virginia's father still writes vaudeville-type comedy skits, and her sister has two books in print. Virginia Lee Hart says reflectively, "With my sort of background, I should have begun writing a long time ago, but I've always been timid and unsure of myself."

148

Like many romantic authors, Virginia can't remember when she *didn't* want to write but her lack of confidence kept her from trying. People who sold books and stories, so she thought, were different from "us ordinary people." Wasn't wanting to be a writer like wanting to be a movie star? "Manuscripts sent off to editors—unless you had pull and knew somebody—might as well have been addressed to Santa Claus at the North Pole," says Virginia with a deep sigh. She's glad that the pangs of shyness have not prevented her from becoming a productive writer. Another shy author, Emily Dickinson, is someone she understands.

"I once read that Emily Dickinson was such a recluse in her later years, that she didn't want to see anyone. Not even her family or friends. She would lower her poems out of a window as someone waited below. Freddie, my husband, accuses me of looking to that as my ambition," she smiles, a faraway look in her indigo blue eyes.

Perhaps her March 5th birthday, under the sign of Pisces, the most mysterious sign of the zodiac, accounts for her infatuation with neat little puzzles that have to be unraveled. She adores mysteries—all mysteries. And she had completed writing two mystery novels. Virginia writes in her living room with a foldaway table in front of a picture window. That way she doesn't *feel* isolated. "I can watch people go by and not have to worry about being pestered by them. My friends have learned that when they see me at my typewriter, with a Coke at hand—I am a Coke-aholic—to keep going."

When Freddie Hart is in the house, he is very *much* in the house and Virginia finds it difficult to concentrate. "My husband is usually composing on his guitar and singing at the top of his voice, hoping I'll listen and comment," she confides. "I would prefer writing early in the morning, but there is terrible chaos at that time. Animals to care for and my youngest son to get out to school. By the time I've delivered Andy to school, my husband is up wanting companionship. He is not a loner."

On the contrary, Freddie Hart is an extrovert and loves everybody. His lifestyle is gregarious and revolves around the happy, cozy home. His philosophy enables Virginia to spend more time on writing books than managing a formal household. When the Harts' living room walls began filling up with awards for hit records, friends asked, "When are you going to move to Beverly Hills?" (And away from Burbank?)

Virginia laughs heartily at the image of her family in Beverly Hills. "Recently we saw a movie where the couple returns to their home to discover that someone has broken in and ransacked the place. 'If that was our house,' Freddie whispered to me, 'we would never have noticed.' As to our moving to Beverly Hills, people would probably get up a petition to kick us out again. Our grass always needs mowing. Our house is usually in need of repair, and the inside is even more in need of work than the outside. I don't think we would change our style of living if we had to build an extra room just to store our money," comments the author. "My husband was one of fifteen children and sometimes had to sleep five or six to a bed—crosswise. He'd feel lost in a big house. He has friends with seven and eight bathrooms and they are a real puzzle to him. Here in Burbank, we'll remain."

Wherever Freddie goeth, so goes Virginia. Both of the Harts are eternal romantics; he's written several songs about her and about their relationship. He and she are direct opposites and Virginia supposes that's why they're so suited. She's been with him to every state in the Union, except Alaska, and many glamorous places throughout the world. "I've been to England, which I love," recalls Virginia, "to Scotland, Wales, Ireland, Germany, Thailand, Hong Kong, and Arabia—all my foreign traveling was in connection with my husband's entertaining. But, my own venture in show business took me through the United States."

So why does she write the stories of romance when she's living them? "I write," she says, "because I am a romantic, married to a romantic. My husband recently wrote and recorded a song called 'Why Lovers Turn to Strangers.' The lyrics explain that people stop loving each other when they stop doing all the things that made them fall in love. This is his philosophy."

As for fulfillment of sexual fantasy through novel writing,

Virginia's soft, pretty face lights up and she beams. "My husband still chases me around the house and is game for everything. That may explain why I write romance."

When the Harts entertain, which is frequently, they love barbecued spareribs. "I simmer them first," explains Virginia, "bake them awhile without sauce, brush them with Chris and Pitts barbecue sauce to bake awhile longer, then brush over a layer of maple syrup and bake still longer. The result is the best sort of eating I can imagine."

What does she prepare for Freddie Hart, when he's strumming the guitar and composing love songs for her? "Freddie loves hush puppies. Cornbread batter with chopped-up onions and no sugar, please, rolled into balls and fried in deep fat. *Terrible* for the waistline, but delicious."

Brooke Hastings

"Fortunately for me," Matthew said, nuzzling her neck, "I've had a rocky time with you as it is." His lips brushed her mouth. "I'm going to split your company, Mrs. Lyle. With a little help and an end to certain fraudulent practices, I think your nonmilitary products will be very well."

It was difficult for Caroline to concentrate on what he was saying, given the fact that his hand had wandered underneath her shirt and was lightly stroking her breasts.

—Winner Take All

"My life has been nothing *like* a Silhouette Romance," sighs Brooke Hastings. "My husband Dave wasn't a dynamic business man many years my senior when we met. He was an eighteen-year-old college student, just like I was. And our fifteen-year marriage has had its share of family crises and personal problems, just as most real marriages do." The name Brooke Hastings is her pen-name.

Brooke, an Aries sun sign, known for exhibiting unusual leadership qualities, was born March 31, 1946, in New York City. When still a child, she moved with her parents and older brother to the suburban town of Yorktown Heights. "Unlike kids today," she recalls, "we had to make our own amusement. Yorktown was very rustic. I spent my time tramping around in

153

the woods, skating on the local pond in the wintertime, and playing sports on homemade fields."

"My focus in life changed pretty drastically once I started college," she admits. "Basically I decided to major in two things: political science and Dave."

She and Dave Gordon married after their junior year at Brandeis University in Massachusetts. Brooke graduated a semester early, earning a Phi Beta Kappa key in the process, and went to work for two of her professors who had started an academic publishing firm. "I typed their first book for them, for photo-offset reproduction," she says. "It contained a group of essays on Slavic linguistics—I had taken several years of Russian in college—and was written in every language from Ukrainian to Old Church Slavonic."

After Dave finished school, he and Brooke moved to New York City, where Dave found work as a teacher in the area later depicted in the Paul Newman movie, *Fort Apache, the Bronx.* Brooke's job, as a researcher with a Columbia University "think tank" was considerably less hazardous. When the organization's funding expired, she put in several months with the now-defunct Book and Educational Division at *The New York Times.* She later used some of her experience at *The Times* in her first book, *Playing for Keeps.*

In the meantime, Dave had decided that he wanted to make education his permanent career and had applied for admission to a doctoral program in educational administration at Harvard University. "If he wasn't accepted," Brooke recalls, "we were going to take the summer off and go to Alaska. Otherwise, we figured it would be a good time to have a child." Dave entered Harvard in September, 1970, and Jennifer was born six months later.

When Dave's course work was completed, he and Brooke decided that he should look for a job in California. "We knew that if we didn't make the move when we were relatively young, we'd never make it at all. We'd taken a trip out here a few years before and loved it," Brooke explains, "but even so, it was very hard at first. In three years at Cambridge, I'd worked part-time,

154

with Dave and I sharing childcare. We'd left behind close friends, as well as both our families. I didn't know a soul. I was pregnant with our second child, and Dave's mother was terribly ill. He had to make several trips back to Florida that first summer, leaving me alone." Brian, born in 1973, is named for his late grandmother, Dave's mother Beatrice.

Brooke admits that it took her a few years to get used to California—the life style and the people are very different, she says—but now she'd hate to leave. While her children were little, she was an active volunteer, eventually serving as a local president and then California State Public Affairs Chairwoman for the National Council of Jewish Women.

Her first exposure to contemporary romances came when she was helping collect used books for a local organization's annual sale. "I read them, enjoyed them, and figured I could write one, even though almost all of my writing experience was in academic-type research," she recalls.

Brooke began work on *Playing for Keeps* during a difficult time in her personal life. Brian was proving to be a handful—he had twice Jenny's energy and a temper to match. Dave, preoccupied by problems that almost broke up the marriage, could offer no help. Reading romances—and writing them— was a form of escape.

"In retrospect, it was a horrible few years," Brooke recalls. "But when you're living through something like that, you just try to get through each day. There's an old saw about adversity making you a stronger, deeper person, and I think there's a lot of truth to it. I wouldn't want to change the past. There have been times in our marriage when I've been working through problems, and Dave has tried to provide support and under-standing. The reverse is also true. My experiences are reflected in my current writing—I hope I've learned something about what people really feel, and why they act the way they do."

What does the future hold for the woman who writes as Brooke Hastings? "I hope to write a longer novel, which would have overtones of high finance and adventure as well as a strong romantic plot. Maybe a literary novel set in the sometimes

155

incomprehensible state of California will be the fulfillment of my second ambition. But for the present, I'm happy to remain one of Love's Leading Ladies."

There are days when she likes to cook. Banana Bread a la Hastings is one of her favorites.

BANANA BREAD

1½ cups sugar
½ cup soft butter
4 ripe bananas, mashed
2 eggs, well beaten
4 tbs. buttermilk
1½ cups flour
1 tsp. baking soda
1 tsp. baking powder
⅛ tsp. salt
1 cup walnuts

Cream sugar and butter; add bananas, eggs, and buttermilk. Sift together flour, soda, powder, and salt and add to liquid mixture. Add nuts. Bake in a well-greased loaf pan for 65 minutes (or until toothpick comes out clean) in a 350 degree oven.

Victoria Holt

*Her masquerade succeeded—too
well. Too late, Suewellyn learned the
true character of the woman she had
chosen to become. Caught in a web
of her own creation, she found herself faced with a final, desperate
choice—risk losing the man she
loved, or face the terrifying chance
that she would be trapped forever by
the tragedy that haunted every Mate-
land bride. . . .*

—*Mask of the Enchantress*

As Victoria Holt, she is considered one of the supreme writers
of the Gothic romance, a compelling storyteller whose gripping
novels of the darker face of love have thrilled millions.

As Jean Plaidy, she has won the accolade, "One of England's
foremost historical novelists."

As Philippa Carr, she has earned acclaim for producing the
bestselling family saga, "Daughters of England," a series which
follows the fortunes of one English family from Tudor time to
the present day.

But what about Eleanor Hibbert, the woman behind the
bestselling authors? She was born in London, September 1,
1906, the daughter of Joseph and Alice (Tate) Burford. Victoria,
as her readers call her, was sickly as a child (throat problems)
and was privately educated in London. Having learned to read
even before she began attending school, the petite brunette
decided very early in life that she, too, would become a writer
some day. In view of her childhood obsession with books, and

her unwavering determination, it's no wonder that she now requires three different pseudonyms to account for all her efforts!

"In my teens and early twenties I wrote several novels, none of which achieved publication," she confides. "But this was not quite as depressing as it might have been, for in the meantime, I wrote short stories, which were published in the *Daily Mail,* the *Evening News,* and other papers."

In college she studied shorthand and typing and also languages, at which she is unusually fluent. After leaving college she held a variety of jobs, ranging from handling opals and pearls in London's famous Hatton Garden, to acting as an interpreter to French and German patrons in one of London's chic cafes.

Meeting George Hibbert and eventually marrying him, gave her the impetus to launch her writing career in earnest. "There was no question that I would try my hand at writing a historical novel," she recalls. "They were the type of novel which had always attracted me."

Right from the beginning she realized she would have to work very hard to become a successful writer. "I soon found that the best method was to work steadily and consistently. The method I adopted is to write for about five hours a day—but not at one stretch." She likes to rise early and arrive at her desk ready to start work at eight o'clock each morning. She works until ten; then has a half-hour break. During this time she attends to tasks around the house and broods on the characters she is involved in. "They are so real to me that I often talk to them," she admits. At ten-thirty she resumes work for an hour. Then she takes a long break until five in the afternoon. At five, she settles down to another two-hour stint, finishing for the day at seven o'clock in the evening. "This method, combined with singleminded enthusiasm and determination to succeed, has meant that I have become prolific and books appear at regular intervals."

Prior to the birth of Victoria Holt (a name suggested by her agent) she had published over thirty books under the names of Eleanor Burford, Elbur Ford, Kathleen Kellow, and Ellalice Tate. She began with publishers Mills and Boone and was for a time one of Harlequin's most popular authors. *Beyond the Blue Mountain* by Jean Plaidy was a 1951 selection.

In 1960, no one was writing or publishing novels of romantic suspense. But in that year, Victoria created a contemporary feeling for romance with the great Gothic tradition of brooding suspense. *The Mistress of Mellyn* became an immediate best-seller. By the time her fourth novel, *The Legend of the Seventh Virgin*, was published, the phrase "romantic suspense" had become part of the language and an important category of fiction in bookstores.

Why the name Victoria Holt captured such a large readership, no one really knows. For eight years, Doubleday kept the Victoria Holt pseudonym a well-guarded secret. Was Victoria Holt really Daphne du Maurier, people have wondered? "I have heard her name mentioned in connection with mine and I think it is because we both lived in Cornwall and have written about this place. *Rebecca* is the atmospheric suspense-type of book mine are. But I don't think there is much similarity between her others and mine," she says.

Research is a vital part of her life. "I prefer to do all the research myself," she explains. "I have never thought it wise to employ researchers because delving into the past is not merely collecting facts, but actually absorbing the spirit of the age. I feel it is very necessary for me to capture that. It is something vague, intangible, which must be suggested; and is entirely a personal feeling that I have to discover and impart to the readers."

She is fortunate to live in London, surrounded by libraries, where she is so highly esteemed that she is allowed into the special archives. "There are thousands of books on my subject," she explains, "some are very rare, and I'm permitted to take them home and keep them as long as I need them. This has been of the greatest possible help," she adds.

Her research and absorption begin some time before the actual writing. "I read the history of the period and then as many biographies, memoirs, and letters as I can—not only leading characters, but of anyone who lived in that age."

Victoria works and lives in a penthouse overlooking London. She reluctantly sold her second home, a thirteenth-century inn.

"The house had provided lodging for Henry VIII and Elizabeth I," she says. "I named that house the King's Lodging, naturally. A Tudor staircase was put in and part of it remains today. Later, when Elizabeth I stayed there, special carved fireplaces were put in for her. I restored it to make it as much like it was in their day, so you see, the Tudors mean something special to me."

Looking back over her books, she feels the richest yield came from the Tudors, though, "I have ranged from the beginning of the sixteenth century to the start of the twentieth. I then went back to the Norman Conquest with a Norman Trilogy, and followed this with the Plantagenet Saga. I shall go writing books in chronological order until I catch up with the early Tudors."

It is always the personal, or human perspective which attracts her most and it is the very tone of the human voice, heard in past eras, she strives to capture.

"Happily, there seems always to have been those people who hide behind the arras, secreting themselves in boudoirs and peeping through the keyholes and then going away to report what they've seen and heard." And it is this kind of fossilized gossip Mrs. Hibbert calls "a tremendous boon" for a writer such as herself.

When she's relaxing, Victoria Holt, now a widow, enjoys seeing friends, playing chess, and working needlepoint. She has taken numerous cruises—more than sixty!—which provides wonderful solace for writing time.

"Writing excites me," she reveals. "I live all my characters and never have any trouble thinking of plots of how people would have said something . . . because I'm them when I'm writing. Obviously," she teases, "I only do one at a time. I couldn't switch from Victoria Holt to Jean Plaidy to Philippa Carr just like *that!*"

She's right, nothing comes that easy. Particularly cooking. Victoria devotes herself more to developing her characters' eating *habits* than developing recipes. However, she does have a favorite she is pleased to share.

160

PORK CHOPS WITH SWEET AND SOUR SAUCE

Grill 4 loin chops in a little oil and keep warm.

For sauce, combine 2 tbs. vinegar, 1 tbs. sugar, a good tsp. of tomato ketchup, 4 tbs. water, 1¼ tsp. cornstarch and boil together, stirring well until thick and smooth. Add salt and pepper.

Stir in very finely sliced spring onion, a selection of Chinese pickle which includes ginger and chilies, a little finely sliced celery and a fresh red tomato.

Pour the sauce over the chops and serve garnished with watercress.

Florence Hurd

Not until one of them threw back her hood and curtseyed low to the king did I see the golden hair, the exquisite, creamy-skinned features, the face of the woman who had filled me with such pain, such guilt and such love. Thaisa.
Forget her? As if I could.

—*Fountains of Glory*

The meals and house payments of Encinitas, California, novelist, Florence Hurd, hang on a sentence, the single sentence that begins chapter one. She knows the sentence must intrigue the browser in front of a book rack, encouraging the reader to continue—then buy one of her books.

That is why, after seventeen years as an author, Florence still believes in that first line. Once she captures the reader, the rest is easy. This quiet, professional writer has held the reading public's attention through twenty Gothics, three romantic suspense novels and five historical novels.

A living that depends upon a sentence is somewhat risky, because just ten percent of America's writers support themselves solely by writing. But, writing under the names of Flora Hiller, Fiona Harrowe, Florence Hurd, and Florence Howe, she has managed to sustain herself by her words for a quarter of her life.

"I stopped 'piddling around' with short stories and writing classes in 1965," admits Florence, who recently moved into a new house bought with her book royalties. Her new three-bedroom ranch has a charming enclosed garden, filled appropriately with plants and trees—a perfect place for this hard-working novelist to spend a relaxing hour. But though the rewards of hard work are sweet, they did not come all that easily.

"Publishers were looking for Gothic novels and offering $4,000, a remarkable sum in those days," Florence recalls. "I decided to live on my savings for three months and wrote a 45,000 word Gothic novel titled *Secret of Canfield House*. Fawcett published it the following year." Reprinted three times, the book has been published in Sweden, France, Germany, Australia, as well as the U.S. She went on to write twenty-seven more novels, sometimes writing three a year.

Born November 4, 1918, in Chicago, Illinois, Florence attended the University of Chicago and obtained a Bachelor of Arts degree. She worked for several years as a social worker, and then a housewife, and raised two children. Daughter Susanne is a schoolteacher and Steve, the youngest, is a restaurant manager. Florence's marriage ended in a divorce.

"My first thirteen years as a writer," she recalls, "were very, *very* chancy, I earned $2,500 a book, just enough to eke out a living. I don't like that idea that nothing's assured. Now I can see a year ahead. Before I couldn't see further than a few months . . . whether I was to get another contract or not. Competition's *murderous*."

In 1978 she signed a contract to write two books for $25,000 each. A *giant* step for this tenacious personality. It's not unusual for a Scorpian nature, such as hers, to exhibit extraordinary discipline.

"There are a lot of people far more talented than I who just don't have discipline. That's what kills them off. It's not lack of talent."

Florence Hurd's technique of writing is to revise extensively, She's never satisfied, and always makes three drafts, sometimes four. And she can't work with noise or interruption of any kind. She tries to finish at least 2,500 words a day, an output which is hardly excessive considering the mornings and afternoons spent at the typewriter, sometimes seven days a week.

"Loneliness is an occupational hazard, but I like to write. Sometimes I would rather be doing something else, going to a party, having friends in, walking on the beach, but on the whole I cannot think of another profession that is so satisfying and absorbing. And in my own case . . . financially rewarding. Success has bought me a new house, but otherwise hasn't changed my life style."

Friends call, and occasionally so does her New York agent, but essentially she is alone in a "very lonely occupation that gets to you."

As she adjusted to the early years of living on a meager budget, she now accepts loneliness, fierce competition, and the ache of daily writing. "It was either write or get a job," she confides. "I think that was one of the reasons. I can't tolerate boredom. To me, it'd be *dreadful* having a nine-to-five job. Even though I'm pretty well disciplined, I have a great deal of freedom with my writing. It's the idea that I have freedom. It's wonderful not having a boss."

She gives other reasons. "Once in a while, you do something really good, and you're really pleased. It's like anything creative. You feel you've done something, and it's done out of your head. In a way, it's terrifying to think the groceries and house payment come out of your head. But in another sense, it's very satisfying. I bought this house on my imagination. It pleases the ego."

Unfortunately, she doesn't have time to travel, although she has been to England and across country on various occasions. She enjoys plays, the concerts and the art exhibits the metropolitan areas offer, but she lives in what she calls, "a beautiful part of the world."

"I am never tempted to move. Everything that is said about the California climate is true. Fantastic. After almost forty years of living here, I still find it fantastic, still find the beaches and the blue, blue Pacific a source of pleasure."

When it's dinnertime, she *may* stop and fix a lasagne platter. Here's her favorite version of an entree which is assembled before guests arrive, then cooked during the cocktail hour. To accompany the main dish she prepares a salad of spinach and watercress.

MOCK LASAGNE

8 oz. noodles
2 3-oz. pkg. cream cheese, softened
1 pt. dairy sour cream
½ cup chopped onion
1½ lb. ground beef
1 6-oz. can tomato paste
6 tbs. dry red wine
½ cup sliced mushrooms
½ tsp. oregano
1 tsp. salt
½ tsp. pepper
8 pitted ripe olives, cut in halves
¼ cup grated Parmesan cheese

Cook noodles according to package directions and set aside. Combine cheese, sour cream and onions, blend well and set aside. Brown meat in skillet, stirring to keep meat crumbly. Drain off excess fat. Add tomato paste, wine, mushrooms, oregano, salt and pepper and stir to mix. Cook 6 to 8 minutes. Place 1½ cups sour cream mixture in 12 x 8-inch casserole. Add layer of noodles and top with 1½ cups meat mixture. Repeat layers. Top with olives and cheese. Bake at 350 degrees 1 hour. Makes 8 servings. Serve a hearty red wine, toasted garlic bread, and spinach salad with the lasagne.

Kristin James

Nick's lips brushed Morgan's soft and warm, undemanding, then returned, pressing against her mouth, suddenly hot and urgent. His arms tightened around her, crushing her against his chest.

Then she heard the trill of Cara's laugh in the distance and a few indistinguishable words in Alexis's firm voice. Morgan jerked herself from Nick's grasp and faced him, one hand nervously smoothing her hair.

"You've got the wrong sister, remember?" Her voice trembled slightly.

"Not wrong, never wrong."

—*The Sapphire Sky*

The names Kristin James and Lisa Gregory are the pennames of a young lawyer by the name of Candace Camp, who lives in central Texas. She started writing her historical romances in law school, and it was soon after graduation that her first paperback novel, *Bonds of Love*, was sold to Jove. Today she doesn't have time to practice law. "I preferred writing and finally have reached the point where I can make a living at it," she says with pride.

Candace-Lisa-Kristin was born in Amarillo, Texas, which is in the vast flat land of the historic Texas Panhandle. Her birthday, May 23, 1949, places her under the sign of the Gemini twins—duality. These people usually make fine judges and journalists, and this author embodies her sign to the hilt!

167

"I came from a newspaper family; my mother was a reporter and my father the business manager for the local paper. Ever since I can remember, I have loved to fantasize. Even before I could read and write, I was making up long, involved stories and acting them out with my mother's kitchen utensils and my playthings. I was very shy. As I grew up, my favorite pastime became reading. During high school, I wrote poetry, short stories, and bits and pieces of novels. I never could finish a novel," she amends, with a shy smile, "because I'd get bored with it and think of a still more interesting plot, and I'd be off writing on another—in those days."

Kristin, as her fans call her, is 5′3″ with light brown hair, green eyes, and a very pale complexion. She was married in 1979, at St. Luke's Catholic Church in Temple, Texas, to Pete Hopcus, a former priest, whom she met while she was in private practice as a lawyer. Their first child was born in October, 1981.

"My husband is a great help," she says with a glowing smile, "in that he *expects* me to be a writer, not a housewife; he doesn't complain about missed meals, dirty dishes, and all that. Also, he listens to my ideas, and that's important. He helps me with my research as well, and aids my attempts at discipline on those blah days.

"I have found that if I make myself start writing in the morning, even though my output isn't as much as later in the day, I am much more likely to stick at my typewriter in the afternoon and produce more then. Not considering anything else, the best time for me to write is the afternoon and evening, even into the night. However, since I like to spend time with my husband, I arrange my work schedule around his. Consequently, I usually work until seven or eight in the evening, since my husband, a marriage counselor, frequently has evening sessions," she explains.

How did a teacher become a lawyer and then a historical novelist? "After I graduated from the West Texas State University I taught school for a year, or tried to—I was not a shining success as a teacher. I liked children well enough, and I loved the English and history courses I taught, but I was lousy at

168

discipline. A teacher of eighth and ninth graders really needs that ability.

"My brother was a lawyer in Winston-Salem at the time, and he encouraged me to go to law school," she recalls. "So I applied at and was accepted by the University of North Carolina Law School, from which I graduated in 1977. Before I went into law school, I read *The Flame and the Flower,* by Kathleen Woodiwiss. It occurred to me that I ought to try my hand at writing historical romances. During my first year at law school, I wrote *Bonds of Love.* Whatever else it did for me, law school finally gave me the time-organizing ability that I had always lacked," she states. "And for the first time I was able to really *finish* a novel! A good friend of mine typed it for me, since I was a terrible typist, and I sent it to a publisher. After several months, I got it back with a note that they had too many books of this type.

"Discouraged, but still game, I mailed it off to another publishing house. I heard nothing from them, and in the meantime, I graduated from law school and moved to Paris, Texas, to work as an attorney for a trust department there. One day, not long after I moved, I got a letter from Jove Publications and they said that they wanted *Bonds of Love.* Of course, I started shrieking and calling everyone I knew to tell them the good news. That first novel came out in June, 1978. I had written about three-fourths of another book while in law school, and I managed to finish it and sent it in. *The Rainbow Season* came out in 1979. While I was finishing the last chapters, I realized that I simply could not work full-time at a demanding job and write a novel every year or so, especially since I had gotten very involved with the local civic theater group and spent a great deal of time on it.

"So I quit my job and went into private practice as a lawyer, working part-time and writing part-time. I also met my husband in Paris—Texas, that is—and we married the same month that *The Rainbow Season* was published. Then we moved to Temple, Texas, a town of about 40,000 people. We have been living here ever since and intend to remain."

Has she ever been sorry that she gave up law and the civic

theater for writing, or for what could be an insecure career? "Oh, no! I started writing historical romances because I read them and enjoyed them. I love romance and fantasy, and I thoroughly enjoy thinking up the stories. Besides that, they sell very well, and I make a better living now doing what I love best," she insists.

Kristin lives in a fairly large, older, one-story house that has a shady beautiful yard. It is in a quiet neighborhood, with manicured lawns and many trees. "I grew up in Texas, and I love it here. That's why I returned when I got out of law school," she explains. "I picked this area of Texas because my husband wanted to live here. He had lived here before and loved it."

Kristin writes in a study in her home. In fact, the study was the feature that most made her want to buy the house. "I do my actual writing there," she explains. "But I quite often do my plotting sitting on a couch in our den, which is more comfortable than my typing chair. And my thinking," she adds, "goes on wherever I am. Two of the best places are in a car on a trip or lying in my bed at night, before I go to sleep."

Many times, authors that she enjoys reading stimulate her to write. "I don't care what type of book it is—mystery, romance, adventure, modern, historical. I can't quite explain it," she says with a mysterious smile, "because it is a process I don't understand myself, but writing depletes me, and reading gives back some life to my imagination."

Kristin adores baking when she's not busy writing. "This is a chocolate cake recipe that is divine, I think, and also terribly fattening!"

DOUBLE RICH CHOCOLATE CAKE

2 cups sugar
2 cups flour
3½ tbs. cocoa
½ cup Crisco
1 stick butter or margarine
1 cup boiling water

Pour boiling water over the above ingredients. Add 2 eggs and beat until blended.

Add:
½ cup buttermilk
1 tsp. soda
1 tsp. vanilla
¼ tsp. salt

Mix together well. Grease large baking pan and pour in mixture. Bake for twenty minutes at 350 degrees. Put icing on cake as soon as you take the cake out of the oven. Don't wait for it to cool.

Icing:
1 stick butter
2 tbs. cocoa
1/3 cup sweet milk

Bring milk to a boil and pour over butter and cocoa. Add 1 small box powdered sugar and mix together. Then spread it on the cake.

Johanna Lindsey

She watched the iron muscles ripple on his back when she tried to move her arms and he stayed her. Brenna admired strength and courage; she always had. But this man's strength was unbelievable. He held her with such ease when she tried her mightiest to move him. Though such a powerful body was magnificent to behold, that she lay at the mercy of its strength was unbearable.

—*Fires of Winter*

At first sight of Johanna Lindsey, one is mesmerized by her *four feet* of long, straight blonde hair! One imagines Alice-in-Wonderland in Hawaii! Then her intelligent hazel eyes, fair complexion, and attractive 5'4" figure catch your eye. She hardly looks old enough to be the mother of three school-age boys.

Johanna was born in Frankfurt, Germany, on March 10, 1952. Compassionate, friendly, sensitive and introspective are the attributes of the Pisceans. Generous and trustworthy to the degree of their sentimentality. A sensitive intuition provides them with psychic tendencies.

The daughter of a Master Sergeant in the U.S. Army, Johanna remembers little of her infancy spent in Germany and France. The family returned to the States where she spent her early childhood in Kentucky. "The most memorable experiences of those years," she recalls, "were visiting my grandmother in Chicago, and my father's family in Harlan, Kentucky.

173

Now those trips I *can* remember, especially driving over the magnificent mountains of Kentucky. I've been fascinated by mountains ever since and was delighted to find so many in Hawaii when my family moved to Oahu in 1964.

"I spent the rest of my childhood in Kailua on the windward side of Oahu, going to intermediate and high school there. I met my husband, Ralph, on a blind date just after graduating from Kailua high school, and married him four months later. We live now in a lovely valley with Koolau Mountains just outside my windows."

Johanna is and has always been a romantic. "Since I was old enough to appreciate a good novel, I've been a romantic," she says. "I enjoy happy-ending love stories more than any other type of reading. Romance is what comes out of me."

Johanna was just twenty-five years old when Avon published her first attempt at writing, *Captive Bride*, in 1977. Her first book seemed to write itself. The second, *A Pirate's Love*, was almost as easy. "I do not use an outline to write, but start with a basic idea," explains Johanna, "and let the story develop by itself. I take care of research before I begin my story, once a century and continent are decided upon. I would love to visit the areas that I write about, but unfortunately, the only traveling I do is to the library."

She prefers to write in longhand, "which is easiest for me, curled up on my bed or couch in the afternoon while my kids nap, and then at night once the house is quiet. In the mornings, between a few soap operas that I became addicted to years ago— 'General Hospital' and 'One Life to Live'—I type up whatever was written the day before. Writing occupies all of my spare time when I am not taking care of my home and family. I love it," she admits. "I get so involved with my hero and heroine and whatever is happening to them, it's like I'm living in two different worlds. I would be literally *lost* if I had to give it up," she states sincerely.

While she writes, Johanna has learned to tune out the noise of her three active sons, who range in age from eleven to six, which is frustrating for them when they get around to asking her something "and have to *scream* to get my attention. The one thing I can't manage to tune out, though, is the TV, which blares a good part of the day and that is why I have to escape to my bedroom, far away from the noise."

Johanna's husband, Ralph Lindsey, is very patient and understanding, and she says, "That's all the help I need. But my mother's encouragement, criticism, and praise has been invaluable."

If she had another hobby besides reading and writing, it would be painting. "I have a few paintings hanging in the Federal Building in Honolulu—but not on exhibition," she hastens to say. "They're in my mother's office there. But I don't have much time for other passions. I enjoy dancing, playing a friendly game of poker or chess, and watching my children grow up on such a beautiful island. Our spacious four-bedroom townhouse overlooks the Valley of the Temples on the windward side of Oahu."

What does success mean to a young writer, wife, and mother who never worked at any other career than writing? "Seeing my work in print is thrilling, but the emotional satisfaction is beyond description," she confides. "Other than a change in family finances, and the pride of accomplishment, success hasn't changed my life."

Johanna Lindsey's three sons love her Hamburger Potpies and always ask for seconds, she says. Here's a detailed recipe for an easy-to-make family dish.

HAMBURGER POTPIES WITHOUT THE POT

1 lb. hamburger (crumble and brown in skillet, then remove)
Dough Mixture
3 cups flour
4½ tsp. baking powder
1½ tsp. salt
1 cup milk
½ cup oil

Place flour, baking powder, and salt in large bowl. Add milk and oil to bowl and stir until ball forms, then knead 10 times and divide into 5 parts, flattening each into 8″ rounds.

White Sauce
1 tbsp. butter
1 tbsp. flour
1 cup milk
5 slices American Cheese

Melt butter in skillet, medium heat. Mix flour and milk, then add to butter, stirring until thickened. Pour into measuring cup.

Divide hamburger between the dough rounds, placing in center. Crumble one slice of cheese on top of each. Pour one-fifth portion sauce over hamburger and cheese of one round. Fold edges of dough over top, sealing it, then place on cookie sheet. Go to the next round, pouring sauce again and sealing, etc. Bake at 375 degrees for 15–20 minutes, until top of pies begin to brown. Remove with spatula. Serves 5. With vegetable and salad, makes a full meal.

Morgan Llywelyn

Brian's strength was so far beyond hers that it no longer seemed necessary to challenge it. More than anything else, she found herself wanting to melt into boneless surrender. As the thought came to her, something gathered itself in her body that had never been there before; a heavy, unbearable sweetness, an intense concentration of pleasure almost identical with pain, a maelstrom spiraling downward into a total loss of self she had never imagined and could have never surrendered to until this moment. She ground her hips together, squeezing him with the female power she had never fully appreciated before, drawing from him the explosion of ecstasy that must be had at all costs. It was impossible that there could be so much, but there was, there was, there was!

—Lion of Ireland

What does it mean to be psychically attuned? To have life abound with occult phenomena? And then write about it? For Morgan Llywelyn, a ravishing brunette, who has "more than her share of prophetic dreams," such experiences add depth and meaning to her life.

The petite, 5'3", 110-lb. author was born in New York City,

177

but she credits the abundance of mystical occurrences that permeate her novels to her Welsh-Irish ancestry.

"I've always had experiences outside the everyday," Morgan says. Her mahogany eyes shine with intensity when she speaks. "I've seen things, and known things; I feel I can communicate with animals and trees.

"Almost anything is possible in life," she believes. "The longer I live, the less I doubt. We are all like tadpoles in the mud at the bottom of the pond, thinking we know all there is to know about the world—we, who have never been up in the sunlight."

When Debrett's Peerage announced that it had traced Ronald Reagan's ancestry back to the eleventh-century Irish King Brian Boru, Morgan, a lifelong Republican, sent him a copy of *Lion of Ireland,* her novel based on Boru's life.

President Reagan called the author Christmas, 1980, to compliment her on the book, saying he was "sneaking away every chance I get" to read it. He also recommended the story to some movie producers who liked historicals as much as he. *Lion of Ireland* is the first historical novel to be brought to the screen in recent years.

Lion of Ireland, Reagan's choice of light reading during his first month in Washington, landed twice on *Time* magazine's national bestseller list, and appeared as the number two best-selling book in Ireland in 1980.

An only child, Morgan was born on December 3, 1937. True to the astrological sign of Sagittarius, she delights in danger and excitement. Significantly, she has the archer's love for horses.

"I was born horse crazy," she recalls. "I used to cut school to ride to the end of the busline, and from there walk four miles to a polo field. At the polo field they let me clean stalls in return for teaching me to exercise polo ponies."

And why didn't she grow up to write *Black Beauty* or *Flicka* novels? Morgan's interest in horse flesh was primarily physical and when she grew older, all she dreamed of was buying her first horse. She worked as a fashion model to support her hobby. In 1953 she held the U.S. high jump record for a woman. Then the day came when she was crushed beneath a horse—her arms, legs, ribs, collarbone and pelvis broken.

Her husband, Charles Winter, whom she married in 1957, encouraged her to change to Dressage, which she explains is "like figure skating, except one performs the stylized movements while riding a horse."

After she came close to making the 1976 Olympic team in Dressage, she decided it was time to go on to something else. "I had my adventures in my head," Morgan said, "and I wanted to use a typewriter to share them with others."

She began to write in 1975 at the age of thirty-eight. At first she wrote short stories for minor magazines. Then her writing career began to flourish, and when it did, she and her husband made a major decision about their lives. Morgan would become the breadwinner.

"My husband retired from being a charter pilot to stay home, keep house, manage our finances, care for our pets, spend time with our college-bound son and leave me free to do *nothing* but write."

Women libbers cheer her role reversal, although such a domestic arrangement is becoming quite common among women writers. Morgan has found that she can "have her cake and eat it too." She and Charles are happier than ever pursuing the things they really enjoy.

"Charles has proved to be a first-rate cook," Morgan says proudly. "He has even learned to like soap operas! And now he's enjoying and caring for our horse. He plans to take up competition riding. Most important, he's a *perfect* companion for a writer. We travel everywhere together; he is my strongest supporter, severest critic, and my proofreader."

Morgan's house in Annapolis, Maryland, has a special chocolate-brown office for her writing hours, with floor-to-ceiling bookshelves and a view of the Chesapeake bay. With this soothing backdrop, Morgan plies her craft six days a week, spending from four to ten hours a day in solitude. "Absolute quiet is essential when I'm working—no exceptions!" says Morgan.

Writing has never been drudgery or painful for Morgan, although she concedes that to be good at it you must work very hard. "I write the kinds of stories I write because they appeal to me; they say things about people that excite me; they shed light on ages and civilizations that fascinate me. I write for my own enjoyment first. I think if I enjoy it, then others will," she asserts.

This visionary writer has had a lifelong interest in all things Celtic. Her first novel, *The Wind from Hastings*, evoked a journey in nostalgia for those of Irish, Welsh, and Scottish or English heritage because of Morgan's scholarly research into Anglo-Saxon history.

In *Lion of Ireland: The Legend of Brian Boru*, author Llywelyn researched old Gaelic Ireland and the life of King Brian so thoroughly that one critic suggested that the story "may very well be as close to an accurate biography as any writer has published so far on the life of Brian Boru," the immortal High King of Ireland, who defeated the Norsemen at the Battle of Clontarf in the tenth century.

Her research into these ancient histories and religions has convinced Morgan that once we were closer to the secrets of the universe than we are now; that we had wisdom and abilities we have lost. "We were closer to the tremendous force of life itself, that power we call God, and we recognized our place in the scheme of things," Morgan believes. "Now we feel dispossessed and frightened, and the world seems to have gotten out of control."

Somewhat in awe, Morgan boasts of her ancestors who did not fear death, and who recognized it as a mere transition state. "The ancient Celts, ancestors of the Irish and Scots, the Germans, and French and Welsh, and some of the Spanish, did not even think that death existed. It was just a door to go through; it had a power to terrify them. They understood the indestructibility of the life force and trusted it. I'm sorry that we've lost that clearsightedness," Morgan declares.

As an author, Morgan Llywelyn hopes to reacquaint her readers with some of the knowledge of those times, and to give them a feeling of pride in their heritage as human beings.

"I have had, so far, a life chock-full of adventure, romance, some danger, a lot of tears and laughter, and I have an endless fund of stories to tell, both my own and those from other times,"

Morgan muses. "I want to think I can offer my readers escape and knowledge; a doorway leading into other times and other lives; a chance to meet, and to be with fascinating people.

"When I can, I like to visit the places I will write about, feel the ground under my feet, breathe the air, look at the views, store up the impressions that will enable me to create a sort of time machine, so that I can always take the reader back there with me."

Not that Morgan paints life as unrealistically idyllic. "As for difficulties, everybody has them," she says philosophically. "A sword must be tempered in fire. But," she adds, "I think of life as a test and a problem overcome. Pain and loss and grief can all be borne—millions of people have done so, and everyone must sooner or later. It's the way you meet them that counts."

As for recipes? Charlie is the cook. "He makes delicious cocoa muffins," says Morgan. "But he won't divulge the recipe. Professional secrecy and all that. He likes to be the one who can make them. I like to be the one who gets to enjoy them," she smiles.

Amii Lorin

"Be brave, Jennifer," Adam whispered invitingly, his hands moving slowly, caressingly over her back. "Take that one tiny step necessary to bring your body against mine."

—*Snowbound Weekend*

One of the new names in category romances is a Pennsylvania writer who helps make Dell's Ecstasy line of romances live up to its name! When her novel *The Tawny Gold Man* appeared, the ever-alert readers sent up "romantic" smoke signals to tell all their reading friends that a new writer was on the scene—one who understood that women want sensuality to exist between more realistic characters.

Amii Lorin writes under a pseudonym that combines the names of her two teenage daughters. The author's real name is Joan Hohl and she lives quietly with her family in a row-style house in Reading. It's a happy surprise to her that readers call her the "new romantic wave."

The high praise she receives is still amazing Amii. "Although I have been indulging in the mental exercise of plotting stories all my life," says the 5'6" hazel-eyed brunette, "I didn't begin writing seriously until five years ago. I reached the age of forty and figured, what did I have to lose? I sat down and thought I'd give it a try. I've always enjoyed category romances, especially the Harlequins and some of the Dell Candlelights."

Her first completed work was *Morgan Wade's Woman,* and it was published in 1981. "Fortunately, I've sold everything I've written to date," she remarks with a contented sigh. "I have an outline in my head and it builds from there. Quite often I don't know what I'm going to say until it gets on the paper. I write the way I feel. I'm a realist, so it surprises me that I'm also considered such a sensualist. My ideal is Ayn Rand, because everything she writes hits me as truth. I want to write the way I like to read. And I like an adult story. But nothing," she emphasizes, "is based on anything true or has what has happened to me in it. I don't know where the ideas come from."

Her husband, Marvin Hohl, is quite proud of his wife's accomplishments, but he's not overly impressed. "Marv *is* Mr. Conservative and he's the force in the family. We have a marriage of opposites and it has been very successful. We don't share many likes. He says very little, but when he talks, the girls and I listen," she says.

The couple love the ocean. Marv has "a thing for lighthouses." Amii loves the seashore the sunset, lilacs, summertime, trees, the white trail of a jet plane across the blue sky, and even the skyline of New York City. "I think of it as a monument to man's potential," she explains.

Amii grew up in Reading, Pennsylvania. Born there on June 13, 1935, under the sign of Gemini, a sign noted for duality of character. She believes she has led a very uneventful and staid life—just the opposite of the lives of her characters! "My father was a cabdriver and my mother was a homemaker," says the author. "I have an older sister and a younger brother, and our childhood was exceptionally uneventful. I was always referred to as the dreamer of the family, living in a world all my own, my head in the clouds."

Life has been very good for Amii. "At seventeen I married Marvin (who now works in a used car parts business), and have had no regrets. I worked after high school. First as a sales clerk and then as a knitting machine operator. But I always dreamed of writing fiction. I thought for years that it was a little presumptuous to think of it, I just couldn't see myself doing it. But turning forty changed all that!"

The royalties are just beginning to affect her lifestyle. "We've invested a little more in the house. We have a little more freedom and leeway in our spending these days, I'm glad to say."

Amii exists during the day "on the coffee pot" (she drinks twelve–fourteen cups). Her writing desk is her kitchen table. She works in longhand, with a pencil. "I write at all times of the day but—being nocturnal—I do my best work at night. By now my family is used to my hours. I've always been nocturnal. I would read at night before I became a writer."

Like every author the glimmer of writing the great American novel exists in Amii's dreams. "I only know that I want to write an original something. Probably it would be a love story because I believe in romantic love, that it exists. My novel would definitely take place in America because it's what I know. I love to travel but so far my forays have been close to home. Someday I hope to be able to travel extensively and who knows—I may go to the South, an area with great historical significance, and write my great American novel. The only title I can think of would be 'In Search of Patrick Henry,'" she remarks humorously. "Because he was fiery, he fires my imagination!"

Her favorite recipe is for a cheese cake that is easy to make. "It's so simple to bake that I'm almost ashamed to accept the compliments I always receive when I serve it."

AMII'S CHEESE CAKE

Grease 9″ pie pan or glass baking dish. Pre-heat oven 350 degrees.
Mix:
1 lb. cream cheese
3 eggs
2/3 cup sugar
Beat until light and fluffy and lemony in color. Pour into pan or dish, bake 25 minutes. Cool 25 minutes.
Mix:
1 cup sour cream, 3 tbs. sugar, 1 tbs. vanilla.
Pour over top of cooled cake and bake 10 minutes.

Elizabeth Mansfield

After he kissed her, and kissed her a second time to make sure it was not a dream, and a third time just because it seemed a perfectly sensible thing to do, she buried her head in his shoulder. "I don't suppose you'd care to tell me that my very flattering sentiments are quite equally reciprocated," she suggested in a very small voice. "It is supposed to be the polite response to the sort of declaration I've just made."

—*Her Man of Affairs*

Readers of Regency novels say that Elizabeth Mansfield is the heiress to the literary crown of Georgette Heyer, the high priestess of Regency novels. But Elizabeth only smiles at the appellation. After all, she's the writer who admits, "I received a Master's degree in English lit, but I secretly read Georgette Heyer in the bathtub."

She believes that the love story has been with us ever since people began telling stories, and it will continue to be with us until the world ends.

"I was born and grew up in New York City," says the fresh-faced blonde, who was born on March 13, between the years of the Depression and World War II. She's a Pisces, one of the most sensitive of the zodiac's sisters. Music and the arts are a marvelous outlet for their creativity; they should stay away from the more rigid careers and Elizabeth Mansfield does just that.

"I teach freshman students in a local community college

one day a week. I used to teach full-time, but now I have too many deadlines to meet. At the moment I'm teaching Jewish-American literature of the twentieth century. Writing is so quiet; I need to teach to get me out of the house and talking," she adds with a grin.

Elizabeth Mansfield's happiest girlhood hours were spent sitting out on a fire escape in the Bronx, eating apples and reading. "I had to practice the piano an hour a day, but I kept a book in the piano bench in case my mother stepped out of the apartment."

She majored in English literature at Hunter. "But," she confesses, with a shake of her blonde curls (all Regency heroines have curls, you see!), "I guess those early romances remained in my blood even though I believed I'd grown out of them."

Elizabeth married a metallurgical engineer and had two children, a boy and a girl, now in college. She taught English in the New York high schools as they were growing up. "Then I went into college teaching," she explains, "where the hours are somewhat shorter and more adaptable to the demands of motherhood. All during those years—since childhood, in fact—I dreamed of being a writer. I used to write movie and theater reviews for local papers, angry letters to editors, and jingles and limericks for contests. Then, one semester, when I was teaching *Anna Karenina* to a class at NYU, I had a sudden, gut-level, born-again realization of the depth and magnitude of Tolstoy's genius and knew with a terrible certainty that I was no Tolstoy. I gave up hope of being a writer."

It was several years before it dawned on her—so great was her awe of the superb writers whose works she taught—that not everyone who writes is a Tolstoy. "Slowly," she recalls, "I began to notice how many of the current books being published were less than marvelous. I began to whisper to myself, 'I can do better than *this!*' By this time, my husband had transferred to Washington, D.C. (as part of the Corps of Engineers) and we were living in Virginia. I was teaching at Dunbarton College. When the college failed financially and closed its doors, I decided to try my hand at writing before looking for another teaching position. In 1975, when Georgette Heyer died, I won a prize for an article I had written about her work. An editor friend who read the article suggested that I try writing her sort of book myself. I did. I am now working on my tenth Regency and enjoying every minute. Incidentally," she adds, "both my children are good writers and, in the true American style, will no doubt surpass their mother before long!"

Was it luck or fate or just a great appreciation for Georgette Heyer that led her to competing for a prize? "It started with a prize," says Elizabeth, "The Irene Leache Memorial Award for Best Essay. Heyer had died the year before, and I noticed that she was given just a couple of paragraphs on the bottom of *The New York Times'* obituary page. I realized that the editor just didn't know who she was; if he had, he would have given her front-page attention. After all, many thousands of American women were faithful readers of her books. As a result, I called my essay 'The Last Secret Vice.' It was about romance fiction in general and Heyer in particular. When I won the competition— a college president who was as dignified, intellectual and *unromantic* as it is possible to be—said that the essay made him wish, for the first time in his life, to read a romance. 'If an essay can do that,' he said, 'it deserves an award.'"

Flushed with pride, and with the helpful friend's suggestion to "try a Regency novel too," an idea for a Regency began buzzing around in Elizabeth's head. "Writing it was the most fun I had ever had in my entire writing career. But the editor," she went on, "thought it was too 'tame.' I didn't think it was, but I took his word for it and sat down and wrote another, hoping that the second would be more exciting. Without telling me, my friend submitted both manuscripts to an agent in New York. Two weeks later, my phone rang. It was the agent, telling me she'd sold both manuscripts in one week. I then adopted the nom-de-plume of Elizabeth Mansfield, a more beautiful sounding name than my own.

"Selling a first book is one of life's great moments for a writer. Selling *two* was almost too much to bear—I walked several feet off the floor for weeks afterward. And, to tell the truth, though it is now ten books later, I am still slightly tinged with the afterglow," she admitted.

Elizabeth's plans for the future are varied. Her son is going to graduate school in England; he has been accepted at both Oxford and Cambridge, but hasn't made a final choice. She's looking forward to paying him visits there. When her current Regency manuscript is concluded, she's going to start a saga of a Jewish family. She once wrote a musical version of Jane Austen's novel, *Persuasion,* and the Jane Austen Society of America is hoping to present it at one of their conventions. And she's always looking for Regency antiques to add to her growing collection; along with fashion prints of the period on the wall of her study, she has acquired a clock which was made in 1815. "It bongs while I work," she admits laughingly.

Would she have enjoyed living during the Regency? "I don't think so," she remarks. "I probably would have been a member of the lower classes, and they had *dreadful* lives!"

TEA AND SCONES

As any Anglophile knows, English tea (high or ordinary) is a very special repast. There are any number of accompanying delicacies which one can serve with English tea, but hot scones are always, in Elizabeth's view, a "veddy Brrritish" and very tasty treat. There are several different recipes for scones, but one which is rare, different, and quite delicious is the one made on a griddle (called "girdle" in Scotland), instead of being baked in the oven. For an old-fashioned, authentic English tea party (with a touch of Scotland added) do try it.

4 cups unsifted all-purpose flour
2 tsp. each of baking soda and cream of tartar
1 tbsp. sugar
½ tsp. salt
1 egg
2½ cups buttermilk

Mix all dry ingredients. Beat the egg well and add buttermilk to it. Add to dry ingredients and mix to a fairly soft batter. Grease the griddle and drop mixture on by the tablespoonful.

When brown on one side, turn and brown on the other. Wrap in clean towel to keep warm.

This makes about four dozen 2½ inch scones. They are very light and tasty because of the buttermilk. They may be served with butter, jam, powdered sugar, or just as they are.

Patricia Matthews

Swept by a desire so powerful that it drove everything else from his mind, he put his mouth to hers, gently at first, prepared to draw back instantly if she resisted. There was no resistance, and his kiss grew steadily more demanding. Charlotte was passive at first, but soon she was returning the kiss with an ardor that matched his.

—Embers of Dawn

Patricia Matthews and her husband, Clayton, have been heralded as "the hottest couple in paperbacks," by *People* magazine. The name Patricia Matthews appears with astounding regularity on bestseller lists. Five of the ten historical romances are in the one-million category of paperback books. To date, Patricia's Love series for Pinnacle Books has sold over fifteen million copies. Clayton's successful titles include *Dallas, Harvesters,* and *The Power Seekers.*

Despite their sky-rocketing success, Patty, 54, and Clayton ("Matt"), 61, who prefer their shortened names, haven't slackened their pace.

"We spend our time either traveling to research our books and publicizing them—last year it was a cruise on the Mississippi River, a car trip through Austria and England, and several short trips to New York City—or at home writing them. We invest all our earnings in a corporation titled Pywacket Inc., named after our black cat, and we pay ourselves identical salaries."

Home for Patricia is a comfortable, split-level California house. It is built on a hillside and is surrounded by greenery and a pool. A path leads to a neighboring house, which they purchased two years ago for the purpose of having additional office space, guest rooms, and a game room. All the windows overlook a spectacular view of Los Angeles.

Patty's office is in the main house and Matt's is in the "second" house. "Now we both have two separate offices for all of our material," says Patty. "The second house is wonderful for visits from my sons and their families, and the large game room on the top floor is furnished with a regulation-size pool table, pin-ball machine, pachinko, darts, and a small slot machine."

Relaxing in her hot tub alongside the pool, or sitting in her quiet office, overlooking a canyon and trees, with her typewriter facing the view, Patty is serene these days. She writes approximately 1,500 to 2,000 words a day. When she isn't working on a historical romance or a romantic suspense novel, she's composing songs and poetry. Her collection of poems, *Love's Many Faces*, was published in 1980 by Pinnacle Books.

A native Californian, Patricia Ernst was born on July 1, 1927, a moon child, a dreamer with a penchant for creativity. She was raised in San Fernando. According to her, "The valley then was nothing but cattle ranches and tumbleweeds, and the area was used by film studios to film Westerns." A child performer, her mother thought she might become another Shirley Temple and enrolled her in a famous Meglin Kiddies school. "I still enjoy music today," says Patty, who recorded two of her songs professionally and sang them for the demo tape.

Her parents divorced when she was five and her younger sister was three. "My father received custody of us. Life after that was a succession of boarding schools or foster homes," Patty discloses. "I became very close with my sister and we continue even now to be good friends. (Sadly, Patty hasn't been in contact with her mother for at least thirty years.) Reading and daydreaming became my favorite childhood pastimes and formed the basis for my later becoming a writer."

In 1946, the nineteen-year-old Patricia married Marvin Brisco. During their fifteen-year marriage, she raised two sons—Michael and David. It was while the boys were young that Patricia began writing fiction. Following a move to Oregon, she sold her first work. "Two poems for a dollar each to a Portland newspaper which printed a weekly column of verse," she remembers. "Next, I sold a science fiction and fantasy story to *Escapade,* a men's magazine.

"When my husband and I divorced, I began to work at the California State University during the day to support myself and my sons and continued writing at night. I worked there for seventeen years altogether, starting in the accounting office and later becoming office manager for the Office of Associate Students. I thoroughly enjoyed my job and it wasn't until 1977 that I finally left the university. The bestsellers were calling me," she states with a wink.

Patricia met Matt at a local writer's group in California. It was a collaboration at first sight and their meeting soon resulted in two novels: a fantasy and a juvenile tale. Real-life romance followed and after his divorce from his first wife, the couple married in 1971 and moved into their present residence with new cat, Pywacket.

The Patricia Matthews historical romances came about in 1976 at the suggestion of the Matthews's agent, Jay Garon. "Until this time Patty had been content writing Gothic mysteries, fantasy and mystery short stories, juvenile books, a play, and poetry using the name Patty Brisco and P. A. Brisco," Matt recalls, his eyes clear and thoughtful behind his spectacles.

"Realizing that I could write an adventure story, using the romantic format popularized by Rosemary Rogers and Jennifer Wilde," Patty continues, "the writing began on *Love's Avenging Heart.* Seven months later it was on the best-seller list. I used Williamsburg, Virginia, as the locale because we had visited there and it had really captured my imagination."

The ten-book Love series for Pinnacle is completed and still selling successfully around the country, with such titles as *Love's Magic Moment* and *Love's Avenging Heart.*

Although Patricia Matthews's name will be appearing for

Bantam Books on future historical romances, the joint name of Pat and Clayton Matthews signals a series of contemporary suspense novels, also published by Bantam. *Midnight Whispers* was the first release.

As Patty explains, "I'm very interested in other genres. Under the pseudonym of Laura Wylie I wrote an occult novel titled *The Night Visitor,* for one of my hobbies is witchcraft and occult objects."

The effervescent Patty also surrounds herself with other hobbies, collecting things she can buy on her travels: frogs, unicorns, and netsukes. On her shelves and coffee table is a wide variety of mystery novels, for both husband and wife belong to the Mystery Writers of America Association. In the midst of her eclectic decor in the living room and in her study, is the cover art from several of her historical romance books, framed and hung like posters. "We finally make enough money to buy the original art from the illustrators," Patty says with a grin, verifying a known fact that the price is high, sometimes as high as $3,000.

The Matthews's successful writing careers have enabled them to buy a vacation home in Pacific Grove, California, and to trade in their Volkswagen bug for a Porsche 924, with LOVES on the license plate! But they still have the same comfortable lifestyle and friends; they enjoy good neighbors on the beautiful winding canyon road, and Patty's two sons are frequent visitors.

Currently, Patty's interest in composing has increased. "I'm becoming more involved in the writing of romantic songs. I've recorded some records for possible promotion. And if others like my voice, I may be heard singing my own songs over the radio. Who knows? That would be another dream come true."

Besides the monetary success, the satisfaction of knowing that her work is read and appreciated is particularly gratifying for Patty. "I am continually touched and warmed by the lovely letters I receive from my readers telling me how important my books are to them. It is very rewarding to know that you can bring enjoyment, and sometimes even encouragement, to other people."

Patty, who describes herself as a large woman (5'7"), is

196

steadily losing weight. A typical Cancer cook, she is always creative, but these days, however, she's using no salt and noncaloric sweetener for all her gourmet dishes. Her bread pudding is a perfect lo-cal example.

OLD-FASHIONED BREAD PUDDING

4 eggs

2 cups scalded milk (she uses skim milk for her diet)

4 slices dry bread, buttered on both sides (she uses diet margarine)

1 tsp. vanilla

1/3 cup sugar (she uses honey or noncaloric sweetener, or a mixture of the two)

cinnamon to taste

raisins, if desired

Scald milk. Butter bread and cut into small squares. Place bread in quart sized baking dish. Add sweetener and vanilla to milk, and pour over the bread, stirring well. Sprinkle surface with cinnamon and bake in low oven approximately 1 hour or until set. Serve with dollop of whipped cream.

Barbara Michaels

She spoke cheerfully, but she could not bring herself to look at Carlton. Knowing her heart at last, the thought of leaving him was almost more than she could bear. However, she was not totally despondent; from some of the things he had said, she thought she could guess why he had arbitrarily removed her from the unenviable position of chief suspect.

—The Wizard's Daughter

When it comes to Gothics, Barbara Mertz, who writes under the pen names of Barbara Michaels and Elizabeth Peters, is the lady with the answers. She's included in all the anthologies and scholarly works on the subject of Gothics and romantic suspense.

"The term Gothics is all wrong, of course," says the charming, outspoken author. "I still call my books romantic novels of suspense. The suspense is the most important element; I do not care for, nor can I write, the standard 'love story.' The part I enjoy is the mystery; I read books like this long before I started to write them, but I do not enjoy pure romance."

People ask Barbara why she writes under two different names. "I think it's legitimate, since E. Peters and B. Michaels write different kinds of books," she explains with spirit, her brown eyes sparkling. "One reader," she goes on to say, "indignantly informed me that Peters had an excellent sense of humor, but Michaels had none. This is not strictly true; Michaels does

199

interject humor, because I think this is an important element in pacing a suspense story—if Shakespeare did it, it's good enough for me. However," she continues, "with the Peters' books I can let myself go, indulge in crazy plot devices and silly puns, and in general have a good time with the plot. Michaels is more inclined to write of the supernatural. In this sense, the Michaels' books are more like the true Gothics, which were heavy with mystic atmosphere."

Barbara was born in a small town in central Illinois, where she lived until she was eight. A September 29 birthday places her under the sign of Libra, which is ruled by Venus. However, the scales that are the symbol of the sign stand for the balance, accuracy, and inborn harmony of the Libran character.

Attending high school in Oak Park, a suburb of Chicago, she majored in history, but it was in a creative writing class that she first discovered that she loved to write. "I had my first writing thrill then, when my teacher called me out of class—really a no-no in those stricter days—to ask me whether I had copied a sonnet I had turned in for an assignment. It was called 'To a Book,' and I prefer not to remember anything else about it—except that I wasn't insulted at being accused, however delicately, of plagiarism. I was so thrilled she thought it that good. Not until she had sent it to *Saturday Review*, and found that none of the readers recognized it, did she really believe I had written it myself. I don't suppose any of my later triumphs ever surpassed that moment, because it was the first time anyone took my writing seriously."

Barbara did not write for years after that. In college she was supposed to major in education, since she came from a family of excellent teachers. "But I found it very boring," Barbara says with her habitual frankness, "and I had fallen in love with ancient Egypt—and by a strange coincidence there was the Oriental Institute, right across campus. Before long I was majoring in Egyptology instead of education: I went straight through and got my Ph.D. I was unable to work in the field, however," she recalls with a sigh, "because I had married and my husband's occupation took us away from any area where I might have hoped to teach or excavate. Two children also kept me busy."

With her husband's work taking them abroad several times, Barbara was given the chance to pursue her interests in history, art, and architecture. She collected a lot of material that was later useful for backgrounds to her books.

"It was at this time," she says, "that I started writing again. Once the children were in school I had a little time, and I needed to do something to stretch my mind. My first three books were popular nonfiction—two on ancient Egypt, one on Rome, under the name of Barbara Mertz. Writing these books was a learning experience. I loved doing them, but they were a lot of work.

"I also loved reading romantic suspense, and at about that time the genre became more popular, so I decided to try my hand. *The Master of Blacktower* was the result—very derivative, but again very educational, because I learned a lot about plotting and character development. I also learned that writing is hard work!"

She wrote three or four books before one was finally accepted. Those unsuccessful attempts, she thinks, were not a waste of time. "I learned how to write by writing, by recognizing the kinds of problems I had to solve, and by figuring out various ways of solving them," she admitted. "Later I rewrote one of the earlier ones and sold it. But at the back of one file drawer there are still several of the failures—which is where they deserve to be."

When Barbara was younger, she did write out her fantasies. "Most women have fantasies about dark, handsome, brooding lovers—though the sensible ones," she says, with a quick grin, "know men like this are only fun in fantasy; they would be awfully hard to live with. Now I identify with my heroines only in the sense that they are all, I hope, intelligent, independent women who fall into the hero's arms *only* because they fall in love. They don't need men for financial or emotional support. They are capable of making it alone and would rather be alone than settle for second best. Not all my heroines marry the heroes;

one turned down both her suitors and got a job at the end of the book."

Barbara and her husband were divorced in 1968. "He was the dark and romantic sort," she muses, "broody and melancholy." She feels that the E. Peters' heroes are the type that she really enjoys. "Funny, modest, and not chauvinistic!"

For many years she supported her children, "plus a number of cats and two dogs," and wrote two books a year—"full-time work, I assure you," she adds. "Three years ago, when the children were grown, I decided it was time for me to indulge in the one thing I wanted and not yet attained—that beautiful old house in the country which I had written about in so many of my ghostly stories. (There are over thirty romantic suspense novels under her pen names.) After looking at dozens of houses and exhausting two kindly realtors, I found my house in the Maryland woods. The oldest part of it is pre-1800; the main house was finished in 1820, by a man named John Jones whose young wife, Phoebe, is buried in the backyard. Some of the neighbors say Phoebe haunts the house. Maybe she does. It is the friendliest, warmest house I have ever lived in, so if Phoebe is still here, I guess she doesn't mind my being with her. I hope to stay here, with my animals and my plants and my fine neighbors, until my arthritis gets so bad I can no longer climb my spiral staircase. In the meantime, I have material for several more ghost stories. I don't believe in ghosts, but I love to read about them, and write about them."

Barbara writes in her study, which overlooks the plant-filled solarium. "It's draped in Indian Sari cloth—black, red, and gold—and extends over the ceiling," she describes. "There's a fireplace, an Aubusson rug on the floor, leather chairs, and many bookshelves. I'm just enamored with it," she admits. It had been designed by a previous owner, an interior decorator.

When Barbara first started writing she didn't insist on peace and quiet because she couldn't get it. "I did most of my work, though, after the children were in bed—from eight or nine P.M. till two or three A.M. Now, I cop out earlier. My children are grown up so I can work during the day. I find it hard to work when anyone else is in the house—but that may be because I am easily distracted and would much rather go and play."

What about romance in her own life? Is there a handsome hero on the horizon, riding a horse, ready to carry her off in the sunset or a manor house in England? "No," she says, smiling. "I write about heroes and life as I *wish* it was like. If I ever meet anyone as great as the heroes I write about, I'll stop writing!"

At present, Barbara, as Elizabeth Peters, is writing a sequel to *Crocodile on the Sandbank.* Another, as Michaels, is an occult-type book. She's also working on a short story, a historical novel set in Ancient Egypt, a nonfiction book on Egypt, a film on Egypt, and she's writing for *Reader's Digest*—a long chapter for a book on "real ghosts."

As for recipes, Barbara admits, "All my favorites are fattening. This is one I got from a friend of my daughter, who is a super cook."

MARLENE'S DATE CHOCOLATE BARS

For a 13 x 9 pan:

Mix and cool:	1 cup chopped dates
	1½ cups boiling water
	1 tsp. soda
Cream together:	½ cup butter or margarine
	1 cup sugar
	2 eggs Add date mixture when cool.

Alternately blend date mixture with:

     1¼ cup flour
     ¼ tsp. salt
     ¾ tsp. soda

This makes a very thin batter. Pour into greased pan. On top sprinkle one package chocolate chips (6 or 12 oz. size, depending on degree of chocolatiness desired) (either semisweet or milk chocolate does well), plus ½ cup chopped nuts and ½ cup sugar. Bake at 350 degrees for 35–40 minutes.

Fern Michaels

She mocked him with her eyes and beckoned with a slow, sensual smile. His arms slipped around her, and he pulled her close, so close. There was that need, the hunger for her. His lips clinging to hers, he pressed her down.

Valentina tore her mouth away, gasping. "There is a difference between lovemaking and ravishment!"

"Only a slight difference," he breathed, and imprisoned her body beneath his hard, lean strength. His mouth became demanding, savage in its urgency. Her struggles were futile, she was no match for his power. His fingers traveled hotly down the length of her body, caressing, arousing.

—Valentina

Mary Kuczkir

Roberta Anderson

The pen-name Fern Michaels belongs to two irrepressible and talented housewives from New Jersey, Mary Kuczkir (pronounced cut-skit) and Roberta Anderson. Their unique pen-name is derived from a plastic fern sitting in one of their living rooms and Mary's son and husband, both named Michael!

Sometimes known as the Laverne and Shirley of the romantic novelists, because of the good time they exhibit writing together (they've been known to roll on the floor in laughter while working out some of their romantic clinch scenes), these two authors have appeared on many major television programs. "We never watch ourselves," they say in unison, and with mirth, "or else we'd never agree to be on another show."

These are the same women who are so down-to-earth that when their publisher sent them on a first-class, all-expenses paid book signing tour, they made their beds in the hotel every morning. "That's the truth," giggles Roberta, raising her right hand to swear.

The two women met in the fall of 1972. They both felt a restlessness and a desire to get out of the house and do something besides being housewives. Both arrived at a meeting run by a local market research field agent. The product to be tested was a device for unclogging drains using compressed air. The agent assigned Mary and Roberta as a team to test the product. At the first house they went to, a disaster occurred because the product worked too well: pipes burst, tile was blasted off the bathroom walls, and three rooms flooded. Both husbands arrived at the local police station to free their wives. This was the beginning of a beautiful friendship!

Mary and Roberta proceeded to try other jobs. "We catered children's parties, trimmed Christmas trees, painted house numbers on curbs, and worked in the school lunchroom," recalls Roberta, the mother of two children and the wife of a warehouse supervisor. "But one day we paired off for a survey in a local drugstore, handing out women's personal hygiene products . . ."

Mary finishes the sentence. "The only thing that saved the day was a bookrack in the store crammed full of Gothic romances. Bored to death with our job," she grins, "we began to skim the books. . . ."

"And read fourteen of them," adds Mary.

"It turns out that both Roberta and I had been Nancy Drew addicts as kids," reveals Mary. "Bumping into telephone poles as we read them on the way home from school and walking miles to borrow copies from friends." Roberta nods her head in instant agreement. "It wasn't surprising that we liked the books. And after reading fourteen of them, we decided we could write romances as well as the professionals."

"So we quit our 'job,' if you want to call it that," says Roberta, "and decided to give it a try. We gave ourselves two years to be a success."

Neither Mary nor Roberta had a college education; neither owned a typewriter or knew how to type. Neither knew anything about the publishing business, or how to go about getting a book published. But they believed they could do it.

"First," says Roberta, "we had to get rid of our sexual inhibitions. We were two women who couldn't write the word thigh or breast without being horrified."

"I'm glad we decided to write a real pornographic-type book the first time out. We needed to learn to free ourselves and this first book, which has never been published, did the trick. We call it *The Liberated Stud*. Actually, although it's graphic, it's quite pretty in its sexual passages. The story is about five housewives of varied backgrounds who are sexually frustrated. They place an advertisement in a local newspaper for a playboy and they get an answer."

"Naturally, he's the liberated stud," laughs Roberta. "He's the world's greatest, and sexiest, and tenderest lover. He liberates all five of our housewives. We used this book as a guide to future love scenes in our other books."

Will *The Liberated Stud* ever be published? "Only at a price we couldn't refuse," they say.

Roberta, who is very happily married, remarks, "Our husbands are still as straight as they used to be. Mary's husband Mike, a draftsman, is *so* straight that to this day he thinks *The Liberated Stud* is about horses." The two of them laugh uproariously. They are obviously at ease and feeling on top of the world.

The way the two authors work is akin to how they talk. "We

207

are very much in tune," admits Mary. "I can start a sentence and Roberta can finish it and vice versa. It works for us writing together. Sometimes one of us will miss a point, but the other one will catch it. We make a perfect team and this prevents us from making mistakes in plot points in our stories."

Their actual work routine is to talk for several hours a day on the telephone, kicking around ideas for possible books. Roberta may tell Mary a story off the top of her head. Mary interrupts with suggestions, new twists of plot, new characters, and after several days they have a story both are happy with. Then comes the outline. Each makes changes as they go along. Their final outline is the skeleton on which they drape their words.

Both women write equal amounts and which portion of the book each writes is selected more or less at random. Mary writes every day from nine to three, usually at the dining room table. "That way I can keep an eye on my kids," she adds. Roberta is more flexible, sometimes writing during the day, more often at night, doing some of her best work very late after the family has gone to bed. "Of course, this makes it hard when I have to fry hamburgers for my son David's football team at the school sports field," she sighs. "But he keeps me down to earth and reminds me of who I am. He's the great equalizer."

Everyone asks them the same question. "What does it take to write a bestseller?"

Trim, bouncy Mary has a quick answer. "We tell people that our market research experience helped us considerably. We studied the market, asked a lot of questions and found out what women liked to read. We were both somewhat shocked at the time to discover they wanted romance, action, and sex, sex, and *more* sex. This is where our still unpublished sex manual proved useful."

Pretty, raven-haired Roberta adds, "We try to write only those kinds of books that we ourselves like to read, and when we imagine our characters, they are people who are believable to us." She emphasizes, and also repeats one of their now famous quotes: "We write for the woman who wants to read romance at three in the afternoon because she isn't sure it's going to walk in the door at six."

208

"Along with our success came new responsibilities," the two authors recount. "We meet a payroll now: agent, accountant, lawyers, cleaning woman. We've had to become corporations. But basically success hasn't changed us. We're still involved in PTA and Little League, and Mary is now a grandmother. We still live in the same houses we've lived in for over twenty years and don't intend to move. Our husbands have now recovered from some minor ego crises, so everything is running smoothly."

Their careers have taken on new dimensions since their early days. "Ballantine Books taught us everything we know," confides Mary. "We had great help and encouragement along the way. When one executive went to Macmillan a few years ago, it was he we turned to when we decided to write our hardcover suspense book, *Panda Bear Is Critical.*

"We think of writing as an art and in some ways we compare it to cooking. As much as we love historical romances and will always write them, we wanted to try writing other genres. One can't excel in desserts all the time; a little bread baking keeps the chef's talent fresh," smiles Roberta.

"A hard cover book is prestigious, and that was in our minds. Our books for Macmillan are suspense thrillers. However, we are also writing contemporary novels for Silhouette and Pocket, and that's fun and interesting for us, too. Last year we signed a half-a-million dollar contract with Ballantine to write four historical romances in two years, so we haven't forgotten our roots."

"We really love romance. Honestly!" says Roberta sincerely. "It's redundant, but it's true."

Mary once entertained the thought of writing a syndicated column a la Erma Bombeck; she has that ribald, down-to-earth sense of humor. "I tried it a bit when I lived in Pennsylvania, but with five kids and a husband, it was too hard. And now with all of our book contracts, it's impossible to find the time."

Roberta, a Leo, was born on August 22, and Mary, an Aries, was born a few years earlier, on April 9, 1934. For astrological purposes, they are the perfect match. Two fire signs with the abilities to take on huge and demanding projects, and the will to carry them out.

Roberta, who saw her only daughter married in 1981, but is still coping with a teenage son, is enjoying their various genre writing. "And it has given us two costly indulgences. Our first extravagances were elegant imported cars with individualized license plates. And we share a cleaning woman."

By now, everyone in the romantic field knows they like to send their families off on a holiday when they get ready to write the sexy scenes for their books. "Some of the foreplay may last twelve pages! We have a great time working on *these* chapters," Roberta concludes with good humor.

Roberta Anderson's favorite recipe and one that she and Mary have incorporated in their historical romance, *Wild Honey*, is a crab dish. "It's delicious and easy to fix. When we're at our vacation place on the Pamlico River in Bath, North Carolina, we catch the crabs ourselves," she says.

FRIED CRAB

Clean crabs. Remove legs and save claws. Break bellies in half. Roll in cornmeal. Fry with an onion in oil until brown.

Virginia Myers

The deep fatigue was gone, the long journey forgotten. There was only now, this moment, in the silent afternoon. Slowly she stood up before him and let her heavy hair— dark golden honey—cascade downward. She knew her eyes—which he called "topaz"—were darker now with desire, and she sensed his quick and violent response. The bright warm air between them seemed to pulse with their sudden surging need. He must not turn away. He must not. She could not stand it if he turned away.

—A Lady of Means

Once, on an Oakland, California bus, Virginia Myers sat next to a girl who was reading Virginia's first book, *Angelo's Wife*. The author watched as her reader kept sniffing and blotting her tears. "I peeked over," admits the brown-eyed *saftig* Virginia, "and saw she was at the part where Angelo dies, and for a few minutes I simply loved her for her response. I wanted to tap her on the shoulder and tell her not to worry, that Petra got over her grief, but I didn't have the nerve."

Virginia Myers is a "real ham" about what she writes. She loves reading her own work, and sometimes when she's written something that pleases her, she reads it over and over, thoroughly enjoying it. "A form of absolute conceit, I suppose," she says. "And I derive such gratification when I hear from people who have read my books and laughed or cried over them."

211

Virginia has known much laughter and tears, both in her personal life and in her writing career. Her published works fall into two phases of her life. The first writings were printed when she was in her twenties. She had three novels published, including *Angelo's Wife* (now reprinted as *Californio*), short stories in slick magazines, and some radio and TV work in the 1940s. The second phase of her career began after many years of being saddled with a tough day-time job.

She has recently resumed writing and seems to be having an astonishing amount of success at it. Dell bought two of her new romances, *The Winds of Love* and *Come November*, and Pinnacle reprinted *Californio* and *This Land I Hold*. She also completed a 90,000 word romance novel, as an original paperback *Ramona's Daughter*, intended as a sequel to the classic *Ramona* by Helen Hunt Jackson. At the moment, she's deep in a two-book multigenerational saga, *A Lady of Means*, for Pinnacle Books, as well as a Harlequin Superromance.

Virginia was a "Depression child," and fortunately, she had the capacity to see the funny-sad things of life. Such things as never having had quite enough money, of always looking forward to payday, and making do, never overwhelmed her. Those days are over, but Virginia never forgot the lesson.

"I grew up in a one-parent household. We were a small, tightly knit family; my mother, my little sister and myself. My father died when I was three and a half, my sister eighteen months. My memories of my father are sketchy—little loving cameos of memory. He was a very good and kindly man. My mother never remarried.

"Our life wasn't easy as my mother had to support our small household on stenographer wages in the Depression years. But we had an enormous amount of fun in those days, too—even in the worst of times—I would never trade my life for anyone else's. I started writing very young—I was always writing, it seemed."

Virginia had little formal education. "I would have nothing of college, preferring to go to work. Later I would regret this, but one lives with one's decisions," she says pensively.

Dozens of jobs fell her way, usually in some clerical capacity, and she usually did well because of her command of the language and her ability to write coherent letters—which many business people can't do," she comments.

No matter at what level she entered a firm, she usually worked her way up, without too much trouble, to be in a letter-writing situation. "I was never keen for office work, and several times I quit," she explains. "When I would quit, I'd spend my time— for a year or more usually—writing, or amusing myself."

Rootless and content to be so, Virginia walked the road of the nomad. She never married or raised a family. "During my early life we lived in a number of places in California and Texas. I'm now living in Seattle, Washington, a delightful city, but I'm feeling the urge to move on," she adds, with a definite twinkle in her deep amber eyes. "I am a sojourner, I think. Not sure where I'll go next."

One of the shattering and saddest episodes of her life concerned her sister, who died an untimely death. "My sister and I were best friends. She took a great interest in my writing and gave me much valuable advice and help all of her life. After our mother died, we shared a flat for several years, and later bought a home together . . ." she breaks off with a sigh.

Like many a Leo, Virginia, whose birthday is August 17, 1918, is comfortable being a leader and usually forging new trails. The travel urge mixed with her interest in history, leads her down many a new and exotic path, and she attracts followers—and helpful natives. "My travels hinge on my historical interests in a place," the author says. "I've traveled quite a bit in England, and rather extensively in Egypt. I have taken a boat up the Nile twice, traveling for eight hundred miles to Aswan and then I made that short flight in a small plane to Abu Simbel. I am most delighted now that mainland China has opened up to Westerners. That is my next travel target, I think."

Virginia has seen more than half of the exotic foreign places of this world; she's experienced life deeply and realistically, and she has all the natural gifts of a writer. But will writing dominate this second phase of her career? She thinks so. She's confident at this period in her life. But her thoughts on writing are still extremely sensitive. "Writing, because it is so personal, has special difficulties. The disappointments seem to be keener

213

and the successes more satisfying, I think. I have had both, and probably will have more of both in the future. But now I fully realize that writing is my passion and one I *can't* escape from again."

One childhood anecdote gives her a special strength these days. It's a memory that all writers could treasure. "I wrote verses and fairy tales as a very small child. I was lucky in that my mother always took my little efforts seriously. I can remember when my sister and I were 'helping' Mother clean house, my mother would say, 'Be careful with that now. Don't throw it away. That's Ginny's little poem.' Or, 'Ginny's little story.' I think," says Virginia, with a faraway smile, "this early appreciation of my efforts gave me an inner sense of security about writing that has helped me a lot."

Today, she is handling the short category romances as well as the full-blown, complicated sagas. "Some books are easy to write, some are difficult," she concedes, knowing that her former experiences, many years ago, prepare her for today's assignments. "I wrote *Come November* (a politician-love story. The heroine is 'hired' to act as a candidate's fiancée for the campaign) easily, with continuing enthusiasm. *This Land I Hold* went through three very complete revisions. *Ramona's Daughter* needed very few revisions, but was still a difficult book to write—I think possibly because of the sadness and underlying sorrow of the basic story. There is one book which I wrote four times. From scratch. I love it."

Like many a fictional heroine, Virginia Myers has made a comeback, and her happy ending seems to be assured.

Here's an old family recipe that Virginia claims is the greatest. She calls it a fried cheese sandwich; but she warns that it's as fattening as it's delightful.

FRIED CHEESE SANDWICH

Make a cheese sandwich—any kind of bread and cheese you fancy—then carefully, so it doesn't fall apart—dip it, first one side then the other in beaten egg. Fry this slowly and gently over less than medium heat, on both sides, until the sandwich is golden brown on the outside and melted inside.

Diana Palmer

Oblivious to the sharp, jagged blade of lightning that shot down on the horizon like a pitchfork, and the tremor of the very air that followed it, he bent to her trembling mouth. His teeth caught the full lower lip, nibbling at it sensuously.

"Open your mouth for me," he growled huskily, his fingers hurting her head, "show me how grown up you are, Tish."

—Now and Forever

Diana Palmer has raced down the Chattahoochee River in inner-tubes, leaned out of private planes to snap pictures, and she married the man of her dreams after one week of courtship. Adventurous? You bet! And she loves every exciting minute of her life.

This author of four romances and one science-fiction novel is also a reporter for the *Tri-Country Advertiser* in Georgia. Susan Spaeth (who took her favorite figure in Greek mythology, Diana the huntress, as the first half of her pen name) began her nonconformist life in a hotel in Cuthbert, Georgia, on December 11, 1946.

"I had no choice," she explains. "The local hospital burned down before I was delivered. I bear no responsibility for that—I was far too young to play with matches," she says with typical humor.

During her elementary schooling in Atlanta, Diana was plagued with a feeling of shyness. She preferred her solitude to the company of other children. It was a preference that extended through high school where Diana discovered, "I didn't like the normal pastimes as much as I like writing."

Inspired by *Indian Love Call*, starring Jeanette MacDonald and Nelson Eddy, she wrote her first ten-page novel at age thirteen. "It was a little short for publication," she remembers and her eyes sparkle behind her glasses. "So I decided to run off with a Royal Canadian Mounted Policeman instead. Unfortunately, I didn't have bus fare!"

The little girl grew up to be a tall handsome teenager, 5'7". Her olive complexion, dark brown hair, and green eyes hint of a Gypsy in her past.

Diana agonized about a college education. Just as she disliked the regimented routine of high school, she equally dreaded a similar routine in college. Without regret she forfeited two scholarships in exchange for a job as a legal secretary in a small town north of Atlanta.

"To me it was a new and exciting grown-up life," she recalls, "and finally my life afforded me the time to write."

At age eighteen, Diana wrote her first real novel, which was rejected by the first publisher she contacted; prompting her to turn her creative energies to poetry. A few of her poems were published by a small New York press.

During this period of her budding career, she sent a poem to a columnist on a South Carolina newspaper, "which to my surprise was published." Shortly after that she was contacted to do feature stories for the paper.

"Actually I didn't know a feature story from a hole in a wall," she admits, "but I was young and willing to learn all I could about writing. Eventually, I began reporting political stories, and then news stories. A few years later, I became a full-time staff writer for my local weekly newspaper."

It's her editor-publisher, Amilee Graves, the elected mayor of Clarksville, Georgia, and the first woman to ever hold public office in her section of the country, who greatly inspired her.

"Through her shining example," says Diana, "I've seen what a woman can accomplish, if she's willing to work for it. And that's how I'm approaching writing my books."

Her first novel, *Now and Forever,* was rejected by two publishers. "I was crushed, Amilee Graves or no Amilee Graves! I didn't want to send it out again and be rejected. But a friend advised me to mail it to McFadden Romances. A few weeks later I received a telephone call informing me that they were interested in my book. I was nearly thrown into shock," she recalls.

Shortly thereafter, Susan (aka Diana) received a check and began to work on plots for some other books. Her editor at McFadden, Anne Gisonny, encouraged her to submit a manuscript to Silhouette and it was accepted almost immediately.

"When I look back at those first feeble efforts, I wonder at the patience that guided me in the right direction when McFadden first accepted my premier effort. I knew so little, and I've learned so much. I'm still learning, every day."

Cradling her bouncing baby boy in her arms brings smiles to Diana Palmer's face. "I write anytime at all, but mostly at 5:00 A.M. when my son wakes me up for his first feeding of the day. When I've finished feeding him, I put him back down for another hour and a half, and go immediately to the typewriter. Some days I barely get one page done," she admits. "Another day I may write two chapters without stopping. With my constant deadlines for publishers, I don't have the luxury of being moody, or waiting for inspiration. I have to produce, and I do," she declares. She types 110 words a minute. Ironically, typing was the only subject she failed in school.

Although Diana claims she'd rather work at night, she had no difficulty writing at her newspaper office, with a conversation going on, both lines of the phone ringing off the hook, and her police scanner running wild on the desk in front of her.

"Reporting taught me to partition off my mind and use only the part I need—I can blot out anything," she says.

Unlike most writers, Palmer does not like to write rough drafts.

"I once read an instructive book by Dean Koontz, who wrote *Demon Seed,* which recommends the completion of a manuscript without revisions. I've done it that way ever since. It saves time and frustration," she believes.

Diana Palmer spins out her stories in the den of her small home in Cornelia, Georgia. Her husband has encouraged her writing all along, foregoing television to mind the baby so she can concentrate in a peaceful atmosphere.

"We both like easy-listening music, classical music mostly. It's extremely soothing, so we don't have any problems with our musical atmosphere around the house," she says and smiles.

As an adult, Diana is a gregarious individual, and loves to collect people: artists, poets, other writers, scientists, farmers, etc.

"I also collect books, fiction, nonfiction, poetry, anything and everything, I might need as reference material. I must have every issue ever written of *Progressive Farmer!*" she confesses. "I write a lot of my stories with farm and ranch backgrounds. My only problem is where to store my reference material. I'm thinking of stacking the magazines together and throwing a table cloth over them—who'd ever guess?"

Along with her graceful facility with the English language, Diana has studied French and Spanish, and speaks enough German, Russian, and Hebrew "to get me arrested." She's also a talented classical guitarist and painter.

"I completed three paintings once, sold all three, and never had time to arrange a show after that," she says and sighs, gesturing as if to touch the fleeting space of time she lives in.

Being the typical, light-hearted, fun-loving Sagittarian, Diana Palmer exudes a healthy enthusiasm for life, looking upon it as a grand and glorious adventure.

"I don't think I live vicariously through my characters," she says. "I have enough excitement in my own life here in Georgia. Reporting gives me the challenge and the opportunity to constantly meet fascinating people. But my parents see it all differently. They wish I'd do something 'sane' for a change. However, I tell my mother that her influence was important. *Foxes of Harrow* was her favorite novel and mine, too. And now my mother reads *my* books," she adds proudly.

When asked what motivates her to write romances, Palmer becomes pensive for a moment. "I write books because the words well up inside me and I have to let them out or choke to death. I want to write books that give unhappy people, lonely people, a momentary escape from the pains and perils of everyday living.

"I read to get out of myself, to taste another person's dramas and visit the people who populate a private world. To share their heartaches. I write for the same reason—to share my private world with others.

"I write love stories because I like to read them. Romance brings all the emotions into play—love, hate, greed, sacrifice, loneliness, pain, joy. I especially love creating unlovable characters and then making them slowly become lovable."

Diana Palmer, born Susan Spaeth, is working these days on a long, racy, contemporary romance, and a recent-history romance. "I only wish I had more time," she says and groans. "I could write twenty-three hours a day if I didn't have other responsibilities. Writing is the air I breathe."

As for a recipe from this writing flying dervish of Georgia? "I never met a recipe I didn't like. I love French cooking, and my favorite dish is beef *bourbon*aisse!" she says, smacking her lips.

Betty Layman Receveur

The girl had stood up in the open carriage and Adam's eyes focused on a demure yellow cotton print, came level with breasts that swelled at the material and thrust at rows of white lace which tried unsuccessfully to hide the separate and distinct slope of them; traveling upward to a nose tip-tilted slightly, enchantingly, beneath green eyes tawny with speckles of gold. She gave her head a shake and the mane of hair, golden, defiantly curly, swirled about her slender neck, forming tendrils at her cheeks.

Adam stared, heard Josh's voice again, "Adam Kingston . . . this is Molly Gallagher."

—*Molly Gallagher*

The lovely name of Receveur, so French and old-fashioned, like the name of a seventeenth-century romantic heroine, could it belong to a Kentucky girl named Betty Layman? Truth *is* stranger than fiction, and Betty Layman became Mrs. Receveur at the tender age of fourteen!

Betty is truly a Kentucky child. She married young Mr. Receveur, during her first year of high school, and bore a son the next year. Two children appeared before she was of voting age, a third son, now eighteen, lives with her. The marriage ended in divorce, amicably, in 1978, and Betty remarried in 1980. In her case, she can talk about happy endings, and write them, too.

Born and raised, and still residing in Louisville, Kentucky, Betty Layman's chances of becoming a writer were very slim. Almost as slim as her family's meager income. Her formal education, cut short by her early marriage, was never continued, but her burning interest always was reading. Then, in 1978, after many years of feeling discouraged over her writing, Betty found herself a published author of a historical romance at the age of forty-five.

This petite brunette, who stands just a shade over 5 feet, was born on October 25, 1933. Scorpio authors usually prefer to stay in one place, dig deep into their roots, and discover the hidden truths about themselves, rather than sail through life with wings. Little Betty was different from the rest of her siblings, and people in Kentucky really recognize that now.

"I would read everything that had words on it when I was tiny. Tin can labels. Church bulletins. Anything. I was a reader in a family of nonreaders and they thought I was a very strange child indeed," says Betty. Her soft voice, well-modulated, seems to sing rather than speak, because of her slow, sweet drawl.

"My supply of reading materials grew better when I started school and better yet when I discovered a small lending library in the back of a dry goods store about three or four blocks from my home. This happened when I was in the third grade and at that time the distance to the store seemed a very long and hazardous way for me to go alone. But the lure of the books was *so* strong that I went regularly.

"When I was in the fifth grade a most wondrous thing happened," she recalls. "My great-aunt Gertrude had the ill luck to be divorced from her husband and the poor lady parceled out her furniture to various relatives. We got an old-fashioned secretary and, miracle of miracles, it was filled with books! For the first time in my life I had books that belonged to me and I read and reread them. There were wonderful things there, including *Captain Blood, Scaramouche,* and *The Scarlet Pimpernel.* These were my introduction to historical novels, and I loved them though they were old and musty and the pages were turning brown."

Betty's childhood fear was that she would read all the books in the world and there would be nothing left for her to read! And from that there sprung the motivating force for her to write . . . so she could create her own supply. She just knew that the words, the images, were always there in her head and sooner or later they had to be put down on paper.

"My first published novel, *Sable Flanagan*, took ten years to write," she admits. "I was well into the writing of it when I read somewhere that an author shouldn't attempt a historical for their first novel. There's too much to handle with the research and all. I didn't let that bother me for I was too deep into the story. I also remembered reading that the Americans shouldn't have won the Revolutionary War. No one bothered to tell them they couldn't win, so they just went on and fought! That's how I reasoned," she says, with a sly grin.

"When I finally sent it to some publishers, word came back that my writing was okay but they weren't buying historical romances. The market was down. So I put it on a shelf and left it there.

"A couple of years ago, a writing friend heard that the historical romances were back in favor, and to please my supportive friends, I took out what I called my labor of love— *Sable Flanagan*—and took a new look at it. I held a 638-page manuscript. The characters, Sable and Lansing, and all the others were so real to me that I could almost see them walk into the room. I did love them all.

"But the corners of the manuscript were badly curled from being so long on the shelf. I didn't want to rewrite or type another word of it. So I took out my steam iron and ironed each corner flat. Then packed it up and sent it to Avon, and went about my other business and my life."

For the next four months, Betty scarcely gave the manuscript a thought. But all the while in New York, Nancy Coffey and Pam Strickler, Avon's former famous literary duo, were enraptured over the unsolicited manuscript. They sent a note saying they wanted to publish it and offered Betty a healthy advance.

"After I hyperventilated," confesses Betty impishly, "I accepted." The book was published in 1979, and in 1980 a Norwegian edition appeared.

What inspired the name, Sable, for the heroine's name? "She came to me in a flash—and backwards," recalls the author. "First I felt Flanagan, then gradually Sable bubbled to the top. The story always excited me. It's about a seventeen-year-old New York girl who is left in poverty when her doting father dies unexpectedly. She joins a boatload of women who sail for San Francisco, in the Gold Rush days, as eligible wives for the settlers. There was a scarcity of good women in the Old West at this period. Sable is chosen by the Virginia adventurer and business tycoon, Lansing Wakefield, who marries her, and after problems and set-backs, the heroine finds herself in a great San Francisco mansion."

Betty is very glad that she wasn't twenty years old when she sold *Sable Flanagan*. "When you're middle-aged," she reveals, "you know who you are and your sense of self isn't distorted. Now I just know that it is very nice to make money at doing something that you really like to do . . . although I still am a little surprised when I receive fan mail, or when, locally, someone recognizes me and comes up to speak to me in a restaurant or department store. These people are always very kind. I think, for the most part, the changes in my life have been very pleasant."

The new dimension in her personal life is exceedingly pleasant. John Birkitt is his name. He and the author knew each other fourteen years through their local writers' club. When they found themselves in similar personal situations—he had three daughters and she had three sons, and both of their long-term marriages were over—they decided to team up. Their October 1980 honeymoon was spent at historic Beaumont Lodge, in Harrisburg, Kentucky. Their first family Christmas was a happy occasion. All their children gathered and some friends humorously refer to them now as "the Brady bunch." Just before the holiday, they bought a small house together in Louisville.

"John is a very fine writer, mostly of short stories, though he's

224

thinking of writing a novel. It's his hobby, actually. He has taught me that there are more ways than one to write a story. He's also made me dare to try things in fiction that I never thought I could do."

He was by her side as she made revisions on her second published novel, *Molly Gallagher*. This story is set in New Orleans, when the city was Creole, not American. "I have not traveled extensively," says Betty, with some regret. "But I did spend a week in the French Quarter of New Orleans doing research on my book. I absolutely fell in love with the place. It is so colorful and romantic and extravagant. It's like stepping into the past. You can almost hear the clopping of horses' hooves along the narrow streets, the cries of street peddlers from long ago. . . . It is certainly an atmosphere that is conducive to writing about life and love in days gone by. I plan to write a sequel to *Molly Gallagher* very soon."

What are her other plans for the future? "John and I would like to buy a big old house one day, with a lot of space for old furniture and our collection of books. I love old houses. Sometimes I can almost feel the people who were there before. Also historical romances would be great fun to write in such a place. You can just let your imagination go."

Betty's time is necessarily limited in the kitchen. She leans toward dishes that are easily and quickly prepared. Such a dish is:

MOCK VEAL PARMESAN

Begin with slices of *raw* turkey breast (you buy this already sliced and packaged). Dip each slice in a mixture of beaten egg and a little milk and salt and pepper. Coat with breadcrumbs. Fry in hot vegetable oil in a skillet until just done. (About three minutes on one side, two on the other.) You can do this part of the recipe in the morning and put in the refrigerator until mealtime, or even freeze for future use.

When almost ready to serve, put slices on a cookie sheet and top each with a generous spoonful of prepared spaghetti sauce (I like Hunt's Prima Salsa), add a slice of mozzerella cheese and sprinkle of parmesan to each and pop the whole thing into a 375 degree oven until hot through and the cheese is bubbly and just starting to brown. I guarantee this is delicious. I usually serve this with baked potatoes, a green salad, and Italian bread.

Janet Louise Roberts

Morgan was there, holding her tenderly, his mouth moving lovingly from arms, to shoulders, to breasts again. He touched her red-pointed nipple, and tugged at it softly. She felt the now familiar weakness in her thighs, the burning desire flaring up in her in response to his urgency.

Morgan drew back a little. His hands caressed her hair, he threaded several locks through his hand. "Your hair is silver in the moonlight, and you are sweet as jasmine," he whispered.

—*Silver Jasmine*

Janet Louise Roberts, a former librarian, is the best-selling author of more than one hundred novels. Under her own name and three pen names, Rebecca Danton, Janette Radcliffe, and Louise Bronte, she writes Regency, historical, and contemporary romance novels for several publishers. More than ten million copies have been printed and she writes four new novels a year from her apartment in Dayton, Ohio.

She seems comfortable with her multiple identities. She explains that she began using pseudonyms, "to avoid embarrassing her father, a missionary in a rather conservative church. When a number of publishers wanted to develop different aspects of Janet Louise Roberts, I ended up using my own name along with my three pen-names. Now there is a different name for almost every genre—Gothics, Regencies, three-generational family sagas, and historical romances. I used to write six or seven short books a year; now I write four longer novels—one under each name. That way I can plan ahead and keep things rolling," she says cheerfully.

Janet Louise Roberts grew up during the Depression, in New Britain, Connecticut, the daughter of the Reverend Walter Nelson Roberts. "My personal life was shaped by two events of my childhood," recalls the author pensively. "One was the Depression: I vividly remember the plight of the people out of work. So many came to my father for comfort and assistance.

"I had rheumatic fever twice, as a child, which left me with a damaged heart. It is my conviction that many authors write because they do not have the physical strength to live the adventurous lives they would like to."

After living in the Philippine Islands for five years, where her parents worked as missionaries, the family returned to the United States, eventually settling down in Dayton. Janet attended Otterbein College, graduating in 1946 with a B.A. degree. "My major was English, my minors were French and Spanish. I have always loved to read a great deal," she goes on. "I wanted by this time in my life to become an author. I worked in various clerical jobs while writing as a freelancer, mostly short stories and later novels. Also, I traveled, living for various times in Florence, Rome, and London, visiting many places in Europe. My father loved to travel and he encouraged me most about this. My mother read to me as a child, and she made up many of the stories. Later, when I began to publish my stories, my mother read all I wrote and helped me revise. She was very good in English, and my father, who liked to write, produced excellent sermons and many articles for Christian publications."

In 1965, she returned to college, and received a Master's degree in Library Science from Columbia University in New York City. She became a reference librarian at the Dayton and Montgomery County Public Library in 1966, where she was employed until 1979.

"Knowing reference work enables me to do a better job of

historical research for my novels. In a library, one meets many kinds of people, and this is stimulating for writing. I enjoy working with books and people," she adds sincerely.

When Janet Louise began to write, she wrote over two hundred short stories, of which few sold. "I threw away the first six novels. I tell people now, 'Throw away the first million words, they are just practice.'" The most difficult part about novel writing, she says, is "to create the characters, work out a complex plot, make up a good background, and correlate them all into one integrated novel. Many authors of novels do not sell until they are in their forties or fifties, as it is so difficult to get all the elements working together," she concludes wisely.

The author, who is 5'4", with brown eyes and gray-brown hair, works on as many as three or four plots at a time. *No*, she doesn't confuse stories or characters because, as she puts it, "You don't confuse people in your family with people in your office, do you?" Janet Louise's characters take on living, breathing dimensions for her, and for others too.

There are not just a handful of readers familiar to the point of intimacy with Janet Louise's work. Her fans have been known to charter airplanes to be present when she makes her few personal appearances!

Neither is it unusual for her to get a long-distance call from a reader praising her for, "understanding so well what it's like to be a woman." Janet Louise Roberts, Rebecca Danton, Janette Radcliffe, or Louisa Bronte, as she is sometimes known, obviously expresses the feelings and fantasies of a very large group of American women. She creates characters who think the way those women think and who react to life circumstances in ways those in the audience think they might react. In any case, that is what her fans tell her again and again.

If this author's first love is writing, then her second is history. It is in the setting of her novels that she puts to use her knowledge of history and her skills as a research librarian. She speaks eagerly about the study of history, revealing fascinating but obscure tidbits of information discovered while exploring a historical period for one of her novels. It was, for example, an unexpected pleasure for readers to come across a passage in *Golden Lotus* describing porcelain from the Sung and Ming Dynasties of China.

Unmarried, but very much a part of a large, extended family, Janet Louise is a doting aunt to a great many nieces and nephews. In fact, her family is a central topic of her conversation, and she declares, "it is from them that I derive much of my emotional sustenance."

Refined and possessed of a delicately sensible manner, Miss Roberts is, before all else, loyal to the tradition that produces her. "That tradition is born of a strong, solid, highly moral, not always tolerant backbone-of-America Calvinism," declares the author, who is thoroughly convinced of its worth.

Although at first, it seems incongruous that a person so completely a product of this tradition would create such intensely romantic, occasionally torrid novels as *Hidden Fires, Lovers and Liars,* or *Fire Opals,* it is actually a logical result of the absence of romance in that tradition. "Romance is a dimension too often missing from the fabric of some Protestant-ethic American lives," comments Janet Louise. She writes to provide that dimension; perhaps for herself, but certainly for her readers. She likes to think that she gives them momentary release from the muddle of life at no more cost than the price of a paperback.

A Roberts' heroine may make noises about it but, in the end, she won't leave her husband and children to man the barricades of political activism. Rather, in every novel, she will endure misfortune and occasional abuse for the sake of love. The virtuous are eventually rewarded, the wicked eventually punished. The wicked are never married, the state of marriage being the fabric for eternal bliss. Instead of being threatening, Janet Louise Roberts' books reinforce and uphold her readers' values, giving those values, unqualified endorsement.

"I have now written and had published over one hundred novels, all in paperback. Many are now out of print. Whenever I wrote," she confides, "I did as well as I could at the time but I hope I have improved over the past ten years. My ambition is to continue to write novels, and to write them better all the time."

Janet Louise celebrates a January 20th birthday—she possesses the independent characteristics of her Aquarian sign, and the desire to be left alone to make her own decisions.

Cooking is something she rarely has time for, but here's a recipe that even she thinks is worth the bother. It was a favorite of the early twentieth century.

MOTHER'S DIVINITY CANDY

Place in a saucepan over low heat—

2 cups sugar
½ cup white corn syrup
½ cup water

Stir until sugar is dissolved, then cook without stirring to 250 degrees (or until a little of mixture dropped into cold water forms a hard ball). Remove from heat and pour, beating constantly, in a fine stream into

2 egg whites, stiffly beaten

Continue beating until mixture holds its shape and loses its gloss.

Add:

1 tsp. vanilla
½ cup broken nuts

Drop quickly from tip of spoon onto waxed paper in individual peaks, or spread in greased shallow pan and cut into 1-inch squares when firm.

Rosemary Rogers

Flickering torchlights and wine forced between her lips. . . . With a feeling of shock she found her thighs nudged apart. . . . There was a stabbing shaft of agony. Her last thought, as she slipped into a state halfway between sleep and unconscious was, "And I don't even know his name."

—*Wicked Loving Lies*

Rosemary Rogers has a soft, sultry voice with just a trace of foreign accent. It adds the final exotic touch that one tends to expect from one of the most glamorous, leading authors of romantic novels. As her friend Tom Huff, aka Jennifer Wilde, always says, "She's one author who looks and lives like one of her heroines."

Born and reared in Ceylon, an independent island off the coast of India, the slim graceful beauty has written a historical novel that uses her birthplace as its background. "That novel, *Surrender to Love,* starts off in Ceylon and moves to London in the time of Victoria's marriage to Prince Albert, the 1830s," she explains. "I did a tremendous amount of research—and loved doing it. When I first started to write, after my divorce, I couldn't afford decent research books, so I haunted libraries. Now I haunt all the bookstores and places that have old and rare books for my research. I look for biographies and costume books, for books on ships and guns, and for books written in that period which give an idea of how the people talked and behaved."

Rosemary has always been a quick and avid reader. Her friends say that she's familiar with every romantic novel ever written. When writing, she has a tendency to scatter pages all around her room. "I may appear disorganized, but I can put my finger on what I want when I need it," she says with an assured laugh. "It was the same thing when I was a secretary; I had papers all around but when the boss wanted something I found it immediately."

Even as a child in Ceylon, Rosemary loved to spin tales. "I've always loved stories; it's a part of me," she admits. "When I was young, I used to tell stories to my younger twin brothers and to my sister. I'd finish one day and then continue my 'serial' the next day. And that's how I started; I made them up as I went along. Later on, I put the stories down in notebooks. So right through bringing up my own kids, through diaper time, instead of watching TV, I'd write stories."

Rosemary grew up in a sheltered, wealthy atmosphere in Ceylon, where her father was the owner of a group of private schools. She met and married her first husband while she was still in college. He was Summa Navartnam, known in the track and field world as "the fastest man in Asia." "We had two daughters, Rosanne and Sharon," she says. "But when the marriage broke up, my children and I moved to London. It was there that I met and married a black Air Force Sergeant, Leroy Rogers, and later returned with him to the United States where he was stationed at the Travis Air Force Base in Fairfield, California. We had two sons, Michael and Adam."

Following their divorce in 1964, Rosemary changed jobs and became a secretary for the Solano County Parks Department. One of her co-workers was another fan of romantic fiction by the name of Shirlee Busbee. "At this time," she recalls, "I was supporting my four children and times were rough. It was there that writing became a much-needed form of escape." Lunchtime was spent researching in the library, and after work Rosemary would grab whatever hours she could to write. The project was to be titled *Sweet Savage Love*.

"I might never have sent off my first novel to Avon in the early seventies," she recalls, "if it hadn't been for a hysterectomy. It left me feeling so empty; I woke up at night with terrible nightmares of people snatching floating babies away from me. I had willed my children through yoga; I now willed myself a bestseller."

In the wake of Kathleen Woodiwiss's successful novel, *The Flame and the Flower,* Rosemary's manuscript arrived on the desk of editor Nancy Coffey at Avon. She was immediately convinced that Avon had another big hit on their hands. It was published as a "Spectacular"—an original paperback, and was an immediate national bestseller. Since then, Rosemary has continued to publish both historical and contemporary novels with Avon and her books in print figure well over seventeen million copies.

Born on December 7, Rosemary believes she has many typical Sagittarian traits. "I love freedom—that's why I'm single, and I'm going to stay single. I'm an individualist, a lover of justice and fairness. I don't fly into rages. The only thing that can really make me mad," she insists, "is if someone tells me of a complete case of injustice or unfairness. Then I'm up in arms." The author also loves animals, especially horses, and the outdoors.

She's very involved with her family. Besides her four children, she recently adopted her niece. "And I've just been made a grandmother by my eldest daughter." She keeps a stack of baby pictures of little Raina at hand and readily admits that she is a doting grandmother.

The success of her novels have given her many new luxuries. "I can afford to buy what I want and I can take care of my children—send them to college and get them what they need—without worrying." She now has an apartment in New York, two homes in California, land in Arizona, and a wardrobe of Halstons. A full-time secretary takes care of all of her business and domestic affairs. As she says, "I have enough of 'things.'" She is more interested in relationships, longtime friends, and in being a patient listener to problems. She loves classical music and ballet, and is a board member of the New York Opera Association. When writing, she likes music playing in the background, especially Wagner or classical guitar. Other than that she isn't concerned about atmosphere for writing. "My most important consideration is: Is my typewriter functioning? If people are around it doesn't bother me at all. I go into my own world and I'm oblivious to everything else."

Rosemary begins her days in the early afternoon with a yoga session. She also follows a strict health food diet that insures her slim figure. She is a "night person," preferring to be awake through the night and asleep through the morning and early afternoon. She writes all night and into the dawn when she's concentrating on a novel.

"When ideas for stories come to me it is often in dreams or half-dreams," she explains. "I stop whatever I'm doing and jot down the thought before I forget it. In the middle of writing one book, all of a sudden an idea may pop into my head for my next novel. It is in one of those twenty-four-hour periods that I go without sleep, almost in a half dream."

For an ideal romance, Rosemary thinks that atmosphere helps but really isn't essential. "The basic thing is the chemistry," she says. "If you have the attraction, then wherever you are becomes romantic. Society overdoes the candlelight, atmosphere bit. Love is a much abused word, nowadays. I believe in attraction at first sight, but love is precious and doesn't come too easily. It has a lot to do with liking. For love to last, it has to involve liking, friendship, and communication," she says philosophically.

One thing that bothers Rosemary a great deal is the patronizing attitude that some critics take toward romantic novels. "I think it's unfair to label what the present generation is writing as *historical* romance," she says. "They're historical novels, not *just* romance. They combine mystery, adventure, action, and more. After all, they never said that Frank Yerby wrote historical romances. It's become a denigrating term. There's a feeling that they're only for women who have nothing else to do," she says angrily.

"Personally, I can't stand to read something that is only a sugary, sweet romance," she declares. "That turns me off. I like something I can sink me teeth into. Something with action,

236

mystery and suspense." She cites her novel *The Crowd Pleasers* as the type of contemporary novel of mystery and suspense that she favors. It combines shadowy underworld figures, political background and trickery.

When Rosemary used to read historical novels as a young girl she often wondered why they didn't say a little more in the love scenes. "Not that you want to be clinical like a sex manual," she explains. "But I always felt you can go into a bit of detail and at the same time you can leave a little to the imagination." This is what she attempts to do. "By the way," she adds with a smile, "the heroine of *Love Play* was still technically a virgin for the first several chapters. There are love scenes but when the male protagonist finds out she's a virgin, he stops short. It's a funny, frothy, happy, souffle. Almost like Harlequin with a little more depth to it."

And what does the creator of the "Sweet/Savage" style expect of the real men she encounters? "More than anything else I admire self-assurance in a man," she says in her worldly manner—a tone which implies they may be hard to find. "A real man," she believes, "is not the macho type who looks down on a woman. He's so sure of himself and his masculinity that he can accept that I'm a woman and a person. And—he isn't threatened by a successful woman. My particular type of man," she adds, "is also a very good businessman." Since Rosemary Rogers adores first-class travel and European jaunts as much as her heroines, her ideal man must enjoy all the travel and excitement of her jet-set lifestyle.

Brown rice is one of Rosemary's favorite dishes; she swears by its nutritional benefits. She's frequently seen dining with a handsome escort at Maxim's or Regine's in Paris where she indulges in a dinner fit for one of her heroines. No recipes available for all that!

Rachel Ryan

His lips came down on hers once again. His ferocious hunger was tempered only by a desire to bring her as much pleasure as he found in the kiss. Though his tongue coaxed her to kiss in a way she had never kissed before, it was a gentle persuasion.

—*A Treasure Worth Seeking*

With a simple bribe to her two young children, Sandra Brown promised that their names Rachel and Ryan would be seen on book covers across the country. "What I said exactly," explains the 5'7" attractive brunette, "is this—'If you'll let Mom write for a few hours every morning without bothering me I'll put your name on every page of the book!'" Now the two youngsters are her biggest fans. "They've been trained," Sandra says, "to go into any bookstore, drugstore, or grocery store, and look for my books, and then place them at eye level. Unfortunately, they're prone to yell out, 'Hey, Mom, there's only four left,' or whatever."

Sandra Brown writes short contemporary romances for Dell Ecstasy as Rachel Ryan, and longer novels under the names Laura Jordan and Erin St. Claire, for two other publishers. The majority of her books have contemporary settings, but she is beginning to write historical romances, and the first was *Tender Victory*.

The eldest of five daughters, Sandra was born on June 12, in Waco, Texas, after World War II. She learned responsibility early in life, being the leader of her young siblings. "My youngest sister was born when I was in high school," she explains. "My father was a journalist and my mother a special education teacher. I devoured Nancy Drew books, like every other normal girl in town, but never dreamed of becoming a writer."

At Texas Christian University in Fort Worth, while majoring in English, Sandra met her future husband, Richard Brown. "We were both entertaining in the same stage show, *Six Flags Over Texas*, a large amusement park in Arlington, Texas. We were married in 1968, and we've kept the act together ever since," she adds with a happy gleam in her brown eyes.

The Brown family lives in a contemporary house in Arlington, Texas. Last year it was necessary to build an addition to give the author of the family a writing study. "I made it personally mine by putting in floor-to-ceiling windows and bookcases. I also designed a special fireplace. On cold rainy days, I light candles and build a fire, and that's when I do my best writing," she says. She tries to put in at least five or six hours a day at the typewriter.

At first the children couldn't understand why Mother was working, even though she never left the house. "There was no question about it, they were jealous of my time and had trouble relating to what I was doing. Now they're very excited."

It was at the urging of her husband, a former television anchorman and talk show host in Texas, that she launched her career as a writer. "Up to 1980 I held a variety of jobs. I started working in TV doing weather reports, commercials, and even a morning talk show in Tyler and Dallas, Texas. I managed a cosmetic studio in Tyler, and I loved that, too." After eighteen months at the typewriter, she sold her first manuscript. In the first year of her career, she sold six novels to New York publishers.

Always the reader, she feels reading is a requirement for any good writer of romantic novels today. "Once I decided to try my hand at writing the light romances, I bought about a dozen of them to get the feel for the right style. I've learned a great deal since I started writing them; they are not all that easy to write!"

There are a lot of changes in the Brown household these days. While Sandra forges out her promising future as an author, husband Michael has also entered a new field. He's now in business for himself and has become a full-time professional speaker and entertainer, and appears in industrial commercials as an actor. "We're not jolted by this rebuilding of our future," admits Sandra. "Michael and I agree that it's a little frightening when you step into something new and for the first time you don't have a regular paycheck coming in every two weeks. But we're just really happy with what we're both doing. We happen to like challenges," she adds.

As with most Geminis, Sandra is able to adjust herself to any situation. Blessed with personality plus charm, she's a true bearer of her zodiac sign, known for talent for languages and writing. Cooking is also one of her pleasures. "We love Mexican food. Especially chicken enchiladas and homemade guacamole salad. We like our guacamole spicy, so I add picanté sauce. My choice of dessert with a Mexican dinner is vanilla ice cream with Kahlua and almonds on top. Chilled Sangria is the perfect drink to sip on."

Edith St. George

How reassuring was his gentle stroking across her wet back! And then she stiffened as realization struck. Wet, naked back! She didn't have a stitch of clothing on her. Now what could she do! Walk casually to her clothes, exposed to his all-seeing eyes? The prospect overwhelmed her and she buried her face into his shoulder, too embarrassed to move.

—White Water Love

Some authors seem to be born with the urge to write. Others come to it much later in life. When Edith Delatush, more familiarly known to her readers as Edith St. George, Edith de Paul, and Alyssa Morgan, was growing up, she wanted to be a nurse. As a young woman, she fulfilled her dream and became a registered nurse at Long Island College Hospital. It was there that she met her physician husband George—over a blood transfusion!

Tall, dark-haired Edith was born on November 21, 1921, in Brooklyn, New York of first-generation German parents. "When I was nine, we moved to a farm on Long Island. I had a lovely childhood. School to me was a joy—I was consistently on the honor role and excelled in sports, as well as held leads in the Dramatic Club." There was no thought of becoming a writer in those days, but she did have the Scorpio ESP and a penchant for mystery and surprises.

Edith is clearly amazed at her success as a writer. Her latest career began casually enough. "I drifted into painting and became quite proficient at it for a time. But it wasn't until 1978, at age 56, that I found what I was searching for when my husband was away at a medical convention. I had just finished reading a poorly written romance and decided that I could do better. Don't we all at one time or another?" she asks rhetorically. "A glimmer of a plot came to mind so I decided to try my hand at writing. I was immediately hooked! However, I was shy about my new hobby and became a 'closet writer,' hiding it from everyone."

When Edith is writing a book she likes it to move quickly, with a lot of tension back and forth among her protagonists. There is little, if any violence in her books. And no rape. Edith believes that the readers—especially women—want "a joyful meeting between the sexes." A certain chemistry and commitment are two essential ingredients in her love matches. "I'm not a women's libber—I'm very old-fashioned," she says. "I believe men should have the dominant role in a relationship, but that the woman should be dominant behind the scenes."

Happiness and fulfillment are two of her constant themes. "Women must have the right man in their lives to achieve happiness and fulfillment," she contends. "Successful careers supply only a part of women's happiness. As a nurse, I've heard a lot of confessions from many different people, and I've seen a lot of life. I know what it is that women—people—are longing for." Nowadays, Edith still works part-time in her husband's office, but writing takes up most of her time.

The romantic stories that blossom from her fertile imagination probably derive their inspiration from that wonderful love-at-first-sight feeling that she had with her husband. "Ours has been an exceptionally good marriage," she says with a warm glow. "We'll soon celebrate our fortieth wedding anniversary!" The couple have two sons and five granddaughters.

Edith's knowledge of a great variety of human relationships is invaluable to her in plotting her category romances and in guaranteeing the happy endings which she considers an indispensable part of her literary "tranquilizers," as she calls them.

She had no previous training as a writer, but she somehow took naturally to it. Her first manuscript was placed "on the back shelf," as the expression goes. "I'd heard that it was impossible for a beginner to get published, so I turned to short stories and managed to get a few published. But I found it wasn't my thing. I preferred developing my characters and watching them in fascination as they led me through the plot." In fact, Edith insists that her characters take over and tell her what to write. Her heroines and heroes are not based on people she knows. Rather, she may see an individual with beautiful eyes and from there she will build a whole character. "This is why I write," she says. "I get a big charge out of typing and wondering what my characters will do next and how the story will end. When I'm finished I ask myself: 'Did I write all this?'"

When Edith finished her third manuscript, she decided to be brave enough to face the unknown. "The poor thing was returned by publishers twice but then I latched onto an agent. I bless the day I found Arlene Gross," she says and smiles, her large hazel eyes bright. "Dell Candlelight bought the book and Arlene sold the next seven I wrote in rapid succession. Eight novels in one year! I was floating on a continuous high."

Edith is still amused by her husband's reaction. "The first sale brought a disbelieving arch to his eyebrow, which indicated he thought it was all a fluke, and secretly I feared it was so. The second brought forth pursed lips and a 'Well, well!' By the eighth he was reduced to 'My God!' We buy champagne by the case now since each sale gets celebrated with a bottle," she says with a laugh. Nowadays, as Edith's husband makes his hospital rounds, he makes sure to have at least one copy of her latest book to give to patients.

Although her first eight books were category romances and Regency novels, because "I write light things and enjoy it," she is now working on a mystery. Her first published novel *The Beckoning Heart,* was written under the pen-name Alyssa Morgan. This novel is an adventure romance that mixes love and sailing with drugs and hijacking on the high seas. "We once owned a forty-one-foot sloop and cruised from the

Chesapeake to Cape Cod, plus chartering boats in the Bahamas and Virgin Islands," she explains, which accounts for the many nautical touches in her books.

The Delatushs now live in Tequesta, Florida, and Edith's favorite writing place in her beautiful home is in her open kitchen, which has a bank of windows that overlook the lovely Loxahatchee River. She admits that writing has changed her life. Now she gets up every morning at the same time, seven days a week, and writes from 8:30 A.M. to 12:30 P.M. "The first thing I do each morning is tighten the previous day's production. And when the book is finished, I edit and read it aloud to check the flow of sentences and words." Completing a novel is a "real downer" for Edith because she is saying goodbye to her characters who have become close friends. "I get over the letdown by starting a new book," she adds.

Edith has valuable advice for beginners and would-be writers. "Anybody who has any desire to write should sit down and write seven days a week." She used the word discipline often and follows her own advice, though she admits it takes a lot out of one to create all the time. But she claims the rewards are worth it! Primarily she is happy that her husband is so proud of her. "And so are my two sons. It's a whole new world. Life *does* begin after fifty!" she says enthusiastically.

The recipe that Edith wants to share with her readers is for Beer Bread, one of her family's favorite treats.

BEER BREAD

3 cups all-purpose flour
2 tbsp. sugar
1 can regular beer

Mix thoroughly. (I use a wire whisk.) Pour into greased bread pan. Bake 20 minutes in 350 degree oven. Brush melted unsalted oleo over top. Bake another 20 minutes or until golden brown. Be resigned to baking this over and over.

Sharon Salvato

A passion only waiting to be set free, he had said. Only to herself, in one small dark corner of her mind, could she admit the constant hunger to be loved, to be taken and used in love. Was Alain the man to set her free of all the longing?

—*The Black Swan*

Sharon Salvato calls herself the "Day" half of Day Taylor, that's the pseudonym she shares with her near-neighbor in Columbus, Ohio, Cornelia Parkinson. Under her own name, she writes equally exciting historical romances such as *Bitter Eden*. Sharon and Cornelia have made quite a popular name for themselves in the world of historical romance, and as Day Taylor, they are the authors of *The Black Swan*, a saga set in the Civil War South, and the stunning sequel, *Mossrose*.

As the Day-half explains, "We arrived at the name as follows— Day is my mother's maiden name. Taylor is the name of one of Connie's ancestors. We plan to continue being Day Taylor, but each of us will write alone as well. It would be nice to think Day Taylor would appear on every other book, but I'm not sure of that. All I know is that at least one more story is on the boards, and there's a good possibility of more to come. Only time will tell for sure what will happen," she says. Her current writing project is a historical romance under the Salvato name.

Sharon, a sparkling, gamine-type brunette, was born on April 30, but prefers to keep the year a secret, and for strong personal reasons. "I am definitely squeamish about the ideas people seem to attach to numbers. If I am twenty, I'm too young and silly to know anything. If I am thirty, I must be into sex, family, career, or some other thing. If I am forty, I am too old to understand what is happening in the world. If I'm fifty, they're hunting for hidden grandchildren. If I'm sixty, they want to know if I take weaving classes at the senior citizen center, and so on. I'm all ages, which is part of the reason, I suppose, that I'm a writer."

Taurus, the bull, is Sharon's astrological sun sign. Lovers of luxury and fine food, Taureans enjoy indulging themselves and usually make enough money to afford the good things of life. They're also stubborn; so it's quite possible that Sharon Salvato will never reveal her age.

A great love of history, which directed this author into the career of writing historical romances, probably comes from Sharon's insatiable curiosity, evident in her education. She graduated from the University of Cincinnati with a teaching certificate in English, history, Russian language and art. "I studied in college for five years; my father thought I might never leave. I had an insatiable curiosity, and tended to take anything and everything that caught my attention. I went to day school and night school and summer school, ending up with 199 semester hours before I graduated. But I took all kinds of neat things like astronomy, and Chinese literature, ethics, psychology, Russian literature, English literature, economic history, and the in-between stuff, even sculpturing, ceramics and painting. It was tons of fun!

"Once I managed to give up my perpetual education," she adds with a radiant smile, "I graduated and taught in the Columbus Educational System, and got married all in the same year—1961. I married Guy Salvato, a man I had met my freshman year in college and dated during the time I went to school. He was studying advertising design, and now has his own graphic design studio. He spends a lot of his time winning awards, and designing stamps for the U.S. Postal Department, along with all of his regular accounts."

248

Sharon had four sons within a space of seven years, and in 1977, "We acquired our first girl in the family besides me—Nikki, our cat," explains Sharon, her dark eyes alive with merriment. "We are a handful as a family. Talk settles around subjects like soccer, baseball, football, track and rock groups."

In 1980, Sharon and Guy dissolved their marriage, but not before child number five was on its way—another boy. Sharon now lives in the same neighborhood of Columbus, about six blocks from her old house, where Guy still resides. "I live in a house we call the Hi-Ho Nest. It is a big rambling house, has a seven-foot tin knight named Sir Odds Bodkin to guard us, supposedly a ghost named Pam, a dog named Riley, and a rock band that my second son plays in. I still have a special room I work in and it is full of books and plants. This house does not have a greenhouse, unfortunately, but we do have an art room in it. And the house is full of music. The kids live with me, but they visit their father on weekends and stay in their old rooms. Everything is very amicable," she adds.

People often tell Sharon that she has a vivid imagination, and she thinks she does, but it isn't her imagination that gets the workout in writing an historical novel. As she says, "It is my ability to organize facts that gets strained to the taffy-pulling point. The imagination is used primarily in being able to 'see' and 'hear' what is taking place in a time in which I have not physically lived. The rest of it is basically a matter of posing a question and then answering it in the most reasonable way for the particular character, and the particular circumstances I am working with.

"For instance," she says, "if a man climbs onto his roof to paint the third-floor windows and the ladder falls leaving him stranded, I will mentally tramp all over that roof until I figure out the most reasonable way that man will find his way back to the ground. Is he a worrier? Would the gutters hold his weight if he chose to go down that way? Is he courageous enough to take that route? Is he foolhardy enough to leap for a tree? Or, just to risk the whole jump to the ground . . . and on and on. What a *lousy* scene that would make!" Sharon comments. "Anyway, it serves, I guess. I'll think about my chosen situation from the physical aspects and from the psychological viewpoint—what is he capable of doing, what is he likely to do and why? I am forever buried in psychology books trying to find out the effects of depression, elation, neurosis and sometimes psychosis, and then the ordinary machinations of your sort of normal plodders!"

Something Sharon is always asked about is her feeling toward the use of sex in her books. "I let that be determined by the nature of the story I'm telling and the people who are the characters," she is quick to say. "In some stories explicit sex is merely intrusive, and, like description, I don't think anything should be stuck in a book just because it seems to be a place where it can be stuck. If you have a scene where there is a natural passion rising between two characters, by all means bed them down in the outhouse, or in the clover, or on horseback, or wherever they are. If, however, they are reticent people, or the action moves in such a way that you must stop it in order to show the sex scene, keep it out! When my characters have sexual relations in a book they do so for a reason. It does not always have to be love, but it will never be for conquest or a whim— unless it is the villain, and even then I seldom use it, and never describe it in detail."

In Sharon's writing room, there's a shelf for her dictionaries and research books that she uses frequently. Another shelf holds a thesaurus and a well-used *Name the Baby Book,* and a few books of poetry and other "oddments." When she's working on a novel, she works every day, and tries to work at least six hours. "I work best," she says, "when I can take about a two-month rest between books. One month is spent doing things I didn't have time to do when working—like making rugs, or canning vegetables, or just playing. By the end of that time, I'm usually restless and another book begins to roll around in the back of my mind. I just let it simmer, and think about it, dream about it, relish it as it starts to take form. Then one day I'll wake up with a craving for the library and I'll know it's time to do the research and begin to think of the book in a scheduled, serious way. Then comes the living in the time period in which I'm writing, the living with the people who are now as much a family to me as my own are, and the laughing with them, and the crying over them—one of these days I'm going to electrocute myself on my typewriter!''

Sharon's favorite food to treat "a horde of kids" is chocolate chip cookies or chocolate turtles. Turtles look more complicated than they are!

TURTLES

1 lb. pecans or cashew nuts
1 lb. package commercial caramels
8 oz. semisweet chocolate or 1-1/3 cups semisweet chocolate bits

Spread cashews or pecans on a baking sheet or cookie tin to a depth of about ½ inch. Melt caramels in top of double boiler with 2 tablespoons water. (Not too much water or the caramel will not harden properly.) With a teaspoon, drop melted caramel onto nuts. Do not make the drops larger than one inch in diameter or place drops too close together. When the caramel has cooled and set, lift out the turtle centers and place them on a cooling rack until firm. Meanwhile, melt chocolate over simmering (not boiling) water in double boiler (being careful, as always, not to let stray drops of water get into the mixture). Spoon chocolate over the caramel centers and let cool until quite firm. Although these candies are edible as soon as they harden, their flavor is improved if they're allowed to stand for 24 hours. Store in airtight containers, in a cool, dry place.

Yield: 50–60 Turtles.

Jeraldine Saunders

"Aha," Shandor sighed. "How wise you have grown in the ways of the Rom. A gypsy needs the evening campfire the way the flowers need the rain." He turned a smiling face toward her, showing strong white teeth below his dark moustache. Graciela looked into the dark eyes, so impenetrable until now, and found them not mysterious at all. They were warm and understanding and appreciative, filled with an innocence, sweetness, and strength.

—Frisco Lady

Stunning, auburn-haired Jeraldine Saunders has had a number of exciting and glamorous careers in her lifetime, the latest being that of a successful historical romance writer. The author of *Frisco Lady* and its sequel *Frisco Fortune,* this third-generation Californian took her deep interest in California history and produced one strong and exciting heroine. "Most historians briefly contrast the adventurous male with his presumably passive, long-suffering wife," she says. "Few paid much attention to the records left by the women themselves, never stopping to consider the real truths. I enjoy writing about the conflicts women have with their emotions and how they cope with love's problems and the men in their lives, the desired and the undesired."

Jeri, as she is called by her friends, is one of the most *experienced* romantic authors in the field of human emotions.

For twenty years she worked as a high-fashion model, an actress, and then as the first woman cruise director on a luxury line. She admits to meeting thousands and thousands of men and women, of knowing the excitement of being "cheered, showered with gifts, kissed and hugged farewell by all nationalities, and receiving proposals of marriage from so many men it would be immodest to mention."

As the cruise director on the *Royal Viking Star*, two Italian ships, and a Greek liner, to mention just a few of her employers, she saw all the "heavenly ports and sang and laughed at sea for seven days a week, eleven months a year," she recalls. "The hours were long and late, and grueling. I was up at six A.M. every morning, planning the day's activities. But I did get a firsthand knowledge of people and their behavior, under all sorts of conditions." She claims there's always an invisible bin at the gangway of a cruise ship with a sign reading: "Store all your inhibitions here. They will automatically reattach themselves upon disembarkation!"

As a result of these many years of unusual and romantic capers, Jeri decided to sit down and write a semi-autobiographical book, *The Love Boats*, based on her actual experiences as the world's first female cruise director. "I was the one person aboard ship who was responsible for keeping everyone happy," she says. The book was bought by TV producers and turned into the hit television series, "The Love Boat." To this day she receives $1,000 every time the show is seen on television, without lifting an anchor, or even a well-manicured finger. The money has enabled her to buy a sumptuous California home and a brown Bentley, among other luxuries of life.

Three times wed, Jeri is now happily married and living on her estate in Glendale, California with her husband, Arthur Andrews, recently retired as West Coast representative for the U.S. Missiles Command. "We met on land," she explains, "between my sailings in the early 1970s. Arthur, who is also a poet, travels with me now and helps keep my career as a cruise consultant, nutrition specialist, astrological lecturer, and historical romance author, on an even keel." A housekeeper and

254

Jeraldine's mother also assist in keeping Jeraldine free for all of her activities.

After the success of *The Love Boats,* Jeraldine penned the popular *Love Signs,* an astrology book filled with information on numerology, palmistry, plus details on colors and people. There's even a section that figures out if sweethearts are really meant for each other by spending an evening meditating on their favorite color to find out if the colors correspond. "If they don't," Jeri claims, "it's probably already apparent to both that things aren't as close to Paradise as they'd wish!" *Cosmopolitan* magazine readers enjoyed excerpts from this book in 1980.

Born in Los Angeles on September 3, 1926, Jeri's youthful appearance leaves people holding their breath. She looks at least twenty years younger. This astrologer enjoys pondering the mysteries of her own zodiac chart. "The moment I was born," she relates, "Sagittarius was on the horizon—my rising sign, my ascendant—the moon, was in Gemini and the sun was in the state of Virgo. This indicates that my life force is focused on perception, understanding of how people feel and react, and a need to articulate my impressions as well as to be of service." She hastens to add, "My Jupiter is in Scorpio, which is my twelfth house and this gives me an understanding of the secrets of love."

Jeri's astrological knowledge began with one of her former husbands, Sydney Omarr, California's famed star-caster. "I was a major performer in a highly successful review based on astrology. In it I modeled twelve beautiful gowns representing the twelve signs of the zodiac. The review was put together and narrated by Omarr." She flashes a warm smile at the mention of his name. "He's a genius and geniuses are not the easiest people to live with. We had a very short marriage but an eight-year courtship," she explains. "We're still close friends, and my husband and I socialize with him frequently when we're in town. He wrote the foreword to my astrology book." Jeraldine studied astrology, palmistry, and numerology for many years, and this was one of her featured lectures on the cruise ships when she was director.

Taking all of her knowledge and experience, Jeraldine

decided to write her first novel, *Frisco Lady*. "It's a sprawling saga, combining spiritualism, psychic phenomena, and gypsy folklore. The plot focuses on Graciela McGee, the beautiful, conventbred daughter of an Irish father and Spanish mother. I combined my love of mystical arts and gypsy lore to create what the critics have called 'a powerful story of passion and prophecy.' Also," she adds, "it's set in the mid-1800s and it starts out in New Orleans and ends in San Francisco, two very romantic port cities!"

With such an interesting and diversified background, one might conclude that life for the beautiful, willowy (she's 5'7" and wears a size eight dress), green-eyed author has been a bed of roses. "Not so," she insists. For the past decade she's been trying to free herself from the haunting memory of her only child's untimely and tragic death in 1970.

For twenty-seven years her daughter Gail suffered from insomnia, hyperkinesis, bronchitis, and severe drops in energy and withdrawal. No doctor could help her. Jeri attended the International College of Applied Nutrition to find out what she could do to help her daughter. Eventually, she recognized Gail's symptoms as signs of hypoglycemia, a disease that the specialists were refusing to acknowledge. As cruise director at the time, Jeraldine began lecturing on nutrition in addition to her myriad duties. "I don't know how I ever did it," she says. "I was out lecturing on the very disease my daughter was dying from and no doctor could help. That certainly was not easy." The night her daughter passed away, Jeri was scheduled to leave on another cruise. "I returned home immediately to find that Gail had died from hypoglycemic shock." Though memories continue to haunt her, Jeri found her catharsis in writing yet another book, *Hypoglycemia: The Disease Your Doctor Won't Treat*, with co-author Dr. Harvy M. Ross. "I'm consoled by the thought that I'm reaching others who might be facing the same tragic story I lived."

Aside from researching her future historical novels, Jeri and her husband are traveling around the world. As a spokeswoman for the United States Cruises, Inc., an organization which is refitting the *S.S. United States* for use as a Los Angeles-

Honolulu cruise ship, and other seagoing projects, she is still making public appearances.

Does she enjoy the "Love Boat" TV series? "I love it," she says. "It's uplifting! It's happy! Nobody gets murdered or tortured. You are left with the light, happy feeling that life is beautiful!"

All of which, of course, fits in with Jeraldine Saunders' life philosophy. "If you dwell on happiness and love, that's what you'll get," says the fashion model turned astrologer-author. "I always tell people they should dwell well."

A WINTER SUNDAY ROAST

I make this easy roast on Sundays when I have my brothers over for dinner. They are hearty eaters and are "meat and potato" types. This roast is especially good on a cold day when you can appreciate the oven's warmth.

One large seven-bone roast. If it is frozen, do not bother to defrost it, just add an extra 45 minutes cooking time.

Place roast in large roasting pan.

Pour in ½ cup of any cooking wine and one can of beer.

Sprinkle one pkg of Lipton's Onion Soup over the top of the roast.

Cover. Place in preheated 325 degree oven for three hours if unfrozen or three hours and 45 minutes if frozen.

In the last hour, add peeled, whole potatoes and whole carrots. Add water if needed.

Gravy can be made with pan drippings if desired.

Bertrice Small

Her sea-green eyes were enormous in her face, and wonderingly she touched her bruised lips with trembling fingertips. "Is that what men do to women?"

"Sometimes," said Jared. "Usually they are driven to it. If I have frightened you, Miranda, I apologize. Your lips are sweet and I could not resist."

—Unconquered

"I will not tell you that I sprang forth from my mother's womb, holding a Bic Clic—but almost!" quips saucy Bertrice Small, the author of *Unconquered*. "There was never any question in my mind that I wanted to be writer, but how to get there has not been easy," she says with a sparkle in her bright green eyes that assures you this spunky lady gets what she goes after.

Gifted with a vivid imagination, Bertrice (rhymes with Bernice) perhaps had more than her share of childhood reveries. At the age of six she was writing poetry and stories that swept her away from the hundrum. And at thirteen, she came up with her first novel—about an Inca princess who was ravished by an evil Spanish conquistador. "Quite frankly," she admits, "at age thirteen, and as a boarding student in an Anglican convent school, I was not quite sure what ravishing entailed, but it sounded slightly and deliciously wicked," she says and grins impishly.

"There's no doubt about it, I've always been an escape artist;

I'd rather spend my time in the past," she muses. At her antique desk in the gift shop she once operated in the pre-Colonial Long Island town where she lives, Bertrice turns out tales of days gone by—of the fourteenth, fifteenth, sixteenth, and eighteenth centuries, of love affairs engendered by the turbulent events of history, and of heroines who might very well have lived. "I have the habit of getting involved with certain of my characters. For me these people exist, and I believe that possibly once they did," she says enthusiastically.

With enormous insight and imagination, this bestselling author of *Adora, The Kadin,* and *Love Wild and Fair,* writes as if she were there—infusing life and depth into her characters and settings. In October 1980, Bertrice formally graduated to the ranks of the great historical romance writers with the publication of her first trade paperback, *Skye O'Malley,* Ballantine Books' first historical romance in that format. Skye is an indomitable Irish heroine of great beauty who loses her heart to her husband's lord, and her memory in a brutal sea battle . . . who lives one life of happiness and bliss as the wife of an Algerian and another as the wife of one of the most powerful noblemen in England.

History has always had a special fascination for this cheerful woman whose friends call her "Sunny." In college Bertrice most enjoyed history and English, and couldn't make up her mind which should be her major concentration. Happily, writing has provided her with a perfect way of blending the two. "Because I am first of all a historian, I get a great kick out of teaching history through my books. It's a painless way to learn because I do believe that those who don't learn from history are condemned to relive it."

Bertrice's buoyant personality belies the fact that at one time, shortly after her marriage, she suffered from agoraphobia, which she describes as a "severe neurotic disorder which at that time was barely understood by the medical profession. "It is basically a fear of going out," she explains, "and strikes mostly women, manifesting itself in totally unreasonable and illogical terror of leaving one's home, accompanied by physical symptoms such as increased acceleration of the heart, profuse

260

sweating, trembling, and the absolute certainty that you're going crazy—which you're not." She spent four years in therapy and today has regained the ability to function as a normal person.

Born in Manhattan on December 9, 1937, this fair, mahogany-haired author is known to possess salient Sagittarian traits. She is honest and outspoken, with a keen sense of humor. When she feels strongly about something, she doesn't mince words.

Elbows propped on her desk, the delightful author rests chin in hands and stares fixedly with her luminous emerald eyes. Bertrice is about to make a pronouncement on one of her pet peeves: critics who attempt to downgrade authors of romantic-historical fiction. "Those of us writing romantic-historical fiction today are the descendants of those fantastic writers of the fifties and sixties, Anya Seton, Taylor Caldwell, Jan Westcott, and Sergeanne Golon. If this were thirty years ago we would all be in hardcover; but it's the 1980s and paper is expensive so we're paperback original authors. What's wrong with it? And why, when we're responsible for making our various houses a lot of money, are we constantly being put down by the reviewers and publishers alike?" she inquires challengingly.

"I'm a damned good writer and researcher, and so are many of my contemporaries, most of whom are women," she continues, just beginning to warm to her subject. "Our books which no longer go to black in the love scenes are referred to with a supercilious snicker as 'soft-core porn for the ladies.' I personally find this very offensive. There is nothing wrong with a escapism at the end of a long, hard day," she observes emphatically.

Then Bertrice Small's expression changes. The frown lines fade, the pretty face brightens, the lithe, 5'7" body relaxes and conversation turns to family matters—to her husband, George, who reproduces seventeenth and eighteenth century clocks for sale in their gift shop; to their young son, Thomas David, and to their home on one-and-a-half acres of land in historical Southold, Long Island.

George Sumner Small was a history major at Princeton; he and Bertrice have a great deal in common, and she knew from the moment she met him that they would marry. (They did so seventeen months later—on October 5, 1963.) Fortunately, he rescued her from a conventional life, Bertrice confides. As a young woman she had conformed to her parents' expectations, "doing all the right things expected of me, which, of course, meant not writing but getting a job like a respectable person."

Both her parents were executives with major television networks and she gravitated toward allied work in broadcasting. For a while she worked as a private secretary in Manhattan for a well-known advertising firm and also did television spot sales. "I was rescued by my husband who also is a not quite respectable, creative soul," she laughs. "It was he who encouraged me to go back to writing and I have been doing it seriously since 1969, stopping only for the birth of our son in 1973."

Conformity and consistency, those "hobgoblins of little minds," as Emerson called them, now are disdained by this spirited lady. She traded roles with her husband years ago when the demands of a writing career made the switch imperative. After discussing the matter at length, George agreed to take care of the house and their child and to cook half the meals so Bertrice would have time to write. The arrangement has worked out fine.

"My first novel, *The Kadin*, took several years of research, writing, and rewriting," she recalls. "Practice, however, does make perfect, and today I am able to do on the average of a book every nine months, sort of like a pregnancy."

Mood music is essential when Bertrice plies her craft. Other essential props include a battered clipboard, yellow legal pads and a good supply of Bic Clic ballpoint pens. Bertrice always writes the first draft in longhand because "the noise of the typewriter when I'm creating annoys me."

How long will she write? "For as long as I live," she says determinedly. "Like the ballerina in the *Red Shoes*, I can't stop. It's a crazy business but then I'm convinced that all writers are crazy people," she adds with a chuckle.

Asked for her favorite recipe, Bertrice comes up with a most appropriate one. "Since the first romance heroine of them all was partial to apples, here's my recipe for Apple Betty," she quips.

APPLE BETTY

8 large cooking apples (she prefers MacIntosh)
1/2 cup flour
2/3 cup brown sugar
1/2 cup white sugar
butter
cinnamon and nutmeg

Pare apples as for pie. Lay in rectangular baking dish (approximately 9 × 6½ × 2½ deep). Mix flour and sugars with enough butter to make a crumbly mixture, and sprinkle over top of apples, after dusting apples with spices.

Bake at 350 degrees approximately 30 minutes or until it looks cooked, and topping is bubbly.

Cool slightly, and serve with either heavily whipped cream or plain heavy cream. *No* Cool Whip, please. If you're going to go to the trouble of preparing this terrific dessert, do it right, she urges.

LaVyrle Spencer

In those first intimate after-minutes, with his body still warm in hers, she lay thinking that this was the highest accolade a man and woman could give each other and that words were insignificant in its wake. She felt rich with his gift, as if nothing greater could be afforded her.

—The Fulfillment

"I guess this is all too new to me to suddenly find myself on the other side of the fence," says LaVyrle Spencer, avid romance reader turned writer. She is an apple-cheeked, blue-eyed brunette who describes herself as "an unsensational, but happy girl." She is also the mother of two teenage girls, a fact that quite belies her July 17, 1943 birthdate. She looks and acts like a young girl herself. Born under the sign of Cancer, she shows the unyielding tenacity familiar to this sign of the zodiac. The Cancerian may hesitate at the start of a project, but once she has put her hand to it, the grip does not relax.

The Fulfillment was her first book and it was written, she says, "because of one special lady, Kathleen Woodiwiss." As both influence and help, Kathleen has been the entire reason LaVyrle is published. As the story goes: "When I read her first novel, *The Flame and the Flower*, I became quite possessed by it. I reread it—indeed, I still study it—so many times that all I wanted was to be her disciple. Reading her book showed me that it was possible to write a tasteful love story that could make the reader go all giddy with longing, filled with anticipation, and finally gratified by exhilaration. I simply wanted to emulate her," confesses the ebullient LaVyrle.

It was then that her dreams of writing began, and finally the catalyst occurred that forced her into her first attempt to get her work published. "Before my first draft was done," recalls LaVyrle, "I learned that Kathleen lived within an hour's ride of my house. My dream intensified: I began hoping one day to meet her, and I did. At an autograph session at a local bookstore. But I did the most awful thing! I stepped up before her, reached for her hand, and began crying! 'You cannot possibly know what it means to me to meet you at last,' and, feeling like a fool because my face was now buried in my hands, trying to hide those embarrassing tears. But somehow, I believe they spoke for me, because the impossible happened: Kathleen Woodiwiss took the time to graciously answer questions, offer advice, and give me her address in case I needed future advice."

During the following year the two women corresponded. When LaVyrle completed her book, she asked Kathleen, with great trepidation, to read and critique it. Kathleen agreed, although her time had great demands upon it just then, so she said it would be a while before she could get at it.

LaVyrle's eyes light up at the next turning point in her literary life. "Within three days 'success' was to come. Kathleen called to say she'd begun my book and couldn't put it down. 'I read till my eyes were red, white, and blue!' she said, then added that the manuscript was on its way to New York. There have been thrilling moments since then, but none with quite the intense joy that her approval brought," declares the new author.

In the ensuing months, through the Woodiwiss intervention, LaVyrle's dreams became reality. "In the time since the publication of that first book, she has shaken me from the doldrums by forcing me to make myself write when words seemed not to come. She has been and always will be, my inspiration," LaVyrle says sincerely.

The setting for *The Fulfillment* is in the place of LaVyrle's childhood, Browerville, Minnesota, and the time-slot is in the days of the author's grandparents. "During every summer of my first sixteen years," LaVyrle goes on, "I spent sumptuous lavishly wonderful weeks staying on the farm with my Bohemian grandparents, some ten miles or so north of Browerville. When I began dreaming the plot of *The Fulfillment*, it was always played out in that setting. When I wrote, I described a very beloved spot, which is still there today, although my grandparents no longer own it. Gramps is dead now, but Grandma, to whom the book is dedicated, is still spry and independent, and was my one and only resource for background for the book. Later, when the book was published, with a cover and everything, I gave it to Grandma to read, to assess it for errors. She found I had done 'a proper job.' Her reaction was 'Forever more! I don't know how that girl done it! I loved it all!' . . . Then she added shyly, 'All but that sex!' Bless her heart . . . that part of the story was fiction," confides LaVyrle.

"The actual writing time put into this book totaled seven months," says LaVyrle, "but spread out over two years. I worked nine months of the year as an aide in our school district at that time, so I found time to write only during summers. Now I write only during the school year, for I have two teenage daughters and I find that they need me during the summers. I coach their summer softball teams, sew (she was a professional seamstress), and we enjoy gardening and music. I have a great passion for music. My husband, Daniel, with whom I went to school during the last two years of high school in Minnesota, is an excellent guitarist and vocalist. With him I play bass guitar and sing. Our favorite musician is Gordon Lightfoot, whose music we sing, and whose concerts we never miss."

Although LaVyrle did not attend college, she has never regretted it a day of her life. "I was all set to start college in 1961. I was going to teach English as a career. But I threw my mother one of the major setbacks of her life by declaring that I refused to be separated from my beloved Dan by two hundred miles. Sometimes," she says and smiles, "I still can't believe I could have been so smart then." LaVyrle's husband of twenty years is obviously the joy of her life. "We fell in love on a dance floor and heightened that love by singing together, which we still do.

We were married in a tiny service in a huge basilica with only two witnesses present. Never had a honeymoon, but a terrific honey *life*," she adds. "And when people ask me about success, I feel comfortable telling them that I was a success before I got published, for I'd accomplished the far more important goal of creating a marriage and a home filled with love, and raising two neat children.

"I also feel that I now have the means to pay back my husband for the 'good life' he has provided me all these years. He gave me the freedom to write: I'd like to give him a similar financial freedom to do any silly thing he might like to do. But the 'good life' is so much more than financial ease, and I've had it all my married life anyway, so what more could I want?"

More contracts, obviously, for LaVyrle has just signed with Richard Gallen Books to write three more novels, starting with *The Endearment*.

A favorite recipe? "Surely you jest!" she replies and smiles. "The way I love to cook and eat? I could fill the rest of this book! How about this one:

"YUMMY FRENCH BREAD

1 loaf French bread, split lengthwise

Spread with this mixture and bake at 400 degrees, uncovered, for 20 minutes.

1 lb. shredded Cheddar cheese

1 cup softened butter

½ cup sliced green onions with tops

½ cup chopped parsley

½ tsp. Worcestershire sauce"

Danielle Steel

At first she cantered gently toward her destination, and then after a while, sensing the huge beast straining to go faster, she let him lope from a canter into a gallop as he made his way toward the rising sun. It was one of the most exquisite feelings she could remember, and she held her knees to his flanks and pressed harder as effortlessly they cleared a series of low bushes and a narrow stream.

—Palomino

It has been said that Danielle Steel's own life resembles the lives of the women in her novels. The same elements are certainly there; an international background (she is fluent in four languages, and French is her native tongue), opulent surroundings, beautiful clothes, antique cars, and a *hint* of mystery about her personal life.

Ms. Steel was born in August 1948, in New York. The daughter of a German nobleman, her family tree includes the Lowenbrau beer barons on her father's side, and a Portuguese diplomatic family on her mother's side. Their common language was French, although her parents each spoke eight languages. Her father's family had always lived in Munich and the family seat was a moated castle in Bavaria.

"I spent my childhood in French schools and in various parts of Europe," she recounts, "crossing frequently between New York and Europe by ship." She describes her parents as two very "flamboyant" people. "My father, John Steel, was extremely gregarious, very social, an international roue. My mother was an international beauty. Together they were two very spectacular people."

At the age of fifteen, Ms. Steel had her first experience in an American school. Having finished the equivalent of an American high school education, she enrolled simultaneously at New York University (to complete the formal education expected of her) and the Parsons School of Design (to indulge her secret passion of becoming a fashion designer or, as she puts it, "the new Coco Chanel." She studied French and Italian literature at NYU and fashion design at Parsons and fashion remains a passion with her even today.

Though she doesn't practice fashion designing, Danielle is addicted to buying exotic additions to her own wardrobe. At a disco party she gave for friends one year, she appeared in a lavender lamé and red-sequined outfit from Paris. And at a recent party for Richard Avedon, the photographer, she appeared in a 1950 Balenciaga original which is earmarked to go the Costume Institute of the Metropolitan Museum in New York. But, Danielle is quick to point out that she is just as likely to wear overalls and a T-shirt, especially when she is writing.

At twenty, the author found herself in New York starting a promotions and public relations firm called Supergirls with a group of other women. As she describes it, "The entire outfit was based on female talent. We did everything from finding photographers to scouting locations, styling, giving huge corporate parties, and developing concepts for new women's products, or old ones that needed a new and more youthful image. There were articles written about us in the *Wall Street Journal, The New York Times, Look* magazine, etc. As vice-president in charge of New Business and Public Relations, I was the one who thought up the concepts to push Supergirls itself— and we made quite a splash—even in New York!"

The bright star of Supergirls faded after about five years and it was then that Danielle decided to try her hand at writing. She was especially encouraged by the staff of *Ladies Home Journal* whose parent company she represented at Supergirls. Danielle picked up her facility with poetry from her childhood when she had written hundreds of poems, and the *Journal, Good Housekeeping, Cosmopolitan,* and *McCall's* began to publish her. (Her first collection of *Love Poems* was published in 1981.)

She wrote her first novel in the very early 1970s called *Going Home,* which Pocket Books published. Five books and no contracts later, Danielle was on the verge of joining the Protestant ministry when her seventh book *Passion's Promise,* sold to Dell. The rest, proverbially, is history. Danielle has published nine paperback novels with Dell including *Loving, The Ring* (her first hardcover novel), and *Palomino* (her first trade edition). There are over ten million copies of her books in print and they've inspired the formation of the Danielle Steel Fan Club and the composition of two original lyric songs.

On the surface it would seem that Danielle is the consummate modern woman: a professional success and a working mother with five children. But the petite, green-eyed brunette insists she is really old-fashioned, although Danielle was divorced. She is now married to John Traina, a shipping magnate, and says that she would like to have more children.

With all the national notoriety that comes a best-selling author's way—especially one who has such a glamorous past— Danielle Steel has treated her success humbly and modestly. She keeps largely to herself in her home in San Francisco these days where she most often spends eighteen hours a day writing. "I have been known to hand in a completed, full-length novel in six weeks!" she comments. "I don't write overtly about sex and I think that the 1930s and 1940s were the most romantic periods of this century, hence the time period of *The Ring,*" and her 1982 hard cover novel *Crossings* (due to be published in October 1982).

Danielle travels far less frequently now (she only recently overcame a severe year-long bout with a fear of flying, which she finally cured with the help of a "Fear of Flying" clinic) and keeps her personal life a private matter.

But there are signs of the more flamboyant side to Danielle Steel that still peek through her current lifestyle. "I have a

271

wonderful collection of clothing and a secret passion for antique cars. I now drive a 1940 Ford Opera Coupe Deluxe," she says, "and have a 1940 Ford 4-door sedan for the family."

Her home is filled with antiques and family heirlooms (which have more meaning to her than value). On the walls of her San Francisco house, among countless old family photographs, there are photos of her father in white tie and tails, looking very dashing, of the family castle in Munich (much like the von Gotthard "schloss" in *The Ring*), of her grandfather's stables and several family members riding to hounds. Her office and bedroom, seen by few, are by contrast a riot of color, and convey an entirely contemporary decor and feeling, filled with hearts, old dolls, photographs, posters, and clouds painted on the ceiling.

Her office is very small, with one comfy chair for visitors and shelves for books. "I have an ancient Olympia manual typewriter, bought about ten years ago for forty dollars. It's an old friend by now and I love it."

In San Francisco, she attends the opera and theater with her husband and gives a lot of parties. That is, when she's not putting in twenty hours a day at the typewriter or taking care of the children. "When I'm working, I live a solitary life. I don't see anyone or talk on the phone, or open my mail. I would like to meet other authors," she says, "but I rarely do."

Despite the glamor, and what seems to be a striking resemblance to the lives of her heroines, Danielle Steel claims, "I lead a *real* life; changing diapers, going shopping, with everyday heartbreaks and joys." No doubt, it is just this mixture—her extraordinary background and her down-to-earth daily life—that enhances Danielle Steel's heroines.

Day Taylor

*Dulcie sighed, happy once more.
Somehow, in Adam's arms, the worst
situations could be made light of;
freshed by his strength, she would
find new strength all her own.*

—*Mossrose*

Cornelia M. Parkinson met her future collaborator, Sharon
Salvato, the other half of the Day Taylor team, at a writer's club
in Columbus, Ohio, in the mid 1970s. "Our friendship
developed slowly, and we talked of books, as writers do, until
one day we decided to collaborate on a novel under the joint
pen name of Day Taylor."

Connie, as she prefers to be called, and Sharon gave each other
advice about the books they were working on before they
decided to try a book together. "We gave that a trial period of a
month, to see if either of us would want to back out," Connie
recalls. "Neither did. Soon we were talking on the phone every
day about our plot and researching madly. At the end of the first
month of collaboration we began writing *The Black Swan.*"

The two Ohio authors finished the historical romance in
"exactly 369 days," adds Connie, "from the first day we talked
about the possibility until the last day, when we mailed in the

last of the manuscript. Rewriting took us about six weeks, although eight months elapsed before it was finished."

What is the personal chemistry that makes the Day Taylor team so productive and successful? "It's a story of contrasts and complements," according to Connie. "Sharon and I are quite different in most respects. She's about 5' tall and I'm 5'6". I'm blonde and she's black-haired; she has five sons and I have three daughters. I'm a little older than she. We both do the house-keeping routine, but neither of us considers it *uppermost.* Sharon is a night person and I'm a day person! Even though the first name of our pseudonym belongs to Sharon's part of the family," says Connie, smiling at her own joke. "We both are perfectly capable of working for ten to twelve hours with very little time out. My husband is a professor at Ohio State University, teaching Engineering Graphics. Sharon's former husband is a designer and an artist."

The team's working habits and research are irregular . . . but every day. While they were writing *The Black Swan,* they each spent a month alone doing research.

"Then Sherry started writing," explains Connie, "and did the rough draft of the first few chapters. I rewrote them, then she rewrote them. I wrote a few chapters and the same process prevailed. We met at least once a week, we live nine miles apart in Ohio, and went over everything we had each written since the first meeting. We also planned in some detail the chapters to be written in the next few days. During the time we were writing, we averaged a chapter a week. This time included vacations for us both, days out for various reasons, and all the research we did as we went along."

The women read and took notes on approximately 250 books to give *The Black Swan* authenticity. They took notes on even the smallest things to give a sense of immediacy. "We knew we had the factors of universal appeal," claims Connie. "A handsome hero who is idealistic and daring and likeable (Adam). A beautiful heroine who is courageous, feisty, and true (Dulcie). Adventures that part them and bring them back together. Romance. And sex, the ultimate universal appeal if it's written properly. Not to mention done," she concludes, sagely.

"Sherry and I have good imaginations. And I've been married thirty-eight years and I remember a lot." She smiles and you know that line is one of her favorite quotes at the many Day Taylor autograph parties these days.

The hero in Connie's life is Parky, short for Richard W. Parkinson, the father of her three daughters. "My grandmother lived with us when I was growing up. She was full of old lore, like wishing on the new moon that you would see your lover. I did that one night when I was twelve, and dreamed of a handsome black-haired man with a moustache and a blue shirt. I found him—Parky—when I was sixteen, and married him when I was eighteen. He was, and is, an exceptional man, highly intelligent and analytical, with as much beauty in his character as in his face. Our relationship is intensely satisfying, with room allowed both of us for personal growth, and contentment with each other," confides Connie. "Unlike Barbara Cartland, who says she hasn't met the type of man she writes about, 'only the blue-eyed, blonde, stupid sort,' I have met my kind of hero, met and conquered, or was conquered by. I'll probably always write about handsome black-haired men, with an equally handsome blond man to provide delicious conflict for the heroine," she says.

Connie McNary Parkinson was born in Casey, Illinois, in the best bedroom of her maternal grandparents' home, on an October 8th. A typical Libra, the lady with the balance scales, it's not surprising that she is a harmonious collaborator and always supportive to those around her. She grew up on a four-acre farm and romped endlessly with her brother, Fred, and a Spanish terrier, Egypt, as companions. The family was poor. "We moved to Ohio when I was ten. It was the heart of the Great Depression," recalls Connie. "We scraped along on little or no money; but we were kept clean, we ate and we had pride. And my parents loved each other and us. We were a happy family, for we all had the necessary things in life."

Her formal education ended with her high school diploma, and she went on to complete the Famous Writers Fiction Course. She has now been a professional writer for more than fifteen years. Although the Day Taylor novels were her first published books, she has written magazine articles on a wide variety of subjects in *Brides, Modern Romance, Sexology, Ladies Circle,* and *The National Enquirer* (she was their stringer for three years).

"I do my own housework, and even iron, so I have some time for thinking when I'm not at the typewriter," admits Connie who lives on a quiet, residential street. "I spend a lot of this thinking time asking myself *What if*—? about the characters I'm working with. What if she does this instead of that? What if he reacts in such and such a fashion instead of some other? I've come up with some surprising results sometimes. I've also found that the characters frequently take over their scenes and do things their own way. Once you've built up a personality," she adds, "with certain characteristics, that personality won't be shoved willy-nilly; and the writer must be flexible in plotting to allow for this sort of imperial prerogative."

When it comes to cooking, Connie is equally creative, as she demonstrates in the following recipe.

"I don't know exactly what to call my favorite cheese mixture, so that's what it is called. If you grate it coarse as I do, it doesn't stay together especially well, but it's so good it doesn't matter. Those who like a little integrity in their compounds can use a fine grater and a little more mayonnaise.

"This is a very loose recipe which permits the user a lot of creativity. I use a hand grater with holes about ¼″ diameter; but suit yourself. This will turn out tasty no matter what you do."

CHEESE MIXTURE

Grate into a large bowl:
½ lb. Longhorn cheese or any ordinary yellow cheese
½ lb. any white cheese (brick or Monterey Jack, for example)
½ lb. sharp or extra sharp yellow cheese
Add:
¼ to ½ cup chopped English walnuts or pecans
¼ to ½ cup mayonnaise
Stir it up using the smaller amount of mayonnaise first. Depending on the kinds of cheese you have used, it may be enough to stick everything together. It helps to have let the

ingredients get warm *after* grating, but it is not necessary. This can be formed into a ball. Store covered in the refrigerator.

Note: The nuts may darken the mixture but this does no harm. It can be frozen; or it will keep two weeks under refrigeration.

This is good in sandwiches, grilled or not; or in scrambled eggs with some butter, salt, and oregano added. I like it in potato soup or onion soup, or melted over baked potatoes or on rough bread.

Kathryn Gorsha Thiels

Cade was demanding in his quiet masculine way everything Alexis had to give. The sensations were searing as their worlds tumbled about space, soon to collide and burst into the flaming colors of sensuality. With him she would glimpse the ecstasy of the universe as a woman, his woman.

—The Cedar Plunge

Kathryn Gorsha Thiels doesn't read others authors for her sole stimulus to composition. Instead, she says that most of her inspiration for plots comes from her dreams. Take the Civil War novel, *A Judas Love;* the great love scene was the result of one particular dream. "I dreamed that I was in an old-fashioned restaurant," the green-eyed author recounts, "in Philadelphia, and my fiancé comes in with a surprise. He is dressed in the regalia of a Union officer. He tells me that he's leaving the next day. We have our first sensual encounter that night which turns into a glorious night of love-making." The next day after the dream, Kathryn sat down at the typewriter and "let my fingers do the rest."

Very seldom does she use any sort of formal outline when she's writing. "Planning a novel is usually easy for me—if it's a short novel, that is. It has been my acquired habit to dream something so vivid that it warrants being put down on paper and made into a story," she explains. Of course, when it comes to longer novels, Kathryn's best resource is her fertile imagination, aided by her keen ability to research background material.

Kathryn's first novel, *Savage Fancy,* was written in July 1977, after the birth of her third child, Jude. The novel is a historical romance, threading its way through rich and cultural New Orleans, to a plantation in the Bayou Teche region. The astonishing ending almost guarantees a gasp of delight from the reader. "That plot was also part of a dream that I could play back through my mind like a moviola," she says.

Her writing does change gears, from historical periods to the fast-paced world of today. Her second book was *Cedar Plunge,* one of the first titles of Silhouette Romances' Special Editions— a longer category romance. This contemporary romance deals with the glamorous and sometimes ruthless world of cattle and land barons in Texas.

Residing with her husband and three children in her home state of Louisiana, Kathryn divides her time between writing, doing promotional work, guest appearances and touring, as well as helping to guide a new writers' group known as The Writer's Forum. The primary aim of the Forum, says Kathryn, is "to exchange ideas and information and to encourage other would-be writers."

Kathryn was born in a small town in south Louisiana, the oldest of three children. After graduation from Providence High School, a private girl's academy, she entered X-ray training at St. Francis Cabrini Hospital in Alexandria, Louisiana. She says it was there that her education began in learning about human behavior.

After two years, she was certified, then left to get married and start a family. For the next eight years, she worked as a secretary and at assorted jobs. "I suppose those ten years between high school and the writing of my first novel were a time of information-gathering for me," she says candidly. "I had to do some living and experiencing before I was qualified to write about it.

"Prior to my first book, the only writing I ever did was to dabble in short stories for my own amusement. A pattern started early and continues: my stories begin as beautiful dreams and

280

I merely write them down after having them." The charming, brown-haired author makes it sound easy!

"*Savage Fancy* is the beginning of a long line of works that I intend to do. It's lucky that I had the good fortune to see it in print. Had I not," she confesses, "I probably would've put down my pen and never written again. I had decided that this one effort would either make me or break me as a writer."

Was it difficult to get started? Yes, Kathryn says. "There was some struggle in the early months. My son was four weeks old when I made up my mind to try my hand at story-telling." The project took a year and a half to finish. Why? "Because I had to hold down a job for financial reasons. I babysat eight children in addition to my own, I was a seamstress, and I also sewed tiny Barbie Doll clothes and sold them as well."

After a day of sewing, tussling with youngsters, and "going ninety to nothing," it seemed like the evening would never come. But Kathryn wasn't looking forward to rest. Ten o'clock to two A.M. was her time—time to sit alone in the den and weave beautiful fantasies for *Savage Fancy*. In fact, she wrote two-thirds of it in script because she didn't own a typewriter at the time. Philosophically, Kathryn considers the experience as a "time of paying my dues."

"It wasn't until after the writing was finished that my real work began! The greatest difficulty I faced was in finding someone who would take the time to read my story and recognize it as a good work," she declares. "I was alone and had no one to show me the way. I had no idea of how to send a manuscript much less to whom. It took five harrowing months and three rejections to push me to the point where I began to lose faith and doubt if *Savage Fancy* was really good enough for publication."

Depressed, Kathryn called a friend in California who insisted that Kathryn send her a copy of the work. After reading it, her friend persuaded her to give up the idea of burning the manuscript and to give it one more try.

"It worked!" Kathryn recalls gleefully. "An agent took notice of me and we were on our way. I was accepted by Pocket Books and in the ensuing seven months, I passed through more changes than a caterpillar waiting to turn into a butterfly. I now have that sense of confidence that enables me to continue doing well."

Kathryn was born on March 18, 1949, and possesses a number of salient Piscean traits. She is affectionate, has a vivid imagination and is partial to the realm of fantasy. Significantly, she possesses a high degree of ESP. "I have been able to foresee many personal events from time to time," she says. "And much of my idea-gathering for writing seems to come as a sort of psychic inspiration. My friends refer to the talent as 'psychic dictation.'"

She considers herself fortunate to have an understanding and encouraging husband. "My husband has been both the biggest influence and the greatest help when it comes to my work," she says proudly. "He listens to my plots and comments on my wording. He also takes care of the children (Deanna, eleven; Shawn, ten; and Jude, four) so I can steal away and write."

One of the dishes that Kathryn prepares for her family is called "Dirty Rice." She laughs at the name. "Being of French extraction and living the life of a Cajun (a Southern Louisiana Frenchman), we have a no-fail, everybody-will-like-it dish called Dirty Rice. (Rice Dressing.)"

DIRTY RICE

Rice Dressing: Chop up one onion, one bell pepper and two cloves of garlic and saute in one-fourth cup cooking oil. Add one pound of hamburger and brown along with ingredients until tender. Season and salt to taste.

In a separate pot, cook four cups of rice and have it ready when the ground beef mixture is done. Fold rice into meat mixture and mix well. Delicious!

Aola Vandergriff

As her mother's voice echoed in her ears, Martha fled to her room. Now she knew. She was a bastard! *Duke and Mama had lied to her. They must have been waiting for her bad blood to show. Well, to hell with them. From now on, she could do what she wanted, be what she wanted to be—and as bad as she wanted to be!*

—Daughters of the Far Islands

To anyone harboring the Great American Romantic Novel within her soul, Aola Vandergriff has a suggestion: Quit procrastinating and start writing. As the author of many successful Gothics and historical romance novels, including the *Wyndspelle* romantic suspense books and the five-part historical series *Daughters of the Opal Skies,* she knows her advice is sound. Her students trust her opinions, for she is one of the most popular instructors at the Writer's Digest correspondence school, and has helped many budding writers.

"I would advise all people who say they'll write fiction someday to do it now," says the New Mexican housewife and author. "And if someone wants to write historical romances, I have the following suggestions: The historical framework must be authentic. But it is important to remember that the story's the thing. The actions of the characters set against the background are *paramount*. Historical facts must be inserted 'painlessly,' so smoothly that they do not stop the action," she adds. "I believe that anyone with a burning desire and the willingness to work can write these novels."

Heredity and environment are two factors that play an important part in a writer's life, she claims. "I inherited a sense of drama and a funnybone from my Irish mother and the ability to doggedly persevere from my Dutch dad."

Aola—her Indian name means whispering wind among the leaves—was born in Iowa on May 7, 1920. Like most Taureans, she is strong, down-to-earth, and loyal. "I grew up in a time when television did not exist. Imagination had to be home-grown, a do-it-yourself thing. With a younger brother and sister, I soon learned that a good story was balm for bumps and tears, and so began my career of telling tall tales.

"I had a book of poetry published at the age of sixteen and my own radio program for several years in Oklahoma City. Once, at a girl's club, we had a spiritualist, just for fun, to tell our fortunes. I was told that I would be wealthy and famous. 'I see long writings,' the woman said. 'Perhaps books. But it will be when you are middle-aged, at least . . .

"I thought, 'Hah!' I didn't think of writing anything but poetry. And, as for growing old! It'll never happen! But, unfortunately, it did."

In the interim, Aola married—ever so happily—husband Bill, and had three boys and three girls whom she loves dearly. Here, again, environment took a hand. "Old stories were revived," explains Aola. "My children were pre-drip-dry. The long hours spent at the ironing board were times to dream, to create stories in my mind. Stories I would write—if I had the talent to become a writer. In the meantime, I wrote for the P.T.A., for a newspaper when my husband was in the missile program. And when we moved to Sacramento, California, I took an adult writing course, 'just to get acquainted.' I paid three dollars for the course. In return, I received a bundle of confidence from a wonderful teacher. I sold my first short story. My second. My first article. My first confession. Within six years, I had sold more than 2,500 short stories and articles. Then, seeing one of my confessions on a national network show (one sells all rights to confessions!), I decided to write a book. It sold in 1974 and since that time, I've sold dozens of Gothics and historical romances all for Warner Books."

One of the turning points for Aola's writing came when she learned she was writing for a reader. The kind of reader that *buys* books. "I created that reader," she remembers vividly. "She's a woman tied to a desk in the day, with children to care for at night. A woman who cooks dinner, does dishes, gets things in order for tomorrow, then escapes for a little while into a book of adventure. A woman who needs to relax. She's very real to me. I like her and she likes me," adds Aola, with a huge smile.

She also learned along the way that writing is business. "It's important to find the market for the idea and *then* write the story. It's important to know just where it's going. The secret of writing success lies not in writing what the writer wants to write, but what the readers want to read . . . and the readers' needs change with the time," the author adds. "I realize that many of the young people like horror stories today, by authors such as V.C. Andrews, but that's not my genre. I know what the romantic readers enjoy. According to the mail I receive, I could write *Daughters of the Opal Skies* and its sequels forever!"

Husband Bill Vandergriff, now retired from government missiles program, goes along with Aola on the exotic research trips around the world, and takes photographs of the locale in case she needs to recall it to describe a certain scene. "I've seen the slaty waters off the coast of Alaska, the heavenly blue surrounding the islands of Hawaii—and the green, green China Sea with swatches of yellow where the rivers flow into it from the land," says the expressive Aola.

The Vandergriff house is often filled with the many guests they've met on their trips abroad. They have even entertained four aborigines and the head of the Australian Land Council and his wife on a tour of oil and uranium lands.

In between family and guests, Aola does keep a strict writing schedule. "Although I began my writing career from a small desk wedged into the bedroom, I now have my own at-home office, filled with book shelves, conveniently located near the kitchen," she says. "I write on an IBM Selectric II, but recently broke in a computer word processor, learning the operation as I wrote two more of my new Western series," she recalls, wearily. Two books in two months was a more exhausting project than she imagined, and "I'll never attempt so much in such a short time again," she promises.

Her goal when writing is to complete twenty pages a day, although a hectic travel schedule sometimes forces her to work at a stepped-up pace "to catch up on days I've missed." Once the rough draft is completed, her husband reads over the manuscript for technical errors. Aola relies on a daughter's gifted imagination and sense of drama to tell her if she's made the most of a scene. Yet another daughter, a secretary, "can find a lost quotation mark or a misspelled word quicker than anyone. I think I have a pretty good staff behind me," she says proudly.

In addition to acting as their mother's back-up team, the family has another ongoing project. After her first book, *Sisters of Sorrow*, was published in 1974, the Vandergriffs left Sacramento for a canyon near Alamogordo, New Mexico. There they have built an incredibly beautiful adobe house with their bare hands. "Each brick weighed fifty pounds," Aola says, vividly recalling this enormous family effort. "The landscape is still not quite finished, since we can only work in and around the books, but the children love it here. They always wanted animals, and it was impossible in the city, so now they raise cows, goats, peacocks, doves, and rabbits."

High up in the desert at an altitude of 5,800 feet, Aola looks down on White Sands, a desert which looks like a salt ocean. "I've a sixty-mile view from my adobe hacienda, and if I want to go to the nearest town, it's a twenty-mile drive," she explains, happy in her beautiful isolated retreat.

Aola likes to cook by "the handful, the dash, and the glug," in her sparkling white Mexican-style kitchen. Whenever she knows a vast number of guests will descend, she whips up her now famous chili pie. "It's everyone's favorite," she claims.

CHILI PIE

Serves a large crowd.

Start out with two pounds of ground beef, and brown and drain it. Then mix in a large can of tomato sauce (16 oz. size), two packages of any popular chili mix, and a gallon of pork and beans (drain part of the liquid, you don't want more soup than beans!).

Let simmer and finally add two tbsp. of masa (a Mexican corn flour) stirred for thickness into a half cup of cold water, and add it to the mixture. Next put the entire batch into two large pyrex baking dishes and cover with slices of American cheese. Top it with cornbread batter, usually a double recipe. Put black olives all around that, and shake a little paprika for color. Bake at 375 degrees until the cornbread is done.

Serve with a large green salad and dessert, such as pie and ice cream.

Karen Van Der Zee

He began to stroke her hair, softly, soothingly, then he kissed her, just a soft brush of his lips. "Faye, I don't want a giveaway. Don't you understand? I want you, Faye—all of you. Your heart and mind and soul, not just your body. I want your love."

—*A Secret Sorrow*

Karen van der Zee is Dutch, born and reared in Holland. The petite, 5′3″ author had a happy life growing up in Rotterdam and Amsterdam. Though she was born in Sneek, a town in the dairy province of Friesland where her mother and brothers now live, she admits she never learned to milk a cow. "I hope I'm not disappointing anybody by saying I never owned a pair of wooden shoes," the pert, freckled author remarks.

Karen is the oldest of four children. Of her three brothers, she especially dotes on the youngest one, a "little latecomer, as they say in Dutch," she says with a grin. "He is tall, handsome, extremely charming, and single. At the moment he's roaming around New Zealand, where we have aunts, uncles, and a score of cousins."

As a child, Karen wrote short stories and poems in a school exercise-book and illustrated them with pictures in colored pencil or watercolor. "Unfortunately," she recalls, "my two

289

brothers had no appreciation for the arts and destroyed the exercise-books by setting fire to them in the attic of our house."

At the age of eighteen, she received a scholarship from the American Field Service, which enabled her to spend a year in the United States. She lived with a family in Oregon and attended the local high school. "Then I came back to Holland and life truly began: I found a place to live in Amsterdam, a minuscule attic room, got a part-time job as a typist, and attended the University of Amsterdam."

Karen's gray-blue eyes shimmer with delight. "A few months later and true love entered my life," she goes on. "I had thought that a few times before, but alas! I met Gary, who is now my husband of twelve years, in the office where I worked—a most unromantic environment. He was an American exchange student in a Junior-Year-Abroad program and attended a Dutch college near Amsterdam. He was from Oregon, quite a coincidence because I had returned from Oregon half a year earlier."

Pretty, brown-haired Karen was to discover that love is not always bliss. "Five months after we met," she recalls, "Gary returned to the States to finish his Bachelor's. He then joined the Peace Corps and went into training for three months. Kenya was his destination and flying over there he had a one-day layover in Rome. Would I meet him there? Twenty-six hours on a train and there I was! We hadn't seen each other for eighteen months. After dark that night, on a bench in a moonlit piazza, he proposed to me."

As it turned out, love conquered all. Two months after Karen arrived in Kenya, they were married. She was twenty-two at the time. For most of their stay in Kenya, Karen and Gary lived in a small town in a little wooden house, which had water and electricity. Karen found a job as nursery school teacher and was in charge of twenty children from all over the world. For the last five months of their stay they lived in a huge, dilapidated settler's house in a mudhut village. No water, no electricity. "We hauled our water from a muddy stream, let it stand in containers for days to kill the parasites, then boiled it and strained it through a dish towel. Ah, such adventures!" Karen muses philosophically.

Back in the States, Gary went to graduate school and Karen found a job as a respiratory therapy technician. But two years later, they were back in Africa, this time it was West Africa, in Accra, the capital of Ghana, where their first child, a daughter named Roshni (now nine) was born.

They are now back in the States, and have a second daughter, Rona (now two), who was born in Connecticut. The happy family lives in Virginia in one of the newly developed towns in the Washington area. "We have a split-level house with a room just for me—with a lock on the door," Karen says enthusiastically. She writes in the mornings for three or four hours, while the oldest girl is in school and the youngest is at the babysitter's.

"I'm a slow writer," Karen describes herself. "It takes me a while to get the right feel about my story and characters, so I do a lot of thinking and planning before I start writing. My characters have to be real to me, or I can't make it work."

She has also had her share of obstacles. "Until a few years after I got married I wrote only in Dutch and had a couple of small successes. However, I realized I'd probably be speaking English for the rest of my life, so it would be more practical to start writing in English. I can't begin to tell you my frustrations." She shakes her head and sighs.

But she persevered. Several short stories got her nowhere, so she decided to try a romance novel—she's not quite sure why. "It took me over a year," she says. "I was living in Ghana at the time, so I had a ready-made exotic setting at my disposal. I read dozens of Harlequins to get and keep me on the right track. I sent the manuscript to Harlequin. They liked it, but could I please make a few changes? I did, you bet. It was then published, my first published work in English, *Sweet Not Always*." As Karen says, she was off and going.

"I suppose I write contemporary romances because I enjoy contemporary fiction most, and because I feel more comfortable writing about the present time—I'm sitting right in the middle of it, so to speak."

And why love stories? "Well, I like love a lot," Karen answers quickly. "It's a wonderful emotion because it has so many different facets. It can be exciting and exhilarating. It can be

291

dead serious or lots of fun. It can be *extremely* difficult. There's a lot to work with here!"

A true Gemini, born May 26, 1947, Karen derives great satisfaction from creating something spun entirely from her own vivid imagination, feelings, and instinct. "When a manuscript is finished, I look at it and say to myself, '*I* did this. This is all mine.' It's a great feeling."

Karen believes that the greatest help with her writing came from courses she took from the University of Oklahoma, by correspondence, while she lived in Africa. "Without a *doubt,* they were excellent," she says. "Crucial also was and is my husband's support. All through those early years of seemingly getting nowhere he kept encouraging me. If writing is what I wanted to do, then I should do it."

The author enjoys cooking for her family, though she insists she isn't good at following recipes. "I always think I can improve on them, which isn't always the case, as my family and I have discovered." However, she has a recipe to share, which she says is hard to ruin. It's a tropical fruit salad that Karen and other foreigners in Ghana would eat some version of every day of the year—thus it was called "365."

365

Fruits should be ripe and sweet.

½ a fresh pineapple, cut in chunks, whatever size you like
1 large mango, cut in chunks
1 large paw paw (papaya), cut in chunks
1 large banana, cut in slices (do at last moment)
orange and/or grapefruit sections, if you like

Mix the cut up fruit, except the bananas, and let stand for an hour or so. "You can put it in the fridge, of course," she says, "but I find the taste better if it is not icy cold. Add sliced banana right before serving. Serves 8."

Joyce Verrette

*The noise the shredding fabric
made only underlined her need to
resist and she said angrily, "What
else, I wonder, should I have expected from a rebel who's no doubt
used to raping captive women?"*
*He winced as if she had slapped
him. Then he raised his head a little
higher and said softly, "You got love
you didn't expect from this rebel and
now he'll teach you to face its truth."*

—*Fountain of Fire*

Joyce Verrette enjoys a complete self-immersion into the
ancient lore of Egypt and she believes wholeheartedly in
reincarnation, a special subject she respects. Her books, she
claims, are not of her imagination but the result of her past
incarnation in Egypt at the time of the Pharaohs.

As a best-selling author, she has been interviewed by major
newspapers, on TV, by *Cosmopolitan,* and other publications.
Some of the media members have been very sympathetic and
appreciative of her belief in the ancient love princess of her
books. Some people speculate that she wears her hair "Egyptian
Style" as an act. "It's entirely natural," she claims. "it just falls
that way." Joyce's hair is coal-black, cut in a banged style,
falling to the shoulders and curling under—suggestively Egyptian princess. Her eyes are mesmerizing pools of pale blue. The
effect, coupled with her reincarnation convictions is startling.

With an ease that is as certain as the sunrise, Joyce believes
that 4,000 years ago she walked the pages of her books. Her

name, she believes was Nefrytatenen, and she sailed down the Nile, bound by royal command to wed, sight unseen, a crown prince she at first despised, then loved. His name was Amenemhet, and their marriage was to unify divided Egypt, then called Tamera, in defense against Syria, then called Zahi.

"The events, the characters, the desert battles which transpired are recorded history," Joyce states, "and while *Dawn of Desire* is romantic fiction, its details are authentic. I don't even name a piece of fruit or a flower that wasn't there."

Joyce has turned the story of Nefrytatenen and Amenemhet into a series of books, the sequels of which are *Desert Fires*, *Sunrise of Splendor*, and *Winged Priestess*. The last two books in the series, yet unpublished, are *The Lion and the Lotus* and *Dawn's Golden Destiny*. They begin in ancient Egypt, then go on to a contemporary setting, where Amenamhet and Nefrytatanen are reincarnated, find each other again and continue to love—the effect portrays an endless love.

Joyce Verrette (the last name is a pseudonym), was born in Chicago, Illinois, on July 19, 1939. Cancer women, generally, are sentimental romantics who take love affairs seriously, which are Joyce's exact feelings. With her olive-tinted complexion she looks best in soft, romantic colors, usually a Cancerian's fashion preference. Her slim, 5'6" figure is often cloaked in tailored soft lines, a customary choice over angular geometrics by most ladies of the moon.

After a divorce from her husband, Joyce moved to Rockford, Illinois, where she now lives in a condominium near her parents. Professionally, the author prefers to use her grandmother's maiden name as her pen name, but in private life she retains the surname of her former husband. Her Rockford family ties also include a brother and sister-in-law. "They sometimes screen calls when I'm busy," Joyce says. "I'm neither anti-social nor a recluse, but I have no social life at all . . . I'm not really an outgoing person. I wouldn't know how to go about meeting people—Where can you go to meet just plain people? I don't know. So many want only to be the 'friend of Joyce Verrette, successful author,' and that kind of friend I don't need."

There is a quality of shyness about Joyce in person that contrasts to the bold lush adventure of her books, and it also a surprising contrast to the impressive niche she has carved with Egyptian historical romances.

"I know few famous people, and I'm acquainted with only a handful of writers—romantic novelists such as myself—whom I've met at publishers' conventions," she says. As a former production assistant to television newsman, Floyd Kalber in Chicago, Joyce admits that she has brushed lives with the star set. "It sounds much more impressive than it was," Joyce, who is a modest woman, recalls. She went to work after graduation from high school, taking such jobs as clerk, stenographer, secretary and bookkeeper before attaining the "impressive job," as friends and the media have called it.

Joyce's writing career is truly one that came to her as in a dream. "My interest in ancient Egypt had a very unusual beginning," she reveals. "I knew nothing whatever about ancient Egypt until some years ago when I had a very detailed dream about it. This was, in itself, unusual since I seldom remember my dreams. At the time I didn't realize the dream's setting was Egypt, because we never called the place Egypt. I described the dream to a friend, who urged me to write it down as the beginning of a story. This friend knew I'd always had an avid interest in writing. Actually, I'd decided to be a writer when I was ten and was always working toward it. If my mother had locked me in a closet, I would have written on the walls—it was just a need in me, to write.

"Later, while passing time in the public library with a friend who was searching for some special information, I found myself standing near the shelves with Egyptian reference books. I felt compelled to find out who was the ruler of Egypt 4,000 years ago. Why? I didn't know then. I was stunned when I learned that the man in my dream had the same name as the king— Amenemhet. I went home with an armload of books to investigate the political situation in Egypt at that time and found it to be the same as in my dream. That's quite a coincidence for someone who at the time didn't even know that the Nile flows from the south to the north. My dream, ultimately, formed the first part of *Dawn of Desire*. In my dream I was Nefrytatanen going to marry Amenemhet because of the political problems both of our realms faced. I had never met him and I hated to marry someone I didn't love. My dream ended when he and I were seated in his apartments trying to get acquainted. I felt about him exactly as I described Nefrytatanen's feelings for Amenemhet."

Later, she called the University of Chicago and spoke to an Egyptologist to learn the name of Amenemhet's queen. "I'd been unable to find it in the reference books available to me. When he told me, I corrected his pronunciation of the name, explained the reason I pronounced it the way I did—it's a combination of several words—and he accepted my reason. We spent the better part of the afternoon chatting about ancient Egypt—I who had never studied it, and a professor, who specialized in it—and I spoke to him very comfortably, as an equal in knowledge." Joyce had more dreams and kept writing things that later were borne out in her research, including other personal names she later found were the names of people whose places in the royal court were as she'd placed them in her story.

"I learned that Amenemhet's queen was, in fact, a high priestess," Joyce continues. "Finally, I had a nightmare about how Amenemhet died, which involved a rather peculiar and very complicated set of circumstances, and awoke sobbing aloud."

Joyce has not had more dreams since.

"When I visited Egypt," Joyce says, a cryptic smile on her lips, "I found a bit of seemingly insignificant information on a prayer tablet that had a great deal of significance to me, in that it confirmed the circumstances surrounding Amenemhet's death and Nefrytatanen's almost immediate death afterward. There were, needless to say, a number of other experiences I had in Egypt that were quite mysterious, as well as profoundly emotional for me."

Joyce has no children, but she does have one pet, a thoroughbred horse named Chancy, "whom I love, love, love."

She speaks no foreign languages, but she can translate ancient Egyptian, if given a little time.

Her other hobbies, when she's not writing, are swimming, sketching and painting. As to her personal love life? "No," she says with a sigh, "I have not found Amenemhet. If I had, I wouldn't have time to write, I suspect!" she adds, narrowing her slightly almond-shaped eyes.

Joyce's favorite recipe is a blend of ancient Egypt and modern if you use a modern stove. Otherwise, cooking on a charcoal grill will be as authentic Egyptian as you can get.

EGYPTIAN CHICKEN

Marinade for Chicken:
Juice of 24 limes (or frozen lime juice)
1 onion, chopped and crushed to extract juices which you use
2 cloves garlic, crushed
1 cup vegetable oil (oil should really be olive)
2 tbsp. chopped parsley
1 tbsp. powdered coriander
Salt and black pepper

Remove skin from chicken pieces and make one layer of chicken in a pan. Pour marinade over. Cover pan and put in refrigerator overnight. Drain off marinade, but try to keep some of the onion pieces on the chicken when you cook it. Broil as slowly as possible on a charcoal grill or bake in oven at 400 degrees for 30 minutes, then put in broiler and broil until golden brown and the inside tender and moist. If you have leftovers, they will be just as good cold as reheated.

Donna Vitek

Her entire being throbbed with quickening desire at his filling invasion of her innocence. Her parted lips sought his eagerly as he wound her hair round one hand and she abandoned herself to the ever increasing pleasure he created inside her with each slow-rousing stroke of his hard body.

—*A Velasquez Bride*

Donna Vitek is an old-fashioned romantic. The very essence of her novels clearly depicts her deeply emotional temperament. Her heroines are exquisitely beautiful and vulnerable; her men are dashing and virile. Invariably, they meet, have a lovingly passionate escapade, and presumably live happily ever after.

"As a young child, I would pretend that handsome movie stars in Hollywood were falling in love with me," says the green-eyed blonde author of eleven books. "My cousin and I would dress up in long dresses and wobbly heels, pretending to be the most gorgeous women in the world. I loved fantasy, even then," she admits. "At the age of ten, I was madly in love with Pat Boone, and flatly refused to believe that he was married and had four children."

During her teenage years, Donna had her average share of boyfriends. But during her junior year in high school, she fell hopelessly in love with Richard Vitek, her English teacher, six years her senior. Three years later, in 1969, they were married, which inspired her first novel, *No Turning Back*.

The mother of two children (Susan, age twelve; Tommy, seven), Mrs. Vitek recalls her early married years as a home-maker and a mother. "It was an extremely happy time in my life," she reflects. "I wouldn't have missed a moment of my children's earliest years, for all the money in the world."

Born in Winston-Salem, North Carolina, on November 10, 1948, the very mention of her Scorpio sun sign conjures visions of Valentino smoldering beside his open tent-flap, or Mata Hari's lithe body embellished with nothing but bracelets. The great lover of the zodiac, the Garbo of the galaxy, who is more equipped to write romance novels than she?

Her second Silhouette romance is a perfect example of her style; *Showers of Sunlight* takes place in lyric, sunny Italy. "Leigh Sheridan is the heroine's name," Vitek relates, looking much like a lovely child as she sits with long blonde hair flowing over her shoulders. "Leigh dreams of working on an Italian newspaper as a reporter, but her life turns into a nightmare when she fails to land the job. Her seemingly hopeless plight,"—obviously a favorite expression that lights up the author's green eyes—"drives her to the beautiful Isle of Capri to find employment with Marco Cavelli, the enigmatic master of the Villa Bianca. Now, of course, she will be confronted with yet another and another dilemma. The all-consuming question is—will the hero come to realize that Leigh's love for him is as deep and pure as the Mediterranean waters that surround them?"

Paradoxically, Donna Vitek was a tomboy as a child. "I enjoyed climbing trees, attempting acrobatics on a basement trapeze, bicycling and swimming," she muses. In her early teens, despite her 5'3", 110-pound structure, she played forward on the Clemmons School basketball team, in Winston-Salem. "I played on the junior varsity basketball team, which eventually became state champion, and won the coveted medallion as most valuable player." But her tomboyish ways did not dissuade her from using her vivid romantic imagination. "My mind would constantly wander off to faraway lands; it was terribly exciting," she recalls.

Vitek wrote her first novel in 1978. It took her three months to complete the contemporary romance and subsequently it was published by MacFadden Romances.

"Most of my work is done in the study of our nice, roomy Winston-Salem house in the woods," she reveals. She considers her husband Richard extremely influential in her career. He has taught her that expressing her thoughts in a simple and straightforward manner can be both a "challenge and a joy!"

"Writing is an occupation which incites insecurity," she says. "Often I've asked myself why I pour my heart and soul into something that might never be published. I've never found a concrete answer to that question. All I can say, is that after the completion of my first novel, I was addicted. And when my first two manuscripts were accepted for publication in July 1979, I felt a great sense of accomplishment, which I still experience every time another book of mine is accepted," she smiles happily. (Silhouette Romances published four of her stories in 1981.)

Why does she write romance? "Because I am a romantic!" Donna goes on to talk enthusiastically about travel as a very romantic pastime. "My husband and I plan to do more traveling when our children are older. Our last trip was to Bermuda. We especially enjoyed the quaint old town of St. George and of course the crystal blue ocean. The swimming was terrific, the weather beautiful, and we hope to return there again very soon. It was a very romantic island," she remarks with a twinkle in her green emerald eyes.

She laughs wryly when asked if she needs quiet to write. "Are you kidding!" she returns. "I have two young children and a five-month-old Labrador Retriever. I can't even *remember* what quiet is."

Donna, who attended Appalachian State University in Boone, North Carolina, does not feel that success has changed her in any significant way, except that it has added more excitement, and a deeper sense of accomplishment to her life.

"My husband and I have a respect for contemporary romantic novels, and not just because of my success. The good ones explore situations in which realistic characters react to real pressures and passions. The happy ending is predominantly still there, but it is many times flavored with the bittersweet of the struggle in the story, giving the reader lingering thoughts, as well as satisfying relief. Indeed, this realism, we feel, classifies the romantic novel as an art form and one that is here to stay; an art form that pleases so many millions today, and perhaps will be honed to a precise edge, pleasing even the most caustic and ill-informed of its critics."

Donna believes that the fantasties of most authors are eventually incorporated into their writing. "Although," she says with an impish smile, "I prefer living out my fantasies with my husband."

The Viteks entertain frequently at home and this is Donna's favorite party appetizer.

PARTY MELON

Smokehouse cured ham and Swiss cheese rolls with melon balls.

Elizabeth Neff Walker

. . . And then she put her arms about his neck and kissed him. Eventually she drew back, embarrassed, and found he was smiling the special smile that made her insides flutter. "I love you," she whispered. "I have never loved a man before." He pulled her to him, the feel of her firm breasts against his chest, and kissed her until she was breathless. He released her then, curious to see how she would respond. Her eyes and face were softened with desire and he sighed contentedly. "I think, my love, that you should marry me, and be my wife."

—Alicia

To Regency fans, far and wide, the names Elizabeth Neff Walker and Laura Mathews rank among their list of favorites. The woman behind these names, Elizabeth Walker Rotter—nickname Neff—began writing Regency romance in March, 1978. Before that it had been about ten years since she'd dabbled at writing short stories. She'd never tried a full-length novel and had never submitted or finished any other works of fiction, except one story, which was published by the *Saturday Evening Post* when she was in college.

"I've found the Regency period especially appealing as a setting for romances because the possibilities for escapades are so much richer than they would be in a contemporary romance," says the brown-haired, hazel-eyed author. "Also, there is the delight of having Jane Austen's novels available as source material; her books are the real predecessors of this type of story. Having books set in England can necessitate a research trip far more enjoyable, if also far more costly, than one to the library," she explains, with a knowing smile.

In writing her period romances, Elizabeth tries to transport herself as well as the reader back into a simpler era, envisioning what it must have been like to live in the early 1880s, how a woman would have thought and felt, how similar or different from today. Neff finds that dealing with the aristocracy is fun, too, even if only in her imagination.

"When I'm working on a Regency, I occasionally dip into a Georgette Heyer book to achieve the proper frame of mind: her humor, her attention to period detail, and her ability to write a delightful romp are always regenerating to my enthusiasm," she says candidly. "I've collected all of her Regencies," she adds, "as well as an extensive library of Regency research materials—biographies, architecture books and writings of the period. Hunting for these volumes in used bookstores has provided me with many hours of enjoyment." Elizabeth admits to one eccentricity in writing that other authors don't exhibit. "I insist on using old manuscripts for typing paper! This not only saves paper, but provides a hardy stack of reference material handy for those times when I'm unable to find the precise direction for my writing! I've just finished a big Regency, my twelfth book, which used up a *great* deal of paper," she says with a laugh.

Born August 12, 1944, Elizabeth was raised in Pleasant Hills, a suburb of Pittsburgh, Pennsylvania. Her parents are both dead now, but she has an older brother, a geologist, and a younger brother, an architect/carpenter. As a student in high school, she recalls, "My passion for writing led me to produce a work called 'The Mystery of the Missing Plane' (a la Nancy Drew), which my father's secretary typed for me—all twenty pages of it. A great aunt's comment on this tome was that I had used supper and dinner on the same page to indicate the same meal. Undeterred, I continued to write off and on for years (a Leo quality of determination?), but found that most of my efforts were autobiographical. I finally desisted when my daughter, Laura, was born, as though that one great creative splurge was all I had in me."

After attending Pembroke College at Brown University, Neff moved from the East Coast to the West, settling in San Francisco. She held a number of clerical jobs, working for a spice company, an architectural firm, and for a psychology research project.

In 1966, she married Paul Rotter, an architect. The couple left San Francisco to settle in London for two and a half years. "Living abroad was a fascinating experience. I felt right at home! I lived and breathed Regency lore. It provided me with much of the material I was later able to use in my romances," Neff says, and sighs at the wondrous memories.

In 1970, the couple returned to San Francisco to live, and their son, Matthew, was born the following year. "Our house is in the upper Haight Ashbury with a view of the Golden Gate Park, and is surrounded by greenery, which can be distracting when writing, but is restful in the midst of the city," says Neff, who is happy and content with her home. "My husband established his own architectural practice, using a little cottage in our yard as an office, and I tried several jobs before writing again," she recalls. "Selling real estate proved so dispiriting to me that I needed some counterbalancing element to offset its disappointments. I began to notice that there were new Regencies being published every month, so I decided to try my hand at one. In just over a year, I'd written six, found my agent, and sold my first books."

Elizabeth writes in her bedroom, where she has a built-in unit of drawers and cupboard space, as well as shelves for research materials. "When I receive cover proofs, my husband frames them and I have them hung on the wall, along with various writing-related cartoons that I collect, and prints from the Regency period—for inspiration! Another indulgence is photocopying my agent's checks to me for advances and royalties. These are framed with some heather collected on Exmoor in England on a research trip there. You might say I'm as romantic in my own way as my demure Regency heroines!"

Elizabeth finds that ideas for her books often come from some passing remark in a history of the period or from some diary of the time. "I was especially fascinated by the diaries of an English Naval surgeon in the Georgian period whose humor and adventures intrigued me. I immediately made this doctor a character in one of my books," she reveals, with a chuckle. "He was such a rogue." Wit and humor are extremely important in story telling, she believes. "In fact, they're *essential* ingredients in keeping a sane view of the world. Very few experiences are as uplifting as a good laugh and I think humor has a place in almost every type of novel, including the historical and contemporary romance." She pauses and adds knowingly, "Laughter and love go together."

As a toast to her philosophy, Elizabeth offers:

CLARET CUP
One bottle of claret
One bottle soda water
Half a pound of ice
4 tbs. powered sugar
¼ tsp. grated nutmeg
1 liquor glass of maraschino juice

Mix it all together and serve in a claret cup (a silver goblet with handles).

Phyllis A. Whitney

Beyond the dry nook where I sat, rain sounded on the tiles of the courtyard, and I listened to its soothing rhythm. Always I felt more peaceful when I was outside the house. How long I sat there, I don't know, but suddenly the morning was pierced by a thin, high scream. A chilling sound of terror, followed almost at once by a shattering crash. I came to my feet, tense and listening. The morning was still except for the rain.

—*Poinciana*

The name Phyllis A. Whitney is a synonym for romantic suspense. After publishing more than two dozen such best-selling novels, she admits that she didn't start out writing mystery stories because "it is a very difficult field—the plotting is so complicated." But once she started, that was all she wanted to write . . . romantic suspense. "I started out doing period novels, but soon became bored with my Victorian heroines and much prefer writing about young women who are involved in the present," she says with a radiant smile.

Time magazine refers to her as "the only American in her field with a major reputation," and other critics praise her as "one of the best genre writers." In the words of *Publisher's Weekly,* the trade magazine of the book publishing industry, her reputation grows with each new novel.

Miss Whitney, who was born in Yokohama, Japan, of

307

American parents, spent her childhood in Japan, China, and the Philippines. After the death of her father, she and her mother returned to the United States, which she saw for the first time when she was fifteen. America was her dream. When others insisted that her childhood in foreign lands might have come from the pages of a romantic novel, she contended that the lands of her youth seemed commonplace to her. Her idea of an exciting "exotic" country was the United States.

Unfortunately, her mother died a few years after coming to this country after arranging for Phyllis to live with an aunt in Chicago. Unable to afford college, Phyllis took various jobs in libraries and book stores. In her spare moments, she began to work seriously at the craft of writing. She wrote after work and on weekends, when other young people were out having fun. The spunky young woman learned by trial and error. "I made every mistake there was to make," she says, "but I never gave up—even when my stories came back repeatedly with rejection slips."

Today, as she totes up her published works—more than sixty books—she knows well the cost of success. "Any success demands a high price," she says, "and the time and effort and sometimes anguish a successful person gives to his work is that price. For me," she adds with her characteristic exuberance, "the satisfactions have been worth it."

Among the rewards," Phyllis says, "are the letters from readers who have enjoyed my books. There is the pleasure, too, of finding my books in stores and libraries and remembering myself as a young clerk in a book store, looking wistfully at the piles of bestsellers."

Did she ever dream that one day she would be one of the best-selling authors in America? *"Never,"* she says, brown eyes glinting. "I never dreamed I'd be really successful. I just wanted to write well enough so that somebody would read me. After my first book, I simply went on trying to be a little better each time, doing the best I could on each new book."

When Phyllis Whitney married in 1925, shortly after graduating from high school, a woman pursuing her own career interests was not accepted. "The women's movement was years

308

away, but the spark that ignited it was alive in me. I have always been out there doing my thing, even though some people didn't approve it," she says proudly.

"In my early writing days, I wrote hundreds of short stories." In fact, it was her fifteen-year apprenticeship perfecting the short story form that gave her the strong foundation she needed to tackle larger projects.

As one who learned the hard way, Phyllis decided to share her knowledge with aspiring writers. For a year, she was Instructor in Juvenile Fiction at Northwestern University and, for eleven years, at New York University. She is the author of a well-known text, *Writing Juvenile Stories and Novels* (1976), which has helped take the mystery out of writing for publications.

After a number of successful books for teenagers on social problems, the editor of the People's Book Club suggested she try a book for adults. She reluctantly agreed. The result, *Quicksilver Pool,* proved she had underestimated her abilities. It was the first of a long series of successful, romantic-suspense novels.

"My tales are usually set in old mansions against an exotic background. Because locale is so important to the flavor of the intrigue, I like to combine my background research with my love of travel to get first-hand impressions." Indeed, her childhood abroad, and travels to Europe, Africa, and the Orient has exerted a strong influence on her work.

"After I learn all I can about the location in the library, I travel, take extensive notes, and collect snapshots," she says. "I want my background details to be accurate."

Phyllis was divorced from her first husband and then had many happy years in her second marriage to Lovell Jahnke, who enjoyed traveling with her to foreign countries for her research. Now a widow, she lives near her daughter, Georgia, and grandchildren on Long Island. Born September 9, 1903, retiring has never occurred to her. At present, all of her time is given to writing, and she often writes two books a year, one for adults and one for young people.

Though Phyllis hates to cook, she has been interested in the subject of nutrition for many years. "I study how to be healthy by paying attention to my diet," she says, pointing to rows of books on nutrition. The slender, 5'5" author must be doing something right! Her youthful appearance and abundant energy are those of a woman at least twenty years younger. "I also believe in daily exercise, which includes dancing and skipping rope fifteen minutes at a stretch three times a day, usually in front of the television set. This," she says, "is to counteract the effects of sitting at the typewriter all day!"

More than twenty years ago, Phyllis wrote that writers stay young more successfully than other people do. "No one who has a keen and lively interest in life can really grow old," she declares buoyantly. The lovely, zesty author is living proof of her statement.

Phyllis eats primarily raw grains, healthful foods, and nothing fried. She does eat lots of chicken and fish, but no beef. Also, seeds, nuts, fruits, and cheese.

She believes strongly in a nourishing breakfast, and here's her usual morning fare.

PHYLLIS A. WHITNEY'S BREAKFAST
Sliced bananas, with lecithin granules and bran
   sprinkled on it
Poached eggs
A cup of yogurt
Toast or millet
1 cup of coffee or herb tea
A handful of vitamins
   "At my age I need loads of vitamins. There's not enough in food today!"

Claudette Williams

A few moments later the yellow brocade drapes had been drawn and Kate was neck high in bubbles. She put her head back and closed her eyes and her mind found the Earl. His eyes were glinting at her, and his lips were smiling. Then there he was, standing over her! "Branwell, what are you doing here?" she demanded, sitting up with indignation, remembering where she was and sinking back down again.

—*Blades of Passion*

When Claudette Williams, one of the leading Regency authors, decides to do something—whether it be horseback riding, water sports, fox hunting or writing—you can be *sure* she does it with gusto. "I attribute my writing success to the fact that when I'm interested in a project, it compels me to give it my all," she explains. "I've always enjoyed my life, probably for that very reason, and I like my heroines to have the same zest," adds the petite, dark-eyed dynamo.

Claudette remembers that she has always enjoyed writing, "but as a child I was discouraged by my parents. They had hopes that I would do something respectable, such as becoming a teacher." Instead, Claudette left Hofstra University after two and one-half years to work and plan for her marriage. So much for becoming a schoolteacher.

Born in Bagdad, Iraq, in 1946, Claudette came to America with her parents when she was barely walking. The family lived for a while in New York City and later settled in Baldwin, Long Island, where Claudette attended local schools. "My adolescence was uneventful, for the most part," she says. "It wasn't until I was already married for ten years, and in my thirties, that I began to cut loose, as I call it, and to plumb the depths of my own personality."

Her favorite pursuit, aside from writing, is horseback riding, which "I took up with a fervor. It was something I'd always wanted to do. I bought my filly and entered a new, and for me, exciting world."

Her first contemporary novel, *Desert Rose . . . English Moon,* deals with horses and the intrigues at a riding stable. Needless to say, the facts are accurate.

Before turning to a career as an author at the age of twenty-eight, Claudette held a variety of interesting jobs. "After a brief stint in college, I worked for a year in the Port Authority's IBM Department in New York. After that, I went to work in the children's garment industry, as office manager and assistant buyer, and remained there for seven years."

Romance entered her real life in the form of Gordon G.W. Williams, an electrical contractor, and they were married in June, 1966. "It was a big, lovely wedding and I can exactly remember it to this day," she says, with a dreamy smile.

The Williamses have one child, Bambi, who is nine. "My daughter was partially responsible for my writing career," explains Claudette. "She was two years old when I decided to give up my business career. The commuting from Manhattan to Long Island was draining me mentally and physically, and I wanted to play at being mommy. With my husband's encouragement I stayed home and—took up the pen!"

Her first book, *Spring Gambit,* took about three months to finish. "The most difficult aspect of this type of writing is the Regency dialogue. It required many hours of patient research in a Manhattan library to get it down pat." Claudette considers her writing career a lot of fun.

"Until recently I did all my writing in a country kitchen where I'd apportioned a cubbyhole as my sanctum. But in 1981, my husband added a lovely studio to our house, and it's all mine. I'm now building a wonderful library around me," she says. "My husband is obviously my greatest fan, and building a special room for me was his most romantic present."

Romance is important to Claudette and Gordon Williams. "We love to travel together. Before our daughter was born, we spent a month in France, England, Luxembourg, and Italy. Now England and Amsterdam are regular spots on our itinerary, and we make frequent trips. Part of the lure has to do with my interest in history. I use the background information for my novels. And now some of my books are published in England, Germany, Italy, and Norway—so we can see them on the bookstands there!"

The Williamses make it a point to spend hours in smalltown libraries scanning old newspapers, antiquities, and original letters. "At Newstead Abbey (Byron's home) in Nottingham, the guide was kind enough to take us behind the scenes and allow us to peruse some of Byron's original letters not on display to the public. Research," she adds, "entertains both of us, and, of course, it's a very integral and enjoyable part of my writing."

Claudette's contribution to the culinary arts is a mouth-watering quiche. Prepared as follows:

QUICHE

Pastry for 1 crust 9-inch pie (or frozen pie shell)
14 small slices lean bacon
4 eggs
2 cups heavy cream
¾ tsp. salt
⅛ tsp. powdered nutmeg
⅛ tsp. sugar
1/16 tsp. cayenne
⅛ tsp. pepper
1 tb. butter or margarine
¼ pound Swiss cheese, grated
  Prepare pastry. Start oven at 425 degrees.
  Fry bacon until crisp. Drain on thick paper towels. Crumble all but 6 strips. Beat eggs with cream, salt, nutmeg, sugar, cayenne and pepper. Rub chilled pie shell with softened butter

or margarine. Sprinkle crumbled bacon and cheese into pie shell. Pour cream mixture over all. Bake 15 minutes. Reduce oven temperature to moderate (300 degrees F.) and bake 40 minutes longer, or until knife inserted in center comes out clean. Remove from oven and garnish with remaining 6 cooked bacon strips. Let stand 5 minutes.

Makes 6 servings.

Jeanne Williams

He brought up her face to kiss her mouth. For a long tremulous moment he held her matched to his body, and she knew that he'd slept last night as poorly as she. If he'd come to her, she might not have been able to remember she belonged to Shea, for she loved this man, too, and in this time of parting her anguished flesh cleaved to his.

—Harvest of Fury

Jeanne Williams is a rarity among women romantic writers— she writes only romantic Western paperback novels. However, her heroes aren't tall, handsome, slow-talking cowboys in white hats. They're beautiful women, but not the kind found in many Western novels; women who stand around wringing their hands in a crisis.

Jeanne's heroines are strong, independent, and resourceful. They shoot straight, ride hard, and survive the harshest situation, from brutal outlaws and marauding Indians to blizzards and burning deserts.

"They're forced by war or some other catastrophe to take care of families and carry on without a man, which is an image many modern women can identify with," the author says.

While there's plenty of action, conflict and a fair amount of violence in four of Jeanne's most popular books, written under her own name—*Bride of Thunder, Daughter of the Sword, A Lady Bought with Rifles,* and *A Woman Clothed in Sun*—she

315

also includes lots of romance, some unexplicit sex and usually a rape or two.

"But no lust in the dust," she quips, then pauses. "Well, maybe a *little*, but not much and never from the heroines, only the villains are lustful. My editors suggested once that the books would sell even better if I included some calculated, tasteful torture but I told them that was out. If I can't keep my readers' interest as it is, I'll go into another trade."

Jeanne was born April 10, 1930, in Elkhart, Kansas and grew up on her grandparents' Missouri farm. Pioneers and explorers are plentiful under the Aries sign, and to this day the author holds strong convictions about wildlife and conservation efforts. She does not eat meat or wear furs, and calls attention to the use of animals in medical research, mistreatment which she does not condone. Her home is an A-frame cabin located on the Mogollon Rim, southeast of Flagstaff, Arizona.

She's been married three times, first to an Air Force navigator, with whom she traveled around the States and lived for three years in small villages in the German Odenwald. They were divorced in 1969. Their son Michael attends the University of Arizona, as does their daughter Kristin, who loves to write fiction.

Her second husband was English, the famous thriller writer John Creasey, whom she married in 1970. "He had a country estate and a Georgian mansion which was the dower house of the local castle, at Bodenham in Wiltshire," recalls the petite brunette. "I lived there over a year." While residing in England, she wrote twelve Gothic romances. After Creasey's death in 1975 she moved to Arizona.

"I like to get into remote areas and explore them," she relates. "I have a simple life. I don't care for jewelry, and a car is simply transport. I do buy more books and I enjoy having a warm, attractive home and working room. The main ways success has changed my life have been that I can donate much more money to wildlife and conservation efforts, groups that work for people like the American Friends Service Committee, and to causes I believe in; and I can travel and live where I want to. I find, however, that a certain amount of structure in my life is necessary for contentment. I need a base and a place to go back after my journeys."

Writing is the only vocation Jeanne Williams ever wanted to pursue. She attended but did not graduate from the University of Oklahoma, and studied at the School of Professional Writing there with two wonderful coaches and advisers. She began selling short stories to Western and fantasy magazines and *Ladies Home Journal* in the early fifties. She has written more than forty books to date: fourteen juvenile books (four of them written as J.R. Williams); twelve Gothics, under the names Deidre Rowan and Jeanne Crecy; eight Kristin Michaels' light, modern romances, usually in an outdoor setting with an environmental theme; and under her own name, a couple of adult novels as well as the historical romances published by Pocket Books and Fawcett.

Jeanne concedes that a lot of her readers are "reading for the romance" in her books, but feels that they are learning something about the Old West, too.

"I get letters saying they like the detail and background," she says. "There are people who read these who would never crack a history book. I want them to have a pretty good picture of what a certain area of the country was like at the time."

As evidenced by four pages of sources and credits for *Valiant Women,* the author does extensive research for her romanticized history.

She has had surprisingly little disagreement with mixing fact and fiction. "I try to get the facts and weave them in, along with historical characters, in an interesting fashion," she explains. "The more you research, the more conflicts you find. Often you'll find four or five versions of historical events."

The Arizona resident loves to tell stories of her grandmother's homesteading experiences and her father's years as a cowboy, and she laces her conversation with historical anecdotes.

"Americans are hungry for myths and legends, and the West is the best we have," claims Jeanne. For people trying to cope with the world today, she sees her books as "both an escape and a fortifying of values. One of the things I've tried to do is show that the good old days weren't all good. There was valor, bravery, and plain old hard work, but there were both good and bad people."

Jeanne started writing "as soon as I could hold a pencil. As soon as I found out that the stories my mother read to me were made up by someone, I wanted to write stories about my dog, the family, and various animals. When I was nine, I got really ambitious and set out to retell and illustrate the Bible. Alas, I gave out at the Tower of Babel, but I did finish my version of The Volsung Saga that same year. My first published story sold when I was twenty-two to *Ranch Romances*, a publication very good to new writers."

Her first full-length book, which was never published, was a historical romance centered around a strong female character—ironically, the kind of book she's doing very well with now. "I couldn't sell my first book," she reveals. "Publishers said it was too Western to be historical and too historical to be Western, and besides, it had a woman as the heroine. Thank goodness, times have changed and strong women are now acceptable subjects to write about."

As far as Jeanne Williams is concerned, "Women really were the frontier. There were no permanent settlements until they came West," she says.

She's now working on a two-volume saga about Arizona, 1847–1917, which deals with three women's lives from the Mexican War to the Civil War. Under the name of Kristin Michaels, for New American Library, she's writing contemporary romances, with environmental and outdoor themes. There's also a wonderful series in process on frontier women, under her pen name of Jeanne Foster.

"I have wanted to do sequels to all my other books, but I've been too busy," she says. However, her lifestyle in 1981 included time for a private romance and her third marriage to a retired engineer. The couple took up residence in the Chiricahua Mountains.

Jeanne, who enjoys camping and backpacking and spending four days holed up in a cave during a flood in Arizona, says she's explored most of the regions she's written about and has taken courses in native foods and how to survive in the wilderness. "I try to show the daily life of the period as best I can, get to the nitty-gritty so I can convey a sense of reality," she admits.

Jeanne avoids the supernatural and the occult. She is interested, though, in healing, telepathy, preknowledge and such. "I think these things definitely exist," she says, "and would be of great benefit as we learn more about them."

The former president of Western Writers' Association is also the winner of several writing awards, including two Golden Spurs from the Western Writers' Association and a Texas Institute of Letters award.

Mexican dishes are Jeanne's favorite cuisine, but she loves grains, tofu, souffles, etc. One of her favorite recipes is also the simplest and adapts to crowds by adding more cans. Great for camping, too. Take equal amounts of corn (fresh, frozen, or canned) and hominy. Layer between shredded cheese and chopped green chilies. Bake at 350 degrees for 45 minutes.

Fran Wilson

Ramon's cool glance swept over her with insulting thoroughness. "If you'll recall, I never wanted you in any of my vineyards, and I agreed to bring you to Mexico, because I hoped I could force you to give up your idiotic schemes of becoming a wine-maker." He intensified his fierce hold. "Your fair skin and blonde hair may well prove an alluring novelty in Mexico, but keep in mind that in my vineyard, I will not tolerate any disruptive element." He pulled her closer, his blazing black eyes burning into hers. "You're here to learn winemaking, not to portray the enticing amber witch. Is that understood?"

—Amber Wine

Among the first books Silhouette Romances released when they started their line of novels in 1980 was Fran Wilson's *Where Mountains Wait.* The heroine of this contemporary romance, Hensley Travis, bears a name (in reverse) known in early day Oklahoma newspaper circles. Fran's grandfather was Travis Hensley, publisher of the El Reno paper, second in the state.

"My mother likes to think that any writing talent I might have comes from my grandfather," grins vivacious, blonde, blue-eyed Fran Wilson. The tall, slender author continues using a family name in her other books since it brought her luck on the first one.

Born in Oklahoma, on July 31, Fran Wilson is under the sign of Leo, which accounts for her unswerving attention to details and colorful atmosphere in her category romance.

"I do enjoy reading all kinds of romantic novels, particularly romantic suspense," says Fran, as she explains her goals in the romantic fiction world, "and because this is what I like to read it is also what I enjoy writing. More than anything else I want to write stories that will really hold the interest of the reader, make the reader care what happens to the people and share the experiences and emotions with the characters. As I write I see the people and the settings myself, but I want them to come vividly alive also for the reader.

"The excitement and pleasure I've had from my first book can never be equalled for me for it has brought with it many opportunities," she exuded. "As a result of my novel being one of the first books in the Silhouette Romance line, I had exciting autograph parties at bookstores in Oklahoma and appeared on endless radio talk shows." She sighed, remembering the furious pace she traveled and her own elation. "Of course, every writer is thrilled to receive fan letters. My editor at Silhouette sent me copies of letters they received on the launching of their line. Then, when the condensation of *Where Mountains Wait* appeared in both the English and Spanish editions of *Good Housekeeping*, I received even more nice letters from readers around the world. These lovely happenings make me want to stay at my typewriter and write—write—write!" she declares joyously.

As a child, Fran wrote poetry and detailed accounts of summer vacations. Her first effort at a story was a whodunit mystery which she entitled *The Vanbregal Ruby*. "Being nine years old at the time," she explains, "the twelve brief chapters, as I called each page a chapter, were peopled with stock characters and predictable situations—the butler did it!"

She grew up in Oklahoma and went on to attend the University of Oklahoma and the University of Iowa, where she majored in English and took her first creative writing courses. Following college she worked as an announcer and special programs artist for the CBS radio-affiliated station in Tulsa.

Love entered her life in a most romantic fashion—her real-life hero was an Annapolis cadet, Thomas Wilson, who married her in the chapel of the United States Naval Academy in Annapolis, Maryland following his June-week graduation. "Our home is still beautiful Tulsa. Both my husband and I are natives," she says. "Our families are here and we love it. It is the greatest city in the Southwest." The Wilsons have two children; their son is a mechanical engineer and their married daughter earned her Master's degree in business administration.

"I've traveled a good deal in the United States," says Fran, "and have at some time been in every state and most of the Canadian provinces. Travel has helped my writing considerably. Our most recent trip," she relates, "was to a beautiful and charming deep-sea fishing area in Mexico called Bahia Kino. I made it the setting for *Amber Wine*. My husband and I also collect ironwood carvings of the Seri Indians. Those dark, beautifully grained wood carvings that you have to see to believe. I decided to have the Spanish hero of my story buy one of the carvings for the American heroine. That's my way of letting my readers learn some unusual information about antiquities and collectibles."

Fran and her husband spend most of their free time traveling and collecting furniture and antiques. "Over the years," says the author, "some of our most enjoyable summer vacations were spent searching through antique stores, barns, and sheds both on Cape Cod and through Pennsylvania and Ohio, as well as throughout the southern states. We bought pieces 'in the rough,' in need of refinishing and repairing to restore them to their original beauty and use. Tom and I made this project a great bit of joint teamwork. I was the 'stripper,' removing the old finish from the wood. My husband then spent hours of sanding and repairing, then refinishing and the results of our labors we feel have furnished our home with interesting and charming antique furniture." Fran's other hobbies include an interest in all kinds of owls— "porcelain, ceramic, wood, brass, pewter, and glass. I have at present over seventy-five owls collected from everywhere."

Fran likes to write in the sunny, southeast bedroom of the

home. "We converted it into a study-workroom," she explains. "I require quiet to write and therefore I do my writing in the mornings and early part of the afternoon, never at night. I write my first rough draft in long hand sitting in a comfortable big lounge chair. I write every day for the most part and 600 to 1,000 words that I keep is a good day for me for I am not a fast, nor abundantly prolific writer. Reading good books of other authors is vital to me. I read both men and women," she added. Fran is also instrumental in a growing organization of Tulsa women writers, many of whom are publishing category romances. "We help one another," she says with a smile.

When asked to share a favorite recipe, Fran offered the following:

CHRISTMAS SNOWBALLS

"Christmas snowballs have been the traditional dessert for Christmas dinner in our family for many years. One year this recipe served a double celebration, for not only did we enjoy this sweet for Christmas dinner but also I prepared it for the wedding rehearsal dinner for the holiday season wedding of our son and his bride."

1 cup sugar
½ cup butter or margarine
2 egg yolks
1 can (15¼ oz.) crushed pineapple
1 cup chopped pecans
Powdered sugar
Almond flavoring
Angel flake coconut
Vanilla wafers
½ pt. whipping cream

Cream butter and sugar until smooth with an electric mixer. Add egg yolks and beat. Add drained crushed pineapple, then fold in chopped pecans. Make individual small stacked cakes by spreading layer of this mixture on top of a vanilla wafer, add a second wafer and a second layer of the filling and then top with a wafer. The individual cake thus consists of three vanilla wafers and two layers of the filling. This recipe makes twenty to twenty-four cakes. Place cakes in a wax paper-lined pan and chill until firm and easy to handle. They may be prepared ahead and frozen.

Prior to serving, beat half-pint carton of whipping cream and add 2 tsp. of powdered sugar and drop of almond flavoring. Ice each cake all around with the whipped cream and then sprinkle with angel flake coconut. This gives the fluffy appearance of a luscious snowball. Decorate with a sprig of red-berried holly if it happens to be available in your yard. May this recipe add the festive holiday finale to your Christmas dinner.

Kathleen E. Woodiwiss

His mouth eagerly took hers and their bodies strained together hungrily, Brandon's nearly famished for the full draught of love, Heather's just beginning to taste it. She moaned softly under his exploring hands, his fierce, fevered kisses, and clung to him as she gave herself wholly to his passion . . .

—*The Flame and the Flower*

There are over thirteen million of Kathleen Woodiwiss's books in print, yet she remains one of America's most reclusive authors, and makes only occasional personal appearances these days for her popular historical romances. At the time of publication for *Love's Leading Ladies,* Kathleen was turning in her fifth manuscript for Avon Books, a story that takes place in Scotland around 1790.

With the invaluable help of Avon Books' publicity releases, Luce Press Clipping Service, and Kathleen's protegé and neighbor, author LaVyrle Spencer, this profile was compiled to bring you a rare glimpse of one of the world's shyest romance authors.

"Savage passion, blazing kisses, and tender caresses" are part of her everyday writing life, sandwiched between washing clothes and cleaning house, for this rural, Princeton, Minnesota housewife. As the author of five can't-put-'em-down historical novels, she is taken aback by comments that she writes erotic novels.

"It irritates me beyond all coolness for anybody to call it pornography," Kathleen told reporter Bob Lundegaard of *Twin Cities Magazine.* "It is not, and if they want to read pornography, there are plenty of books around. I resent it. I guess if you are sensitive about sex, you can call it that, but I would have to disagree. All the letters I receive say it is very well done.

"I think my books are sexy, but it's a nice sex because the couples are true to each other and they are not falling into bed with every Tom, Dick, and Harry. I get letters from women who say, after reading my books, it has helped their marriages."

A common thread—faithfulness—runs through all her books. Her heroines may be passionate or passive, domineering or headstrong, but the lovers are always faithful to each other.

Kathleen embodies such sentiments in her own life. "Marriage is a very important thing to me," she has said. "We've been married over twenty years, and I think, well, I just can't imagine myself not being married."

When her Civil War romance, *Ashes in the Wind,* was released in 1979, she told the *New York Times,* in a soft, shy voice, "I'm really just an ordinary housewife. I enjoy cooking and cleaning, my family, and my home."

While Kathleen may *sound* like a typical American housewife, she is most definitely not. What other housewife invests her royalties, now in the millions, in an apartment complex, a restaurant, and lives in a lake-front estate in a forest called Tanglewood? (So named for the creek that flows behind it.)

Her home is a stucco-and-wood house, and her three sons fill the rooms with the usual teenage activities. She's often seen at the local football field watching them play with their high school team. "No one would recognize her, although I'm sure most of the women in the stands have read her books," says her neighbor LaVyrle Spencer. "Her boys' names get in the paper for their football exploits far more than hers."

Kathleen is very modest. "And demure," says Tom E. Huff (aka Jennifer Wilde), who met her at a book-signing party in

Texas. "She has a flawless, radiant complexion. And she's very gracious, but reserved. A lovely woman."

Kathleen's career during her early years of marriage was as a model. She worked in Tokyo, appearing in fashion shows. That was all before she began writing. Then she had her third son and became a born-again Christian.

As she explained to the *Twin Cities* reporter, "A born-again Christian is a person who accepts Christ as his Savior. I believe that nobody is perfect. There's no possible way we can get into heaven on our own merits. The only way I believe we can get into heaven is because of what Christ did on the Cross. I just realized there was a better way than just trying to do it all yourself."

She also appears to have definite opinions on other controversial subjects. "I don't agree with the ERA and the women's movement. I enjoy being a woman, and it seems like some of the liberated women want to take over the positions of men, and I don't have any desire to. I guess I'm liberated in the fact that I'm willful and I have a mind of my own and I'm not really put down by what men think."

Kathleen is a very private person, a homebody, and not the mercurial social butterfly one associates with her Gemini sun sign. (Her birthday is June 3, and she was born in 1937.) But her artistic interests have certainly had a mercurial change-about. She originally had a strong talent in art, and painted in oils, portraits mostly, but also woodland scenes. Eventually, she put down the brush and took up the pen.

Born in Louisiana, her childhood had one unhappy and tragic incident. Her father died when she was twelve. Her mother was left to raise her and her four sisters and three brothers. It was while she was attending a "sock hop" as a teenager that she first met her husband, Ross, whom she has described as a lookalike to Brian Keith, with gray hair, brown eyes, about six-foot-two, and on the robust side. Now retired from the Air Force, he helps Kathleen with her writing. In fact, he contributes actively; he wrote the poem at the beginning of *The Flame and the Flower*, the myth at the start of *The Wolf and*

329

the Dove, and the lead into *Shanna.* It's known that she likes to "pick his brain" because he has traveled all over the world, while she hasn't—except for her modeling stint in Japan.

Her motivations for becoming a writer were similar to those of other leading romance writers. She just wanted to write a story because the day had arrived when she couldn't find anything to read. And so she decided to write her own book on a typewriter she'd given her husband for Christmas.

It took her a year to finish the first draft of her "story." Her husband was an instructor-navigator at the time, in Kansas, and there were a lot of distractions. She belonged to the Wives' Club and sat on a number of committees. It was when the Wood-iwisses were transferred to Minnesota that she rewrote the novel, with her husband's and friends' encouragement. It was rejected by eight hardcover publishing companies before Avon discovered it.

Here's how Nancy Coffey, the then senior editor at Avon, describes the event. "I took the manuscript home with me for the weekend. It was the largest on the slush pile—almost 200,000 words. The cover letter described the story as a romance between Heather Simmons, 'young, beautiful, desired by many men,' and Brandon Birmingham, 'handsome, willful Yankee sea captain.'

"I couldn't stop reading it," says Nancy. "She was such a natural storyteller. In this business you very rarely come across someone who keeps you turning the pages."

Avon's other editors agreed with her and offered a contract. They published *The Flame and the Flower* as a paperback original in 1972 and to date it has sold more than three million copies. Her subsequent novels have followed this same pattern of success. Her fresh, vibrant style apparently appeals to older women and younger women as well; those who want something a little racier than Barbara Cartland, but not quite as steamy as Rosemary Rogers.

The only complaint of her readers is that she's the only author who doesn't seem to answer her fan mail. "She may be a born-again Christian," says one fan, whose letter was published in hopes Kathleen would reply, "but when does she become a born-again correspondent?"

A poll taken by over 1,000 readers of *Romantic Times* showed that she is the all-time favorite author of historical romance, and her book, *The Flame and the Flower*, was number one on their list of favorites.

Kathleen does her writing mainly during the school year. (When her three boys are home during the summer, she likes to spend time with them.) She gets up early in the morning to get her sons off to school, then rushes around cleaning up the house or cutting the grass. Once her chores are out of the way, she sits down at a desk in her study, comfortably dressed in jeans and a plaid shirt, with the family dog at her feet, cranks some paper into her typewriter, and heads back to another period of time.

She's frequently asked if her characters are taken from real life, but she denies it. She believes they come completely out of her imagination. Was it just a coincidence then, that one of her heroines, Alaina MacGaren, moved from Louisiana to rural Minnesota, just as Kathleen did in real life? As she said to the *New York Times*, "The only similarity I share with Alaina is a temper, but I try to keep it under control. Actually, the only reason I used those states is that I like them."

Kathleen looks upon her heroes and heroines as children, characters she has created. And she claims not to ever have put herself in their place, wishing she could be like them. She's content.

Cynthia Wright

Her body was so warm, so soft yet firm. There wasn't a woman in the world he desired as much as Court-ney, or one for whom he would submit to this bizarre, late-night chitchat in bed when all he wanted to do was make love. Testing the words "make love" in his mind, Damon realized they didn't scratch the sur-face of what he longed to do with Courtney.

—*Crimson Intrigue*

Cynthia Wright is now living in a wonderful eighteenth-century house in Connecticut and writing historical romances under her own name and that of Devon Lindsay, the heroine's name in *Silver Storm*. Since her first book, *Caroline,* was published in 1977, she has attracted a unique following of loyal readers. She writes sensuous books with accurately described historical backgrounds, and the most romantic of romance readers think she is the successor to Kathleen Woodiwiss.

What accounts for her irresistible style of writing? "I have a rule," says Cynthia, a petite brunette. "I try not to let anything happen to my heroines that I wouldn't care to live with myself. I think the readers need to identify closely with the main characters and that rapes, beatings, and other sadistic treatments make that either impossible or painful."

The success of her novels may very well be due to the success of her marriage. "I married my high school sweetheart and one true love—Richard Wright—on my nineteenth birthday," she explains. So far, they have lived happily ever after.

Cynthia was born in Cedar Rapids, Iowa, on April Fool's Day, 1953. She had a beloved older brother Bill, and the family lived in her father's childhood house while he ran the same pharmacy his father had established. Eventually, they moved to Whittier, California, the first of many, many moves in Cynthia's life. "My father continued his pharmaceutical work," she recalls, "and my mom did the things moms did in 1950s."

As a teenager, this budding author entertained her friends and teachers with her stories of Herbert, The Talking Diary. Meanwhile, at home, she scribbled secretly in a spiral notebook, tapping out "my *Gone with the Wind* sequel.

"Also," admits Cynthia, "I worked myself into a froth over the Beatles. My mom was ready to have me put away! My interest in the Beatles was probably the first clear indication that I would tend to be obsessive in my interests. After the Beatles, I spent two years reading everything written about Abraham, then Mary, Lincoln. Next came John Kennedy, then Jacqueline, then Robert. I was never satisfied until I had read every printed word—usually two or three times. I'm still that way. Currently, I'm a self-taught expert on ballet, past and present."

Cynthia's sixteenth year held a lot of changes. "I suddenly began to date—a lot! I met Rick—now my husband. I had known who he was. A grade ahead of me, Rick was the classic rebel with a wealth of potential and love locked inside. Before we met, he was expelled several times for fighting, drinking at dances—well, there were few rules Rick didn't break. I can remember him showing up at school during his suspension, wearing dark glasses, no less. His parents were divorced and his relationship with his mother was a big part of his problem. We began to date and soon he had given me his ring (wrapped in yarn and the whole bit). I was as in love as any of my heroines have ever been. The sincerity and passion of my love broke down all of Rick's barriers and he returned my love unreservedly. Except for a few normal crises, we were together constantly until our marriage three years later, on my nineteenth birthday."

Although Cynthia's formal education was interrupted, she

did finish one year at the University of Iowa before her marriage, and during the following years, when Rick was in the Navy, she picked up credits from Kansas University—and wrote *Caroline* and half of *Touch the Sun* at the same time.

Cynthia and Rick were living in Lawrence, Kansas, so Rick could attend Kansas University too, when Jenna, their only child, was born, in 1973. "I attended the Lamaze classes (this was before natural childbirth was widespread) and I was the first person in the Lawrence Hospital to go through it. Rick was there through it all," she sighs happily. "Jenna was a gorgeous baby. She's always been a delight, an irresistible child, which is probably the major reason we haven't been in a great hurry to have more. We enjoy Jenna so much. Her career plans include becoming a ballet dancer (Mikhail Baryshnikov's partner) and a paleontologist. She might write a few books on the side," boasts Cynthia with a smile.

After Jenna was born, Cynthia grew restless, not to mention "financially pinched," and went to work evenings at the local McDonalds. "All my coworkers were college students," she says, "which was terrific since I was just twenty-one myself. Rick took care of Jenna all of those evenings, which formed a wonderful bond between them, but the strain of that plus trying to study, cook, etc. was taking its toll. So, I decided to play homemaker again."

All through the previous year, she had been reading historical romances. "I was in need of intellectual stimulation, so beginning with Barbara Cartland and leading up to Kathleen Woodiwiss, I read and read. *The Flame and the Flower* was an incredible experience for me. It was as if she had written it just for me! The books were few and far between then, and over so quickly! I began to explore the idea of creating my own book . . . one that wouldn't be over in a day and one where the characters wouldn't make me angry, as they had in some of the more 'graphic' type of historical romances."

Cynthia then sat down with a spiral notebook and began to write *Caroline*, which turned out to be a complicated hobby. "It was like pulling a thread that goes on forever as I started doing research. That's the reason the book begins in the woods," she admits, "in the middle of nowhere—I didn't need to supply any historical data! Things got worse as I decided to light a fire. Then I realized I didn't know how that was done in 1783. Obviously not with a box of matches from Alex's favorite restaurant! My books about Colonial architecture and furniture were joined by volumes about Colonial cooking, customs, modes of travel, clothing, gardens, and general lifestyles—not to mention history and books that dealt with the areas where *Caroline* took place."

Writing seems to be something Cynthia has always needed to do. If she wasn't writing historicals, no doubt it would be something else, but the historical romance genre seems perfect for her. "I love relationships and the excitement of blossoming romance," she admits freely. "I also am fascinated by certain periods of history, so the opportunity to thoroughly research them has been a treat for me. Finally, I write these stories for the same reason other women read them—and that reason cannot be given easily. It's as complicated as love itself."

Rick was tremendously encouraging. He kept Cynthia believing in her potential success, especially later when they had to deal with several rejection slips. A year went by—and over and over again rejection slips arrived with the returned manuscript of *Caroline*. "Only Rick was convinced," recalls Cynthia.

In the meantime, Rick went off to Officers' Candidate School that summer of 1976. During one of his leaves Cynthia received a call from Ballantine informing her that they wanted the manuscript, which she had renamed *Caro's Quest* for the resubmission. "I rushed down the stairs and told him the news and we held hands and jumped up and down in the living room. I was on a euphoric high for days afterward," she says, remembering the excitement in the Wright home.

"Rick and I had talked about going to Hawaii for his next duty station, but after the news about my book, he agreed that it was time to put my career first for a change. He asked for Connecticut instead, and was assigned to a submarine based in Groton. I had been East once, briefly, but after writing one and three-quarters books set on the East Coast, I felt I had spent most of the past two years in 1780s America. I was instantly at home in Connecticut—we all loved it. I had just finished *Touch the Sun* by then and *Caroline* was being published."

At the sight of her book for sale in stores, Cynthia developed a nagging worry about the reactions of people she knew to the more explicit scenes. "I kept picturing women from my hometown church or the wife of Rick's captain reading those passages," she says, amusement in her brown eyes. "Fortunately, I got over that finally. There are so many books with tones completely different from mine, with brutal sex that seems inserted as a form of entertainment for the reader, that I pride myself on being different. I have a lot of respect for my readers; I remember what made me angry in the books I read. I work very hard to intricate one man–one woman relationships that are the cornerstones of all my books."

Cynthia did learn an important writing lesson in 1981—never try to work on two plots at the same time. "It was exhausting," she recalls. "For me, writing demands a fragile chemistry that can't be manufactured. I'm not a machine and I'll never commit myself to doing two books at once again."

Spring Fires, the semi-sequel to her first three Ballantine books, brings past readers up to date on these characters' lives. The hero is Nicholai Beauvisage, the brother of Caroline, but the heroine, Lisette, is a new character and a very liberated woman who runs a coffeehouse.

Success has brought monetary benefits to Cynthia, enabling her to own her own house and travel. But there are other rewards. "I also have much more self-respect than I used to and I find that Rick sees me in a different light. I've become a feminist since 1977 and Rick admires that. He's much more ready to share—housework, decisions, everything. He knows I won't back down or take second place—and he loves it! There's no telling whether these changes might have occurred anyway, without my career and success, but I do know that my financial independence makes both of us take me more seriously."

As for the following recipe, Cynthia reveals, "I found my recipe for Fish House Punch through my research for *Touch the*

Sun. We now fix it during the holidays each year; friends who have tried it before wouldn't miss coming over for some, but one does learn moderation—usually the hard way!"

FISH HOUSE PUNCH

1½ cups sugar
1 quart lemon juice
2 quarts dark Jamaica rum
1 quart brandy
¼ cup peach brandy

Dissolve sugar in a small amount of cold water; stir well. Stir in lemon juice. Pour mixture over a block of ice in a punch bowl. Add remaining ingredients in order listed; stir lightly. Allow mixture to stand for a few hours, stirring occasionally.

40-50 servings (can be halved)

BIBLIOGRAPHY

(The following data are compiled from the authors' currently in-print works in both hardback and paperback. In cases where the book was originally published in hardback, such information appears on the Copyright page of the paperback edition.)

Violet Ashton

Love's Triumphant Heart	Fawcett	1977
Love's Rebellious Pleasures	"	1978
Swan Song	"	1979
Love by Fire	"	1980

Rita Balkey

Prince of Passion	Pinnacle	1980
Tears of Glory	"	1981

Iris Bancroft

Love's Burning Flame	Bantam	1979
Rapture's Rebel	Pinnacle	1980
Dawn of Desire	"	1981

As Iris Brent

Swinger's Diary	Pinnacle	1973
My Love Is Free	"	1975

As Andrea Layton

Love's Gentle Fugitive	Playboy	1978
So Wild a Rapture	"	1978
Midnight Fires	"	1979

Jennifer Blake

Love's Wild Desire	Popular Library	1977
Tender Betrayal	"	1979
The Storm and the Splendor	Fawcett	1979
Golden Fancy	"	1980

Embrace and Conquer	Fawcett	1981

As Patricia Maxwell

Secret of Mirror House	Fawcett	1970
Stranger at Plantation Inn	"	1971
Dark Masquerade	"	1974
The Bewitching Grace	Popular Library	1974
Court of the Thorn Tree	"	1974
Bride of a Stranger	Fawcett	1974
Notorious Angel	"	1977
Sweet Piracy	"	1978
Night of the Candles	"	1978

As Maxine Patrick

The Abducted Heart	Signet	1978
Bayou Bride	"	1979
Snowbound Heart	"	1979
Love at Sea	"	1980
Captive Kisses	"	1980
April of Enchantment	"	1980

As Patricia Ponder

Haven of Fear	Manor Books	1974
Murder for Charity	"	1974

As Elizabeth Trehearne (with Carol Albritton)

Storm at Midnight	Ace	1973

Parris Afton Bonds

Sweet Golden Sun	Fawcett/Popular Library	1978
Savage Enchantment	"	1979
The Flash of the Firefly	"	1979
Love Tide	"	1980
Made for Each Other	Silhouette	1981
Dust Devil	Fawcett/Popular Library	1981
Deep Purple	Fawcett/Columbine	1982

Barbara Bonham

Diagnosis: Love	Monarch	1964
Army Nurse	Thomas Bouregy	1965
Nina Stewart R.N.	"	1966
Sweet and Bitter Fancy	Fawcett/Popular Library	1976
Proud Passion	Playboy	1976
Passion's Price	"	1977
Dance of Desire	"	1978

The Dark Side of Passion	Playboy	1980

As Sara North
Jasmine for My Grave	Playboy Press	1978

Rebecca Brandewyne
No Gentle Love	Warner	1981
Forever My Love	"	1982

Dixie Browning
Unreasonable Summer	Silhouette	1980
Tumbled Wall	"	1980
Chance Tomorrow	"	1981
Journey to Quiet Waters	"	1981
Wren of Paradise	"	1981
East of Today	"	1981
Winter Blossom	"	1981
Renegade Player	"	1982
Logic of the Heart	"	1982
Island on the Hill	"	1982
Practical Dreamer	"	1982
The Long Escape	"	1982

As Zoë Dozier
Home Again My Love	Thomas Bouregy	1978
Warm Side of the Island	"	1978

Shirlee Busbee
Gypsy Lady	Avon	1977
Lady Vixen	"	1980
Renegade Lady	"	1982

Barbara Cartland

Barbara Cartland is the world's most prolific female romantic author. We are listing her titles for 1981 and into 1982. Beginning in February, 1982, Jove started a new line of Barbara Cartland romance titled Camfield Romances.

An Innocent in Russia	Bantam	1981
Gift of the Gods	"	1981
The Kiss of Life	"	1981
Winged Magic	"	1981
The Lioness and the Lily	"	1981

A Portrait of Love	Bantam	1981
The River of Love	"	1981
Dollars for the Duke	"	1981
Dreams Do Come True	"	1981
Love in the Moon	"	1981
Lucifer and the Angel	"	1981
Signpost to Love	"	1981
Lost Laughter	"	1981
The Waltz of Hearts	"	1981
Afraid	"	1981
Enchanted	"	1981
The Goddess and the Gaiety Girl	"	1981
Pride and the Poor Princess	"	1981
From Hell to Heaven	"	1981
The Complacent Wife	Jove	1981
The Unknown Heart	"	1981
Stars in My Heart	"	1981
The Heart of the Clan	"	1981
A Virgin in Paris	"	1981
Lost Enchantment	"	1981
The Wings of Ecstasy	"	1981
Love on the Run	"	1981
The Kiss of the Devil	"	1981
In the Arms of Love	"	1981
Wings on My Heart	"	1981
Love Is Dangerous	"	1981
Touch a Star	"	1981
The Secret Fear	"	1981
A Ghost in Monte Carlo	"	1981
For All Eternity	"	1981
Love under Fire	"	1981
Love Wine	"	1982
The Vibrations of Love	"	1982
Love Rules	"	1982
Moments of Love	"	1982
The Odious Duke	"	1982
The Audacious Adventuress	"	1982
Smuggled Heart	"	1982
The Poor Governess	"	1982
Sweet Enchantress	"	1982
Love Forbidden	"	1982

The Reluctant Bride	Jove	1982
Love to the Rescue	"	1982
The Pretty Horse Breakers	"	1982
Lucky in Love	Jove/Camfield Romance	1982

Jayne Castle

Vintage of Surrender	MacFadden	1979
Queen of Hearts	"	1979
Gentle Pirate	Dell/Ecstasy	1980
Bargain with the Devil	"	1981
Wagered Weekend	"	1981
Right of Possession	"	1981
A Man's Protection	Dell/Ecstasy	1982

As Stephanie James

A Passionate Business	Silhouette	1981
A Dangerous Magic	Silhouette Special Edition	1982
Stormy Challenge	"	1982

As Jayne Bentley

Maiden of the Morning	MacFadden	1979
A Moment Past Midnight	"	1979
Turning towards Home	"	1979

Elaine Raco Chase

Rules of the Game	Dell Candlelight	1980
Tender Yearnings	"	1981
Caught in a Trap	"	1982
Double Occupancy	"	1982
No Easy Way Out	"	1982
Designing Woman	"	1982

Marion Chesney

Regency Gold	Fawcett	1980
Lady Margery's Intrigue	"	1980
The Constant Companion	"	1980
Quadrille	"	1981
My Lord Ladies and Marjorie	"	1981

As Jennie Tremaine

Kitty	Dell	1979
Daisy	"	1980
Lucy	"	1980
Polly	"	1980

Molly	Dell	1980
Ginny	"	1980
Tilly	"	1981
Susie	"	1981

As Ann Fairfax

Henrietta	Jove	1979
My Dear Duchess	"	1979
Annabelle	"	1980
Penelope	"	1981

As Helen Crampton

The Marquess Takes a Bride	Pocket Books	1980
The Highland Countess	"	1981

As Charlotte Ward

The Westerby Inheritance	Pinnacle	1982

Virginia Coffman

Mistress of Devon	Fawcett	1973
Veronique	"	1975
The High Terrace	NAL	1975
The Ice Forest	Dell	1975
The Alpine Coach	"	1976
Enemy of Love	"	1976
Careen	"	1977
Marsanne	Fawcett	1977
Fire Dawn	"	1978
Night at Sea Abbey	NAL	1978
The Cliff of Dread	"	1978
The Evil at Queens Priory	"	1978
Legacy of Fear	"	1978
The Looking Glass	Dell	1978
Dinah Faire	Arbor House	1979
The Gaynor Women	Fawcett	1979
Lucifer's Cove	Pinnacle	1979
A Few Fiends to Tea	"	1979
Black Heather	NAL	1980
Pacific Cavalcade	Arbor House	1981
The Lombard Cavalcade	"	1982

As Jeanne Duval

The Lady Sorena	NAL	1978
The Ravishers	"	1980

Susanna Collins

Flamenco Nights	Jove/Second Chance at Love	1981
Hard to Handle	"	1981
Destiny's Spell	"	1981

As Susan Ellen Gross

Midnight Fury	Fawcett	1981

As Susana de Lyonne

Six Days, Five Nights	Fawcett	1978

Janet Dailey

No Quarter Asked	Harlequin	1976
		Texas
Boss Man from Ogallala	"	1976
		Nebraska
Savage Land	"	1976
		Texas
Fire and Ice	"	1976
		California
Land of Enchantment	"	1976
		New Mexico
The Homeplace	"	1976
		Iowa
After the Storm	"	1976
		Colorado
Dangerous Masquerade	"	1977
		Alabama
Night of the Cotillion	"	1977
		Georgia
Valley of the Vapors	"	1977
		Arkansas
Fiesta San Antonio	"	1977
		Texas
Show Me	"	1977
		Missouri
Bluegrass King	"	1977
		Kentucky
A Lyon's Share	"	1977
		Illinois
The Widow and the Wastral	"	1977
		Ohio

The Ivory Cane	Harlequin	1978
		California
The Indy Man	"	1978
		Indiana
Darling Jenny	"	1978
		Wyoming
Reilly's Woman	"	1978
		Nevada
To Tell the Truth	"	1978
		Oregon
Sonora Sundown	"	1978
		Arizona
Big Sky Country	"	1978
		Montana
Something Extra	"	1978
		Louisiana
Master Fiddler	"	1978
		Arizona
Beware of the Stranger	"	1978
		New York
Giant of Mesabi	"	1978
		Minnesota
The Matchmakers	"	1978
		Delaware
For Bitter or Worse	"	1979
		Texas
Green Mountain Man	"	1979
		Vermont
Six White Horses	"	1979
		Oklahoma
Summer Mahogany	"	1979
		Maine
The Bridge of the Delta Queen	"	1979
		Mississippi River
Tidewater Lover	"	1979
		Virginia
Strange Bedfellow	"	1979
		Rhode Island
Low Country Liar	"	1979
		South Carolina

Sweet Promise	Harlequin	1979
		Texas
For Mike's Sake	"	1979
		Washington
Sentimental Journey	"	1979
		Tennessee
Land Called Deseret	"	1979
		Utah
Touch the Wind	Pocket	1979
		Mexico
The Rogue	"	1980
		Nevada
Ride the Thunder	"	1980
		Idaho
Kona Winds	Harlequin Presents	1980
		Hawaii
That Boston Man	"	1980
		Massachusetts
Bed of Grass	"	1980
		Maryland
The Thawing of Mara	"	1980
		Pennsylvania
The Mating Season	"	1980
		Kansas
Lord of the High Lonesome	"	1980
		North Dakota
Southern Nights	"	1980
		Florida
Enemy in Camp	"	1980
		Michigan
Difficult Decision	"	1980
		Connecticut
Heart of Stone	"	1980
		New Hampshire
One of the Boys	"	1980
		New Jersey
Wild and Wonderful	"	1981
		West Virginia
A Tradition of Pride	"	1981
		Mississippi

The Traveling Kind	Harlequin Presents	1981
		Idaho
Dakota Dreamin'	"	1981
		South Dakota
Night Way	Pocket	1981
		Arizona
This Calder Sky	"	1981
		Montana
This Calder Range	"	1982
The Hostage Bride	Silhouette	1981
		Missouri
The Lancaster Men	"	1981
		North Carolina
For the Love of God	"	1981
		Iowa
Terms of Surrender	Silhouette Special Edition	1982
		Texas

Celeste de Blaisis

The Night Child	Fawcett	1976
Suffer a Sea Change	"	1979
The Proud Breed	"	1979
The Tiger's Woman	Dell	1982

Jude Deveraux

The Enchanted Land	Avon	1977
The Black Lyon	"	1980
Casa Grande	"	1982
The Velvet Promise	Gallen/Pocket	1981
Bronwyn	"	1982

Joan Dial

Susanna	Fawcett	1978
Lovers & Warriors	"	1978
Deadly Lady	"	1980

As Amanda York

Beloved Enemy	Gallen/Pocket Books	1979
Somewhere in the Whirlwind	"	1980
Echoes of Love	"	1982

As Katherine Kent

Druid's Retreat	Pinnacle	1979

348

Dreamtide	Gallen/Pocket Books	1980
Waters of Eden	"	1981
The Adventuress	"	1982
The Enchanted Dawn	"	1982

Bonnie Drake

The Passionate Touch	Dell Candlelight	1981
Surrender by Moonlight	"	1981
Sweet Ember	"	1981
Sensuous Burgundy	"	1981
The Ardent Protector	Dell/Ecstasy	1982
Whispered Promise	"	1982

As Billie Douglass

| Search for a New Dawn | Silhouette | 1981 |

Julie Ellis

Girl in White	Pocket	1976
Wexford	"	1976
Eden	Fawcett	1976
The Magnolias	"	1977
Eulalie	"	1978
Savage Oaks	"	1978
The Hampton Heritage	"	1978
The Hampton Women	"	1981

Zabrina Faire

Lady Blue	Warner	1979
Midnight Match	"	1979
Romany Rebel	"	1979
Enchanting Jenny	"	1979
The Wicked Cousin	"	1980
Bold Pursuit	"	1980
Athena's Heirs	"	1980
Pretty Kitty	"	1981
Tiffany's True Love	"	1981
Pretender to Love	"	1981

As Lucia Curzon

The Chadbourne Luck	Jove/	1981
	Second Chance at Love	
An Adverse Alliance	"	1981

Barbara Faith

Kill Me Gently, Darling	Manor Books	1978
The Moon-Kissed	Gallen/Pocket	1980
The Sun Dancers	"	1981
The Bitter Wine	"	1982

Patricia Gallagher

Shannon	Avon	19
Shadows of Passion	"	1971
Summer of Sighs	"	1971
Thicket	"	1974
The Sons and the Daughters	Bantam	1975
Castles in the Air	"	1976
Answer to Heaven	"	1977
The Fires of Brimstone	"	1977
Mystic Rose	"	1977
All for Love	"	1981

Dorothy Garlock

Love and Cherish	Zebra	1980
This Loving Land	Gallen	1981
The Searching Hearts	"	1982

As Johanna Phillips

Gentle Torment	Jove/	1981
	Second Chance at Love	
Amber-Eyed Man	"	1982

As Dorothy Phillips

Marriage to a Stranger	Dell	1982

Roberta Gellis

Sing Witch, Sing Death	Bantam	1975
Bond of Blood	Avon	1976
Knight's Honor	"	1976
The Dragon and the Rose	Playboy	1977
The Sword and the Swan	"	1977
Roselynde	"	1978
Alinor	"	1978
Joanna	"	1978
Gilliane	"	1979
The English Heiress	Dell	1980
The Cornish Heiress	"	1981

The Kentish Heiress	Dell	1982

As Priscilla Hamilton

The Love Token	Playboy	1979
Rhiannon	"	1982

As Max Daniels (Science Fiction)

The Space Guardian	Pocket Books	1978
Offworld	"	1979

Jean Hager

The Whispering House	Steck-Vaughn	1970
The Secret of Riverside Farm	"	1970
Portrait of Love	Dell Candlelight	1981
Yellow Flower Moon	Doubleday	1981
Web of Desire	Dell/Ecstasy	1981

As Marlaine Kyle

A Suitable Marriage	Dell Candlelight	1981
Frost Fair	"	1982

As Amanda McAllister

Terror in the Sunlight	Playboy	1977

As Jeanne Stephens

Captured by Love	Dell Candlelight	1981
Mexican Nights	Silhouette	1981
Wonder and Wild Desire	"	1981
Sweet Jasmine	"	1982
Man from Barbados	Silhouette Special Edition	1982
Pride's Possession	" " "	1982

As Sarah North

Evil Side of Eden	Playboy	1978
Shadow of the Tamaracks	"	1979

Anne Hampson

Payment in Full	Silhouette	1980
Stormy Masquerade	"	1980
Second Tomorrow	"	1980
The Dawn Steals Softly	"	1980
Man of the Outback	"	1980
Where Eagles Nest	"	1980
Man without a Heart	"	1981
Shadow of Apollo	"	1981
Enchantment	"	1981
Fascination	"	1981

Desire	Silhouette	1981
Realm of the Pagans	"	1982
Man without Honor	"	1982
To Buy a Memory	"	1982

Virginia Lee Hart

So Wild a Rose	Pinnacle	1980
Where Glory Waits	"	1982

Brooke Hastings

Playing for Keeps	Silhouette	1980
Innocent Fire	"	1980
Desert Fire	"	1980
Island Conquest	"	1981
Winner Take All	"	1981
Intimate Strangers	Silhouette Special Edition	1982
Rough Diamond	"	1982

Florence Hurd

Curse of the Moors	Manor Books	1975
Voyage of the Secret Duchess	Avon	1975
Terror at SeaCliff Pines	Manor Books	1976
Rommany	Avon	1976
Night Wind at North Riding	NAL	1977
Legacy	Avon	1977
Shadows of the Heart	"	1980

As Fiona Harrowe

Love's Scarlet Banner	Fawcett	1977
Fountains of Glory	"	1979
Forbidden Wine	"	1981

As Flora Hiller

Love's Fiery Dagger	Popular	1978

Kristin James

The Golden Sky	Gallen/Pocket	1981
The Sapphire Sky	"	1981
Cara's Song	"	1982
Dreams of Evening	"	1982

As Lisa Gregory

Bonds of Love	Jove	1978
The Rainbow Season	"	1979

Analise	Jove	1981
The Crystal Heart	"	1982

Victoria Holt

Bride of Pendorric	Fawcett	1978
Curse of the Kings	"	1978
The Devil on Horseback	"	1978
The House of a Thousand Lanterns	"	1978
King of the Castle	"	1978
Kirkland Revels	"	1978
Legend of the Seventh Virgin	"	1978
Lord of the Far Island	"	1978
Menfreya in the Morning	"	1978
Mistress of Mellyn	"	1978
On the Night of the Seventh Moon	"	1978
Queen's Confession	"	1978
Secret Woman	"	1978
Shadow of the Lynx	"	1978
Shivering Sands	"	1978
My Enemy the Queen	"	1979
The Pride of the Peacock	"	1979
The Spring of the Tiger	"	1980

As Philippa Carr

The Miracle at St. Bruno's	Popular Library	1976
The Lion Triumphant	Fawcett	1977
Saraband for Two Sisters	"	1977
Lament for a Lost Lover	"	1978
The Love Child	"	1979
The Witch from the Sea	"	1979
The Song of the Siren	Putnam	1980

As Jean Plaidy

Spanish Inquisition: Its Rise	Citadel Press	1966
St. Thomas's Eve	Putnam	1970
Gaylord Robert	"	1971
Murder Most Royal	"	1972
A Health unto His Majesty	Fawcett	1973
Mary Queen of Scots:	Putnam	1975
The Fair Devil of Scotland		
The Italian Woman	"	1975
The Sixth Wife	Fawcett	1975
Beyond the Blue Mountains	"	1976

Madonna of the Seven Hills	Fawcett	1976
The Haunted Sisters	Putnam	1977
Here Lies Our Sovereign Lord	Fawcett	1977
Light in Lucrezia	"	1977
Queen Jezebel	Berkley	1977
The Three Crowns	Putnam	1977
The Captive Queen of Scots	Fawcett	1977
Queen and Lord M	"	1978
The Captive of Kensington Palace	"	1978
The Goldsmith's Wife	"	1978
The Queen's Favorites	Putnam	1978
The Lion of Justice	"	1979
The Passionate Enemies	"	1979
The Queen's Husband	Fawcett	1979
The Widow of Windsor	"	1979
The Bastard King	"	1980
The Heart of the Lion	Putnam	1980
The Plantagenet Prelude	"	1980
The Revolt of the Eagles	"	1980

Johanna Lindsey

Captive Bride	Avon	1977
A Pirate's Love	"	1978
Fires of Winter	"	1980
Paradise Wild	"	1981
Glorious Angel	"	1982

Amii Lorin

Morning Rose, Evening Savage	Dell Candlelight	1980
The Tawny Gold Man	Dell Ecstasy	1980
The Game Is Played	"	1981
Morgan Wade's Woman	"	1981
Breeze off the Ocean	"	1981
Snowbound Weekend	"	1982

As Paula Roberts

Come Home to Love	Tower	1980

Morgan Llywelyn

The Wind from Hastings	Warner	1979
Lion of Ireland	Playboy	1981

Elizabeth Mansfield

Unexpected Holiday	Dell	1978
My Lord Murderer	Berkley	1978
The Phantom Lover	"	1979
A Very Dutiful Daughter	"	1979
The Regency Sting	"	1980
A Regency Match	"	1980
Her Man of Affairs	"	1980
Duel of Hearts	"	1980
Bluestocking	"	1981
A Regency Charade	"	1981
The Fifth Kiss	"	1981
Regency Galatea	"	1981
Regency Wager	"	1981
A Very Dutiful Daughter	"	1982

Patricia Matthews

Love's Avenging Heart	Pinnacle	1977
Love's Wildest Promise	"	1977
Love, Forever More	"	1977
Love's Daring Dream	"	1978
Love's Pagan Heart	"	1978
Love's Magic Moment	"	1979
Love's Golden Destiny	"	1979
Love's Raging Tide	"	1980
Love's Sweet Agony	"	1980
Love's Bold Journey	"	1980
Love's Many Faces	"	1979
	(Book of Poems)	
Tides of Love	Bantam	1981
Embers of the Dawn	"	1982

As Laura Wylie

The Night Visitor	Pinnacle	1979

Patricia & Clayton Matthews

Midnight Whispers	Bantam	1981

Barbara Michaels

Dark on the Other Side	Fawcett	1977
Greygallows	"	1977
Witch	"	1978

House of Many Shadows	Fawcett	1978
Patriot's Dream	"	1977
Wings of the Falcon	"	1978
Wait for What Will Come	"	1979
Ammie Come Home	"	1979
Someone in the House	Dodd/Mead	1981

As Elizabeth Peters

Legend in Green Velvet	Dodd	1976
(Pub. under title	Cassell	1977
Ghost in Green Velvet)		
Crocodile on the Sandbank	Fawcett	1978
Devil-May-Care	"	1978
Street of the Five Moons	"	1979
Summer of the Dragon	"	1980
The Love Talker	"	1981
The Curse of the Pharaohs	Dodd/Mead	1981

Fern Michaels

Vixen in Velvet	Ballantine	1976
Captive Passions	"	1977
Valentina	"	1978
Captive Embraces	"	1979
Captive Splendors	"	1980
The Delta Ladies	Pocket	1980
Without Warning	"	1981
Sea Gypsy	Silhouette	1981
Golden Lasso	"	1981
Whisper My Name	"	1981
Beyond Tomorrow	"	1981
Night Star	"	1982
Panda Bear Is Critical	Macmillan	1982

Virginia Myers

The Winds of Love	Dell	1979
Californio	Pinnacle	1979
(Reprint of Angelo's Wife)		
This Land I Hold	"	1980
Come November	Dell Candlelight	1980
Ramona's Daughter	Pinnacle	1981

Diana Palmer

Now and Forever	MacFadden	1979
Storm Over the Lake	"	1980
To Have and to Hold	"	1980
Sweet Enemy	"	1980
Love on Trial	"	1980
Bound by a Promise	"	1980
Dream's End	"	1980
To Love and Cherish	"	1981
The Morcai Battalion	Manor Books	1981
Cowboy and the Lady	Rendevous/Pocket	1982
September Morning	"	1982

Betty Layman Receveur

Sable Flanagan	Avon	1979
Molly Gallagher	Ballantine	1982

Janet Louise Roberts

Wilderness Inn	Pocket	1976
Island of Desire	Ballantine	1977
The Curse of Kenton	Pocket	1978
The Devil's Own	"	1978
Golden Lotus	Warner	1979
Black Pearls	Ballantine	1979
Dark Rose	Pocket	1979
The Black Horse Tavern	"	1980
Silver Jasmine	Warner	1980
Flamenco Rose	"	1981
Forget-Me-Not	"	1982

As Janette Radcliffe

Gifts of Violets	Dell	1977
The Heart Awakens	"	1977
Hidden Fire	"	1978
Stormy Surrender	"	1978
American Baroness	"	1980
The Court of the Flowering Peach	"	1981
Vienna Dreams	"	1982

As Louisa Bronte

Greystone Tavern	Ballantine	1975
Greystone Heritage	"	1976

Gathering at Greystone	Ballantine	1976
Casino Greystone	"	1976
Freedom Trail to Greystone	"	1976
Moonight at Greystone	"	1976
The Vallette Heritage	Jove	1978
My Lady Mischief	Dell	1978
Ravenswood	Pocket Books	1978
Isle of the Dolphins	"	1978
Her Demon Lover	"	1978
The Bornstein Icon	"	1978
The Jewels of Terror	"	1979
Weeping Lady	"	1979
The Sign of the Golden Goose	"	1980
Love Song	Pinnacle	1980
The Gunther Heritage	Jove	1981
The Landau Heritage	"	1982

As Rebecca Danton

Amethyst Love	Fawcett	1977
Fire Opals	"	1979
Star Sapphire	"	1979
Highland Brooch	"	1980
White Fire	"	1982
French Jade	"	1982

Rosemary Rogers

Sweet Savage Love	Avon	1974
The Wildest Heart	"	1974
Dark Fires	"	1975
Wicked Loving Lies	"	1976
The Crowd Pleasers	"	1978
The Insiders	"	1979
Lost Love, Last Love	"	1980
Love Play	"	1981

Rachel Ryan

Love's Encore	Dell Ecstasy	1981
Love beyond Reason	"	1981
Eloquent Silence	"	1982
A Treasure Worth Seeking	"	1982

As Laura Jordan

The Silken Web	Gallen/Pocket	1982

Tender Victory	Gallen/Pocket Books	1982

As Erin St. Claire

Bittersweet Rain	Pocket Books	1982

Edith St. George

Mountain Song	Silhouette	1981
West of the Moon	"	1981
Midnight Wine	"	1981
Dream Once More	"	1982·

As Edith DePaul

The Viscount's Witch	Candlelight	1981

As Alyssa Morgan

Beckoning Heart	Candlelight	1981
Walk Beside Me, Friend	"	1982
Architect of Her Heart	"	1982
White Water Love	"	1982

Jeraldine Saunders

The Love Boats	Pinnacle	1974
Signs of Love	"	1977
Frisco Lady	"	1979
The Frisco Fortune	"	1981
Hypoglycemia: The Disease Your Doctor Won't Treat	"	1980
The Complete Guide to a Successful Cruise	Contemporary Books	1978
Cruise Guide and Diary	J. P. Tarcher Inc.	1982

Sharon Salvato

Briarcliff Manor	Dell	1974
The Meridith Legacy	Stein/Day	1975
Scarborough House	Ballantine	1977
Bitter Eden	Dell	1980

As Day Taylor

The Black Swan	Dell	1978
Mossrose	"	1980

Bertrice Small

The Kadin	Avon	1978
Love Wild & Fair	"	1978
Adora	Ballantine	1980

Skye O'Malley	Ballantine	1980
Unconquered	"	1982

LaVyrle Spencer

The Fullfillment	Avon	1980
The Endearment	Gallen	1982

Danielle Steel

Passion's Promise	Dell	1977
Going Home	Pocket	1978
Now and Forever	Dell	1978
The Promise	"	1978
Season of Passion	"	1979
Summer's End	"	1979
To Love Again	"	1980
Loving	"	1980
The Ring	"	1980
Love (poetry)	"	1980
Palomino	"	1981
Remembrance	"	1981
A Perfect Stranger	"	1982
Crossings	"	1982

Day Taylor

The Black Swan	Dell	1978
Mossrose	"	1980

Kathryn Thiels

Savage Fancy	Pocket Books	1980
Cedar Plunge	Silhouette Special Edition	1982

Karen Van Der Zee

Sweet Not Always	Harlequin	1980
A Secret Sorrow	"	1981
Love Beyond Reason	"	1981
Waiting	"	1982

Aola Vandergriff

House of the Dancing Dead	Warner	1974
Wyndspelle	"	1975
The Bell Tower of Wyndspelle	"	1975

Wyndspelle's Child	Warner	1976
Daughters of the South Wind	"	1977
Daughters of the Wild Country	"	1978
Sisters of Sorrow	"	1978
Daughters of the Far Islands	"	1979
Daughters of the Misty Isles	"	1981
Silk and Shadow	"	1981
Daughters of the Shining City	"	1982

As Kitt Brown

Caitilyn MacGregor	Fawcett	1981
Laurian Kane	"	1981
Elyssa Deane	"	1982

Joyce Verrette

Dawn of Desire	Avon	1976
Desert Fires	"	1978
Sunrise of Splendor	Fawcett	1978
Winged Priestess	"	1980
Fountain of Fire	"	1981

Donna Vitek

A Different Dream	Silhouette	1980
Showers of Sunlight	"	1980
Promise from the Past	"	1981
Veil of Gold	"	1981
Where the Heart Is	"	1981
Garden of the Moongate	"	1981
Game of Chance	"	1982
A Velasquez Bride	"	1982

As Donna Alexander

Red Roses White Lilies	MacFadden	1979
A Lover's Question	"	1979
No Turning Back	"	1979
In from the Storm	"	1979

Elizabeth Walker

The Nomad Harp	Fawcett	1980
A Curious Courting	"	1980
The Lady Next Door	"	1981
In My Lady's Chamber	"	1981
Alicia	Dell	1980

361

Seasons of Love	Dell	1982

As Laura Matthews

Seventh Suitor	Warner	1979
Aim of a Lady	"	1980
Lord Clayborne's Fancy	"	1980
A Baronet's Wife	"	1981
Holiday in Bath	"	1981

Phyllis A. Whitney

The Red Carnelian	Warner	1974
Fire and Gold	NAL	1974
Seven Tears for Apollo	Fawcett	1977
Sea Jade	"	1977
Listen for the Whisperer	"	1977
The Golden Unicorn	"	1977
The Trembling Hills	"	1978
The Moonflower	"	1978
Window on the Square	"	1978
Black Amber	"	1978
Columbella	"	1978
Hunter's Green	"	1978
The Winter People	"	1978
Snowfire	"	1978
Spindrift	"	1978
The Quicksilver Pool	"	1979
Skye Cameron	"	1979
Thunder Heights	"	1979
The Glass Flame	"	1979
Ever After	"	1979
Domino	"	1980
Poinciana	"	1981
Vermilion	"	1982

Claudette Williams

Sassy	Fawcett	1977
Myrian	"	1978
Cotillion for Mandy	"	1978
Blades of Passion	"	1978
Cassandra	"	1979
Lacey	"	1979
Jewelene	"	1979

After the Storm	Fawcett	1979
Sunday's Child	"	1979
Spring Gambit	"	1979
Passion's Pride	"	1980
Mary, Sweet Mary	"	1980
Naughty Lady Ness	"	1980
Lady Brandy	"	1981
Hotspur and Taffeta	"	1981
Sweet Disorder	"	1981
Desert Rose	"	1981
Silky	"	1982

Jeanne Williams

The Horsetalker	Prentice-Hall	1962
Oh Susanna!	Putnam	1963
Trails of Tears: American Indians Driven from Their Lands	"	1972
Freedom Trail	"	1973
A Lady Bought with Rifles	Pocket	1977
A Woman Clothed in Sun	"	1978
Bride of Thunder	"	1978
Quetzal Lady	"	1978
Daughter of the Sword	"	1979
The Valiant Women	"	1980
San Patricio	"	1980
Harvest of Fury	"	1981

As Megan Castell

Queen of a Lonely Country	Pocket	1980

As Jeanne Foster

The Woods So Wild	Fawcett	1981
Shining Mountains	"	1981

As Kristin Michaels

To Begin with Love	NAL	1975
The Magic Side of the Moon	"	1979
Shadow of Love	"	1979
Enchanted Twilight / Song of the Heart	"	1980
Heart Song	"	1980
Voyage to Love / Make-Believe Love	"	1981
Design for Love	"	1981
Love's Pilgrimage	"	1981

A Special Kind of Love/Enchanted Journey	NAL	1981

Fran Wilson

Where Mountains Wait	Silhouette	1980
Until Summer	Thomas Bouregy	1981
Amber Wine	Silhouette	1982
Winter Promise	"	1982

Kathleen Woodiwiss

The Flame and the Flower	Avon	1972
The Wolf and the Dove	"	1974
Shanna	"	1977
Ashes in the Wind	"	1979

Cynthia Wright

Caroline	Ballantine	1977
Touch the Sun	"	1978
Silver Storm	"	1979
Spring Fires	"	1981

As Devon Lindsay

Crimson Intrigue	Gallen/Pocket	1981